T0384124

SWIMMING
AGAINST THE
CURRENT

SWIMMING
AGAINST THE
CURRENT

FIGHTING FOR **COMMON SENSE** IN
A WORLD THAT'S **LOST ITS MIND**

RILEY GAINES
WITH A.J. GREGORY

CENTER
STREET®

NASHVILLE   NEW YORK

Center Street
Hachette Book Group
1290 Avenue of the Americas, New York, NY 10104
centerstreet.com
twitter.com/CenterStreet

First Edition: May 2024

Center Street is a division of Hachette Book Group, Inc.
The Center Street name and logo are trademarks of Hachette Book Group, Inc.

The publisher is not responsible for websites (or their content)
that are not owned by the publisher.

The Hachette Speakers Bureau provides a wide range of authors for speaking
events. To find out more, go to hachettespeakersbureau.com or email
HachetteSpeakers@hbgusa.com.

All photos unless otherwise indicated are courtesy of the author's personal collection.

Library of Congress Control Number: 2024933348

ISBN: 9781546007449 (Hardcover), 9781546007463 (E-Book)

Printed in Canada

MRQ

Printing 1, 2024

To those who challenged, championed, and fought for the rights of women and to those who will finish what we started.

CONTENTS

AUTHOR'S NOTE

Initially, I believed it was respectful to use preferred pronouns, like they told us it was.

The use of pronouns is natural and something you pick up on before even forming full, coherent sentences. At first, I didn't see the harm in using preferred pronouns when referring to individuals who identify as transgender. I knew it contradicted both biology and common sense, but I wanted to be respectful.

It wasn't long in my activism role before I realized that my understanding of respect was skewed and that I was compromising on my values and the truth. This is why I insisted upon using sex-based pronouns in this book when referring to trans-identifying individuals. Hiding sex behind pronouns hurts women. In the name of not wanting to "offend," we were being gaslit. I have personal experience with this.

As I began working on this book, I also found myself using the term "biological female" when writing about women. A quarter of the way through, I stopped myself. What was I doing? By adding the word "biological" as a prefix to "male" and/or "female," I was compromising the English language and making a joke out of science. I was subconsciously conforming without even knowing it. I was using that phrase as if there was an unbiological alternative to male or female. There isn't.

People are desperate for honesty, and they want to see that it is okay to use clear language. The language I speak and the words I write must reflect that. We can still be respectful, compassionate, and empathetic without disregarding truth. It IS loving to speak the truth.

SWIMMING
AGAINST THE
CURRENT

BEFORE YOU BEGIN:
The What, How, and Why

I never would have considered myself a feminist.

Yet here I am fighting for the rights of women.

There have been two pivotal moments that fortified this advocacy role I've undertaken. The first was on March 18, 2022, when I experienced firsthand the effects of competing against and changing in a locker room with a male at our national championships. The second defining moment was on April 6, 2023, when I was ambushed and physically attacked on a college campus in California for publicly stating that what happened at the national championships was unfair, unjust, and detrimental to women's rights to privacy and equal opportunity.

This experience was the first time I had ever feared for my life.

It also unveiled a scarier truth, scarier than the punches that were thrown and landed that day. Barricaded in a room for hours, listening to vicious vitriol being spewed outside the room that would become my prison through the night, it hit me—when common sense and truth are exposed, people resort to violence

1

and threats to try to annihilate what is true. To these people, violence and threats are all that's left. And that day, despite being in physical danger, I decided I wasn't going to stop speaking the truth.

I won't ask you the question "what is a woman" on the first page of this book, but I do think we should define feminism for clarity. According to the *Oxford English Dictionary*, feminism is "the advocacy of women's rights on the basis of the equality of the sexes."[1] In theory, that sounds wonderful, and like something most of today's society would agree upon. So how did this movement (or lack thereof) end up being the root of one of the most controversial and divisive topics of the twenty-first century?

When you think of late-nineteenth-century first-wave feminism, you probably think of women's suffrage and trailblazers like Susan B. Anthony. This wave had the most clear and defined goals like property, voting, and educational rights for women. I would make the point that 99 percent of the public today is largely supportive of the intent of the original feminist movement: equal rights and opportunities for the two sexes, reiterated by the definition of feminism provided above.

Things escalated during second-wave feminism in the 1960s and 1970s. Second-wave feminism had less delineated legislative goals and is most often linked with sexual liberation and reproductive rights as the dominant issues. Picture the women who torched their bras in protest of beauty pageants, symbolically throwing off the cultural mores that defined and oppressed women. Many women-only groups and organizations like the National Organization for Women (NOW) were created during second-wave feminism, and phrases such as "identity politics" were coined during this time. The development of the Equal Rights Amendment, which aimed to establish legal rights for all

American citizens regardless of sex, and the birth of Title IX, which prevented discrimination on the basis of sex in educational programs that receive federal funding, also occurred during this second wave of feminism. These federal civil rights proposals continue to be legislated and discussed today.

In the 1990s, third-wave feminism began. Further awareness was brought to rape culture and the pay gap. A clear distinction was made between gender and sex as traditional gender roles and the nuclear family came under fire by these activists. The term "toxic masculinity" was introduced as well. Individuality and self-expression among women were fully embraced in a way it hadn't been before. Third-wave feminism paid more attention to how sexuality, race, and gender intersected and the disparities that came with their intersection. This wave was also more radical and therefore polarizing than the previous two waves.

It's becoming clearer daily that we've been thrust into a fourth wave of feminism, the most ironic and contradictory wave yet: the wave where men make the best women. The objective of this wave is equal outcomes for all humans rather than individual freedoms, opportunities, and the ending of sex-based discrimination. This ideology is in direct opposition to traditional American values. The aims of fourth-wave feminism have shifted to combat movements like slut-shaming, fat-shaming, and transphobia, extending far beyond individualism. Internet activism has advanced this movement like wildfire. Fourth-wave feminism no longer just attends to the struggles of women; it's a demand for the elimination of "men" and "women" by rendering them the same and interchangeable.

While many modern Americans wouldn't consider themselves feminists, most still support legal, social, and economic equality between the sexes. The reason most don't identify as feminists is a result of the conflation of the fundamental principles of feminism with identity politics. Real feminism, I contend, is not a concept that should contort itself to fit the politics of the day.

Most of those who openly and proudly call themselves feminists believe men and women are equal *and the same*, which is why I mentioned I wouldn't have previously considered myself a feminist. While I certainly believe men and women were created equal and in God's image, I don't believe they are the same. Men and women are inherently and beautifully different. Neither is inferior to the other, as we each have unique strengths and weaknesses.

I believe that women deserve to be recognized, embraced, and celebrated for their unique contributions and achievements, not overshadowed or overlooked by men struggling with their own gender identity. I believe it's time for a new wave of feminism where we fight to take back womanhood, the language we use, and our sex-based rights as endowed by our Creator and enforced by our constitution.

We are being force-fed the message that women's rights, privacy, dignity, feelings, and safety do not matter. What does seem to matter, however, are the feelings and experiences of men who decide that they are women and subsequently integrate themselves into female spaces. Daily, I hear story after story of men forcing their presence into the spaces of vulnerable girls and women because their self-perceived identity does not match up with their sex and they feel they belong in the female sphere. In the process, women, real women, become collateral damage.

The hard-won rights women have fought for are being erased.

I never could have imagined that being a twenty-one-year-old NCAA swimmer from Tennessee would have ignited a life path to fight for the current and future generations of women. I suppose I have one person to thank for that—Lia Thomas, who was previously on the University of Pennsylvania men's swimming team before competing in the women's category at the 2022 NCAA Swimming and Diving Championships after beginning to identify as a woman. Thomas so perfectly brought to light the reality of the injustice against women that was happening right before my eyes. I began to recognize the subtle devaluing of female athletes and have since experienced the rapid widening of this travesty as it continues. I'm grateful that Thomas sparked this fire in me and in so many others. Gender-critical feminists have been screaming what I've now been able to amplify given my testimony and my platform. I'm grateful for them and their guidance as I continue to mature and adapt.

This book is the story of how I unexpectedly became a nationally known advocate for women and a champion of our uniqueness. I also hope it inspires and empowers you to speak the truth and stand up for common sense in this world that seems to have lost its mind.

Whether or not you have personally been affected by gender identity ideology, or know someone who has, it's important to understand what is happening and what's at stake. If we all wait until we're directly impacted to take a stand, it will be too late. We're already headed down a slippery slope.

Today I'm using my platform to advocate for the bare minimum—privacy, safety, and equal opportunities for both sexes. And for that, I have been physically attacked, verbally assaulted, labeled some of the most obscene things you can imagine, and had many superficial jabs hurled at my reputation. The pain is worth it. As a big sister to a little one and a wife to a wonderful husband who hopes to have a daughter of my own one day, I feel compelled to stand up for them, so they have the same opportunities and chances for success that I was awarded because of the women who came before me and fought relentlessly for my rights. I cannot remain silent and watch as women's efforts and accomplishments are destroyed. I hope to encourage you to find your voice and your stance in these uncharted waters and to swim against the current.

Culturally speaking, to swim against the current entails following the cause of truth despite the slander and abuse we encounter. It is refusing to acquiesce to a false sense of inclusion and virtue when you know it is wrong. It is knowing you may be misunderstood and misrepresented but choosing to stay true to your convictions rather than falling in line with popular opinion. When you swim against the current, unlike going with the flow, you cover less ground in way more time, which can lead to a lot of frustration and the temptation to quit. But it's in those hard moments, when it hurts, that it matters most to sprint.

Swimming Against the Current is about standing up for reality, facts, and common sense. It's my story of how I became a passionate advocate not only for myself as a collegiate athlete but for every woman whose future is at risk of being jeopardized. For me, this is the biggest race of my life. It won't be complete until no young girl or woman is losing out on opportunities or having their privacy and safety threatened by males claiming our identity. I'm nowhere near touching the wall yet.

I'm still swimming.

1.

EARLY STROKES

The first lesson I was taught on mental fortitude took place when I was eight. I didn't realize what was happening until it was over.

I was in the second grade when, one winter, I went with my dad on a weekend business trip to Memphis, Tennessee. On an afternoon with an empty schedule, Dad told me to get up, put on the robe in the bathroom, and follow him. Zero elaboration. *Um, okay, Dad.* I had no clue what his intentions were, but I knew to do what I was told.

While I was flooded with curiosity, Dad was quiet as we took the elevator down to the lobby. The waffle-weaved robe trailed behind me like a train from a wedding gown. We slipped through the lobby doors that opened to the back of the building. Cold air blasted my face.

And there we were, standing on the concrete deck that surrounded the outdoor pool. It was closed for the season. If we couldn't figure out this key detail by the big sign, the pool itself was topped with a vinyl cover. I didn't have time to process what was happening when, suddenly, Dad peeled back a portion of the pool cover, as if it was a totally normal thing for any hotel guest to do in the middle of winter. I stared at the gentle waves lapping against the concrete wall. Dad broke the silence. In the same tone of voice as he used when he'd remind me to brush my teeth every night, he said, "Okay, Riley, jump in."

My eyes bugged out of my head. "But Dad, it's cold!"

"It's not cold. There's no such thing as cold. You just think it's cold. Your body wants you to think it's cold. Now listen, you're going to jump in and wait for me to tell you when to get out. But first, there are a few rules. One, your teeth are not allowed to chatter. Two, you are not allowed to shiver. Three, you are not allowed to say, 'I'm cold.'"

I spouted back, "What do you mean there's no such thing as cold?! I'm cold now!"

"No such thing as cold. There is only the absence of heat. Kind of like there's no such thing as the dark, just the absence of light."

This went right over my head as the color drained from my face. I never wanted to call my mom so bad in my life. This was some form of child abuse. It had to be. At least something like it. A former football player at Vanderbilt University who went on to play professionally in the NFL and who had multiple brothers who were also SEC athletes and NFL superstars, Dad was all tenacity and steel. I remember watching him manage to squat over five hundred pounds with a broken ankle when I was little. I knew he was tough—but this?

"I don't get it, Dad. Why do you want me to jump in?"

"It's time you learned mental toughness, Riley. Look, if you can stop focusing on your teeth chattering and your body shivering and the obvious fact that it feels cold, eventually you're going to realize it's just that: it's a feeling. And we, as humans, have control over our feelings. It's all relative."

I still didn't get it.

"After you get in," Dad continued, "I'll tell you when you can come out, and we'll go back to the room." Then he jerked his head in a curt nod, the sign for me to jump. I don't remember how I managed to throw myself into the pool, but I'll never forget the feeling of being punched in the lungs when I hit the water. The cold sliced right through my bones.

"No shaking or chattering!" Dad yelled from beside a rusty lounge chair. I scrambled to remain calm in a frantic circle of bubbles while I treaded water. I just needed to breathe. And remember the rules. Do you know how hard it is to control reflexive muscle spasms?

"Just one more minute!"

Inhale. Exhale. Inhale. Exhale. My legs churned in furious circles. *I'm not cold. I'm not cold. I am not cold.*

Dad made me stay in the cold pool for three to four minutes. My lips were so purple it looked as if I had eaten a grape Popsicle, a notorious trait I had all the way through college when I would get out of cold pools. Once we got back to our room and my body eventually acclimated to a normal range of temperature, he sat me down and explained the value of a strong mind. "This is something my brothers and I had to learn at a young age. Having a tough mind is important in sports, in relationships, in school, and in your career. Whatever you decide to do with your life, Riley, whether it's sports or not, just know that having mental toughness is going to get you farther than physical toughness ever will."

Dad was right. And although, at the time, jumping in a cold pool would not have been the experience I'd have chosen to illustrate mental fortitude, his words have echoed in my mind ever since. "Success depends less on strength of body than upon strength of mind and character."

• • •

Dad isn't the only seasoned athlete in my immediate family. Mom played Division 1 softball at Austin Peay. My oldest sister, Taylor, was a three-sport athlete; my younger brother, Bradford, is a collegiate football player; and my little sister, Neely, is a Tennessee state champion gymnast. Neely is probably the best athlete of us all, but I would never admit that to her (if you're reading this, Neely, don't let your head get too big). Growing up around Nashville, Tennessee, sports was my thing. My parents didn't have to push me to say yes; I just never said no. And I tried it all—softball, basketball, horseback riding, track. There wasn't a sport I didn't beg my parents to put me in. I was four years old when I started swimming. It was just your typical summer swim that a lot of young kids get involved in.

I don't have a love-at-first-sight story to share with you. I didn't fall in love with the stench of a chlorinated pool at first sniff Nor did I become infatuated with the sport the very first time I won a race at my first meet. In fact, my most vivid early memory in swimming is of six-year-old me desperately trying to convince my mother to not make me swim the mini IM (individual medley) at a meet. All that meant is I had to swim the twenty-five yards (one lap) of backstroke then turn around and swim freestyle back to the wall I started at. I was terrified and used every excuse I could think of in hopes of convincing her to rescue me.

"I can't do it, Mom," I cried through clenched teeth.

"Yes you can, Riley," she encouraged. "And when you do, I promise I'll take you to Target, and I'll buy you whatever you want." This memory perfectly illustrates the philosophical differences between my parents. While Dad would have never stood for my theatrics and likely would have thrown me into the pool himself, Mom was a little more tenderhearted. I mean, at least one parent must have some compassion, right? I don't remember how I did in the mini IM or what I bought at Target, but Mom's brilliant tactic worked.

Despite the deeply rooted trauma from having to swim two laps in a row, every summer my siblings and I came back to swim for our neighborhood team. By the time I was eight, the summer swim coach, Andreea, convinced my parents I had natural talent and should really consider swimming year-round. Coach Andreea was of Romanian descent and relatively new to the United States, so you can imagine I had a hard time understanding her harsh accent at eight years old. It wasn't "kick faster," it was "keek faster!" The number of push-ups I had to do for nodding as if I understood her instructions before pushing off the wall and having no idea what she had just told me is innumerable. Thank goodness having kids of her own softened her, because she would turn into my second mom for the next ten years.

"If you start Riley young," she told my mom and dad, "she could be really good." Ultimately, Andreea prevailed, and I started swimming year-round for a team called Excel Aquatics. Despite being lifelong athletes, my parents never pressured me into swimming. Whether I chose to swim on a higher level or told them I'd rather play the flute (they knew I was the least musically inclined person on this planet, so I guess this wasn't a worry of theirs, but you get the picture), I'd have their full support. At that point, I'm not sure anyone had seismic dreams of me becoming one of the fastest swimmers in the country. But Coach Andreea did point out the good genes I possessed as it pertained to swimming. I had big hands, big feet, and an athletic build. Not going to lie, I was pretty buff for an eight-year-old. According to her, I also had natural abilities that many young kids don't possess. There are certain skills in swimming that are hard if not impossible to teach, such as maintaining a proper body line in the water and being self-aware of what your body position looks and feels like while swimming. I instinctively knew if I was moving my head too much or if my elbows weren't high enough, making my pull inefficient. Recently while coaching my neighborhood summer swim team, I found myself telling the same group of kids to keep their heads down while they swam. Each kid told me they *were* keeping their head down when in reality it was clear to anyone watching that their eyes didn't point to the black line at the bottom of the pool, but rather to the wall they were so desperately trying to reach in front of them. As I mentioned, self-awareness in the water is a hard thing to teach.

It wasn't until high school that I started focusing on things that actually make you faster like form and technique, so until that time, I simply swam laps. I excelled in butterfly and freestyle early on so, naturally, those were my favorites. When I progressed into the 9–10-year-old category, I began breaking team records in various events, most of which I still hold to this day. It still didn't occur to me that I was a pretty good swimmer. Whatever success I was told I had in the pool flew over my head. I never dwelled on the wins. It wasn't something we did, or I guess didn't do, in the Gaines family. Neither Mom nor Dad was the type to celebrate an accomplishment with much fanfare. They used to say, "Don't focus on the past. Don't focus on the future. Be where your feet are." At the time, I didn't understand how broad this advice was, yet I find myself still alluding to it even after finishing my collegiate career. Another one of Dad's favorite lines I've heard thousands of times over the years is "Just keep chopping wood." It's essentially a Southern way of saying, "Keep your head down and don't stop grinding." Remember how I said only one of my parents was tenderhearted and it wasn't him? In fact, I called him a few days ago simply to vent. I was feeling exhausted, overwhelmed, and mentally drained. I don't know what I was thinking expecting even a small smidgen of sympathy. Dad listened before he offered a reply in his thick Southern drawl. "Keep chopping wood, Riley. Just keep chopping."

Other parents would approach mine at meets and say things like, "Wow! Your daughter just got her AAAA time! That's amazing!" Mom and Dad would just smile, nod, and say thank you. They had no idea what the other parents were talking about. "What's an AAAA time?" They were athletes, yes, but not being part of the swimming world, they weren't keen on the lingo. We didn't sit around the table during dinner chatting about best times or fangirling over Olympic swimmers. Nor were Mom and Dad screaming in my ear at every meet ordering me to go faster or demanding that I train harder.

When I was twelve years old, I led the nation in my age category in the 100-yard butterfly. I honestly don't remember much of the details of that race. After I came out of the pool, my coaches swarmed me, alerting me I had just posted the nation's leading time for the event, making me the fastest twelve-year-old girl in the entire country. I just nodded, trying to catch my breath.

By that point, the intensity of the sport had picked up the pace. My life was simple and predictable. Get up early. Swim for a couple hours. School. Swim for a couple hours. Back home for dinner and homework. Ice shoulders if we swam a lot of butterfly that day. Sleep. Do it all over again the next day.

Make no mistake. I've always had a love/hate relationship with swimming. Most swimmers do. Heck, most collegiate athletes of all sports do. From the start and until I finished my career at the

University of Kentucky, I loved being on a team, setting and meeting goals, and being pushed and challenged to keep improving. Weirdly enough, one of my least favorite aspects of swimming was feeling like I was always wet, especially my hair. Despite wearing a swim cap, my hair is still recovering from spending the last eighteen years in a chlorinated pool. Also, though I was used to smelling like chlorine, I can't imagine how the stench hit anyone I passed outside of my swimming circle. Even when I was out of the pool, bleach reeked from every pore. No amount of showers, body wash, or perfume can mask it.

There was one thing I hated the most about competing—losing. I hated losing even more than I loved winning. I'd always been like that. And I still am like that. My husband won't even play Uno with me. I was seven when my family introduced a new Thanksgiving tradition. We figured if we were going to be watching football, we might as well play it. We played our first Turkey Bowl in the backyard, which was just a friendly game of flag football. Football ran in our blood. The Gaines family bred professional football players. Because Mom was an only child, all my cousins came from Dad's side of the family. My dad is the youngest of the brothers, meaning, in turn, my siblings and I were the youngest of the cousins. When it was draft pick time, I and my sister Taylor were chosen last. Shocker.

The absence of puberty, a Y chromosome, speed, power, or experience didn't deter me from giving the game my all. I sprinted until my leg muscles quivered and attempted catches that knocked me splat on my back without much effort. While everyone else seemed to be playing "for fun," I was playing to win. And when my team lost, I took it to heart. You'd think my best friend just told me she was moving away. My world, or at least Thanksgiving that year, imploded. My mom had to shove me into the family photo as the winning team hooted and hollered while holding up their fingers in a "number one" sign. She didn't promise me a trip to Target that day. While everyone else went on with their day after the game, gorging on turkey and stuffing and talking sports, I sulked and scowled. It was at this exact moment when I realized I hated losing more than I loved winning. Losing sucked. But when you play sports all your life, you're not always going to win. It was a lesson I eventually would have to learn.

By the time March 2016 rolled around, I was a sophomore in high school and was a month out from my sixteenth birthday. At this point, I was also a four-time state champion in the 100-yard freestyle and the 100-yard butterfly. When my coaches told me I was on track to qualify for the Olympic Trials, for the first time in my swimming career, a pressure I had never known started living rent free in my head. The "O-word" was filled with magic, untouchable energy, something reserved for superstar athletes. It was real. And it freaked me out. Looking back, I still can't pinpoint the root of my mellow attitude about swimming up to this point. Maybe I was afraid of failing and figured it was better not to care or think about it much. Maybe I wasn't ready to make an all-out commitment to the sport. Either way, listening to my coaches use my name and the words "Olympic Trials" in the same sentence, I suddenly forgot what it meant to "be where your feet are."

The National Club Swimming Association Junior National Championships took place in Orlando, Florida, in March 2016. I was closest to achieving my Olympic Trial cut in the 100-meter freestyle, which had a qualifying time of 56.49 seconds. I had missed it merely by one hundredth of a second three times before, the most recent time by .07 of a second. Not even a blink of the eye. I felt like I was psyching myself out. This event is an all-out sprint. Because it's such a short distance, two 50-meter laps, pretty much the only successful strategy a swimmer has is to swim as fast as you possibly can from the start and pray your legs don't give out before you make it back to the wall again.

I shot off the block and hit the water like a rocket. I remember flip-turning at the halfway point with a feeling I beat my best time in the 50 (I had). As I swam back to touch the wall, my legs burned, starved of oxygen and laden with lactic acid buildup. There was no way I could make them kick any faster. I swum my best time yet, 56.31 seconds. In swimming, it's not just every second that counts. Every hundredth of a second counts.

The trials for the 2016 Summer Olympics were held in Omaha, Nebraska, at the end of June 2016. I'll never forget arriving at the pool a day or two before the meet actually started so I could get acclimated to the pool. I got on the elevator to go down on the pool deck, but the elevator doors opened a floor too early. When the doors separated, my mouth dropped. Michael Phelps stepped into the elevator and stood right next to me. To date, Phelps has won twenty-three Olympic gold medals, the most ever won. It was hard to act cool and not like a fangirl when you're standing right next to a swimming legend. *What am I doing here?* I wondered. *This is crazy!* Without trying to seem like I was freaking out, I hesitantly asked Phelps for a photo, which he graciously posed with me for, and then gave me some great advice. Phelps congratulated me on being at the trials and told me to get this one under my belt; then when I swim at the next trials in 2020 (which turned into 2021 because of COVID), it would be like a weight is off my shoulders since I will have already experienced the hype of this meet. I thanked him and went on my way, still in disbelief. Phelps wasn't the only heavy hitter at this event. Gold medalists from the previous Olympics, including Ryan Lochte, Katie Ledecky, and Missy Franklin, were also qualifying. I added over a second to my time, meaning I was well behind my personal best, but I was just excited to be there, especially being one of the youngest ones on the pool deck. Clearly, I knew I wouldn't qualify to compete at the Olympic Games. I'm hopeful, but not unrealistic. Being at the trials did push me to want to work harder going forward. When I was there, I stalked the top-tier swimmers from afar. I watched what they ate for fuel before they raced and what they ate for recovery after they raced. I observed what stretches they would do before getting on the block. I noticed how long they stayed in the warm-down pool. I was itching to learn their routine and have new skills to learn and tweaks to make when I returned home.

When I was a junior in high school, it was time to choose a college where I could continue excelling in my athletic career. I also wanted to follow the footsteps of my dad and my uncles, who played football in the Southeastern Conference (SEC), the best and most competitive conference, especially in swimming (I know I'm biased, but it's true). Though I was heavily recruited, it was my dream since middle school to become a Florida Gator. Having memorized the university's fight song years earlier, I was ready to "give a cheer for the Orange and Blue."[1] I was always told you would just *know* when you're at the place meant for you. I didn't know what this meant or what it would feel like, but I tried to force this feeling on myself my entire recruiting trip there. You can imagine my disappointment at the end of the weekend when that feeling never came, even when I tried to force it. It's a great school with a stellar academic program and a strong swim team, but I returned home knowing it wasn't the right fit for me. I was so gung-ho on being a Gator that I never even thought about where else I could see myself continuing my swimming career.

I started thinking about the University of Kentucky and the pesky voicemail and email messages Coach Lars Jorgenson of the swim team kept sending me since June 15 of that year. According to NCAA recruiting rules, in most cases, Division 1 coaches are only allowed to reach out to high school athletes via phone, text, and email starting on June 15 after their sophomore year. In fact, the first email I got from any school from any division was from the University of Kentucky at exactly 12:01 a.m. on June 15, 2016. The email invitations to visit the school kept coming. And I continued to blow them off, mainly because they didn't boast a top swim program. Once I realized I wasn't meant to be a Gator, and at the begging of my boyfriend, who at the time was a huge Kentucky fan, I accepted an invitation to visit the school sometime in the late fall. I figured it'd be a nice Christmas gift to give my boyfriend, who would be my plus-one to a Kentucky basketball game the coaches were enticing me with. Don't judge: this was when Kentucky men's basketball was actually good and not losing to the St. Peter's Peacocks. Never in a million years did I think I'd actually fall in love with the school, which, of course I did. And that annoying coach who kept calling and emailing? He became, and still is, one of my best friends. What's the saying, the quickest way to make God laugh is to make plans for yourself?

I remember when Coach Lars, who represented the US in the 1988 Olympics, pulled me into his office on that trip. I was sixteen and a lot shyer and quieter than I am now. He had pictures of some of the UK greats wearing their championship medals all over the office walls. Coach leaned over the desk. "So," he said with a serious face, "are you ready to commit to UK?"

My face turned the color of a tomato in the span of half a second. "Uh, I need some time to think," I sputtered.

It didn't take long. A few days after I returned home, I prayed and thought long and hard about the decision. Kentucky may not have had the finest swim program, but being part of a developing team excited me. Lars had been at the school for five seasons before I got there, and the Wildcats were on an upward trajectory (which isn't hard to do when you start at the bottom). I wanted to help build something great. I also loved the fact that the university had great academic resources and poured into their student athletes regardless of what they accomplished athletically. We were more than just moneymaking machines for the university. Plus, the University of Kentucky was big on community service. While our sport took up most of our time, as a student-athlete, giving back to others and the community was and still is important to me. Once my mind was made up, I canceled the other trips I had planned, and I made the leap of faith. I called Lars and told him I couldn't wait to be a Wildcat.

Unlike most competitive swimmers, I wasn't emotionally or mentally dominated by the sport. Being able to compartmentalize, partially thanks to my dad's relentless lessons on mental fortitude, helped me for the most part to maintain a Zen-like approach to swimming. This wasn't to say I didn't get nervous for big meets, but I internalized the motto "doing your best is the best you can do." Once my suit and goggles were off and I got to leave the pool deck, I tried not to obsess over times I was or wasn't hitting in practice, how I needed to do more dolphin kicks to stay underwater longer after each flip turn, or how sore I felt from squat day the day before. I left swimming at the pool so when I was studying, I could focus on studying; when I was with my friends, I could zone in on them, and when I was sleeping, I could get in my seven or eight hours without monopolizing my snooze time with what I could have done better. This worked, until it didn't.

In the late fall of my senior year in high school, I had seemed to plateau. I stopped improving and getting best times when I would race. I was more fatigued than usual at the end of my races.

I barely had anything to give during that final fifteen yards. I tried tweaking my diet, adding some dryland practice, and changing my technique entirely. Zero improvement. Now, plateaus are common. They usually stem from overtraining or puberty and the body changes that accompany it. This was different. The pressure piled on—of having successful athletic parents, of having to please my coaches and teammates, of having to exceed the expectations of everyone around me. But the source of this pressure wasn't external; it was rooted in me.

There were times at the pool when I'd find myself suddenly out of breath for no reason. It wasn't after a lap like you'd expect, but at random nonactive times like just resting on the wall before a hard set. It felt like a phantom was squeezing my chest in a deathly vise grip. My heart rate would double and the tips of my fingers and toes would feel like blood circulation had just stopped. At times my vision would even start to blur, and I would see stars. These instances started occurring not just during practice, but outside the pool. I noticed the pattern that this would only happen when I thought about swimming and the future I hoped to have as a Kentucky Wildcat.

On December 9, 2017, I had qualified for the Speedo Winter Junior Championships along with other elite swimmers around the nation. The meet was held at the University of Tennessee in Knoxville. Although I was already committed, I knew my future coaches from Kentucky would be there to recruit from the class below me, and I was a ball of nerves. Long story short, I did awful. I added tons of time in every event I swam.

One of the assistant coaches texted me right after I swam a horrible race: "Don't leave before you see me." My heart started beating out of my chest while my stomach coiled in thick knots. *It was over,* I convinced myself. He was going to tell me the University of

Kentucky was changing their mind and was rescinding my offer and scholarship. I was so distraught from imagining my worst fear that I didn't text him back. But this wasn't like ghosting a bad date. Ignoring a future coach won't make him disappear. I tried to escape the pool without seeing him, but he was posted near the door I had to use to leave the complex. He approached the conversation with concern and desperately tried to convince me to graduate from high school in December of my senior year so I could move to Lexington as soon as possible and get training with the team. That wasn't an option. I made plans to move to campus right after I graduated the following year. In the meantime, these breathless episodes continued.

Mom had been scuttling me from doctor to doctor to get to the bottom of what I was struggling with. Though there was initial concern that I suffered from a recurrence of childhood asthma, my physician finally determined there was nothing physically wrong with me. He diagnosed anxiety attacks. Looking back, of course that was it. He prescribed a low and short-term dosage of antianxiety medication, which helped me quell the nerves and reclaim my focus. Between the plateau and battling the burden of pressure I placed on myself, I had to begin to understand that I wasn't always going to get best times at every meet. I wasn't always going to make finals. I wasn't always going to be in lane 4. And that was okay. I could only do my best each day. Go in, work as hard as I could, leave, and don't think about it.

When I got to college and started a new weight lifting routine, I beat the plateau. Coach Lars would always tell us, "Even when you feel depleted, you still have forty percent to give." He never told us where he got the research from or how he came up with that 40 percent number, but I believed him. And somehow, it worked.

But wait, I'm getting ahead of myself. By the time I graduated from high school, I was a seven-time Tennessee state champion, an Olympic trial qualifier, a multiple-time Junior National–qualifying swimmer, a CSCAA Scholastic All-American, and, most excitingly, a future Kentucky Wildcat.

The college drop-off in the summer of 2018 was memorable. My mom stayed home and tended to the little siblings; I don't think she wanted to cry in public saying goodbye to me. My dad had the honor of driving me the three hours to Lexington. We did the typical dorm room shopping spree and bought boring things like a laundry basket, some bath towels, and school supplies. Dad offered to get groceries while I went to a mandatory orientation for student-athletes arriving to campus. We both returned to my dorm around the same time.

Dad carried one grocery bag. In it, a jumbo pack of Oscar Meyer hot dogs, a bottle of ketchup and mustard, and toothpaste. That is it. After he handed me my apparent grocery stash for the semester, he gave me a bear hug, looked straight into my eyes, and said, "Brush your teeth. Say your prayers. And know I'd run here barefoot for you. If you ever needed anything." And that was that.

I was on my own.

2.

SOMETHING IN THE WATER

M y muscles, even ones I didn't even know I had, hated me my entire first year at Kentucky. The weight room was an all-new space, and I was in an endless state of soreness from the training we had to endure. I'd never attempted a pull-up or incorporated squats into my swimming routine, and it took a while before my muscles forgave me.

I arrived on campus in June to start training early and take a few courses. I competed with my UK teammates at national-level meets before the fall semester even began. Once the excitement of being away from my parents wore off, the reality of fourteen practices a week, classes, and feeling like little fish in a giant collegiate sea set in.

As a high-level recruit, I always felt a low-level undercurrent of pressure to prove myself. Every day was an opportunity to learn and adjust, thanks to strength training for the first time, regularly getting lost on campus, keeping on top of schoolwork—which seemed impossible—and not having my siblings and my parents just down the hall. What I had were my best friends, which also, of course, happened to be my teammates, Sophie and Izzy. Sophie was my roommate and had bright red hair. You would never see one of us without the other following closely behind. We were often referred to as Tweedle Dee and Tweedle Dum. Izzy was one of the most intense athletes and hardest workers I'd ever met. When she became a cocaptain in our junior and senior year, she was the one everyone was intimidated of, but in a good way. As freshmen, the three of us were naturally clueless, but as the saying goes, there is always strength in numbers—and we were always together.

• • •

Lars was instrumental in turning a lackluster swim team into champions. When he began coaching Kentucky's program in 2012, the school was consistently ranked at the bottom of the SEC year after year. Within a few years, he and the team changed course. In 2016, Danielle Galyer won UK's first NCAA swimming title in the 200-yard backstroke. The victory charged momentum. The following season the team finished top three at SECs and fourteenth at the NCAA Championships, the best our school had done under Lars and in a decade. The Wildcats repeated the same success in 2018, making another top-fifteen finish on a national stage, two years in a row. Asia Seidt excelled in 2018 when she became a 16-time All-American and won her fourth SEC gold medal. During that same season, Coach Lars was responsible for helping the swim program set a total of thirteen school records.

Lars's goal was to enforce a positive and healthy team culture knowing that it would, in turn, bring athletic success. His mindset about winning wasn't solely focused on swimming. It wasn't just about being the top swimmers in the nation; it was about being women of great character and students who excel in the classroom as well. Take Danielle Galyer, for instance. She didn't just bring home a national title; she also won the Elite 90 award for having the highest GPA at that same national championships. Lars made sure his swimmers were successful not just in their four years as a Wildcat, but for the rest of their lives. As far as the actual sport, his philosophy was that the freshman team had to be better than the seniors who left the year before if we wanted to continue climbing the ladder. To this day, I can count on him for anything. Not that I'm ever expecting this to happen, but if I ever landed in jail, he'd be my first phone call.

All that being said, I didn't exactly mesh with Lars at first. In fact, I thought he sucked. I should rephrase. I didn't think he sucked at his job. Clearly, he was knowledgeable and was very well accomplished in his athletic and coaching career. But personality-wise, he seemed to have no understanding of the adversity that we as student-athletes faced, especially us freshmen. I was used to keeping my feet on the ground and "chopping wood," so I wasn't looking for reassurances or compliments. But I didn't expect utter savagery. In the beginning of freshman year, he continually addressed me as a LOFT. I had no idea what this meant and never questioned it until one day I mustered up the courage to ask. I was told it means "Lack of F***ing Talent." Ah, cool, thanks.

I get the tough-love approach, but constant criticism doesn't do much except break a girl's spirit. At one point in my freshman year, I began documenting all the harsh words he said to me and wrote them down in a journal. It was cathartic. I used it not to feel sorry for myself, but to fuel the competitive spirit in me. And Lars knew this. That's exactly why he did this. He didn't actually think I was a LOFT. This was just his way of seeing how we liked to be motivated. He would test it out on the freshmen once we arrived on campus and pick out the ones who could take it and the ones who required a different approach to reach their fullest potential. While I wasn't his only scapegoat, the whole team observed as I tended to receive the brunt of it. I felt somewhat relieved when one of my teammates and upperclassmen told me, "Don't sweat it. Start worrying once he *stops* being hard on you."

Swimming in college was life-consuming, to say the least. I imagine all collegiate sports are like that, but swimming . . . there are no adequate superlatives to describe the grueling demands it made of us. You don't get the kind of social college experience an average student enjoys—like indulging the freedom to do whatever you want in the absence of your parents, going to parties, drinking, doing stupid things because you're young and dumb. Swimming was my life. It was all our lives. There were a few full weeks each year I couldn't even go to classes because of meets. And unfortunately, these weeklong meets often fell during finals. I was still required to carry an academic load, of course, which is why the university gave the student-athletes tutors and access to additional resources to help us get our work done and understand the material. Some professors were accommodating to athletes, but most were not. Outside of studying and being in the weight room, my life was in the pool. There were a few funerals I couldn't attend, some weddings I couldn't go to. We didn't get to come home for summer, or Thanksgiving break, or Christmas break. Rather than getting time off, the intensity and practice schedule got more extreme over these breaks. Rather than fourteen training sessions a week, it amped up to sixteen. We added two more swim workouts each week into a schedule that seemed like it had no viable room for this. God forbid we had time to even remotely do anything social or take time to recover. We got a week off in August each year and that was it. I was a chlorine-drenched rat for four consecutive years, training to get faster, more efficient in my technique, and stronger in my body. Like all collegiate sports, either you're all in or you're not.

My favorite Bible verse is Romans 8:18. It always has been. "Our present sufferings are not worth comparing with the glory that will be revealed in us" (NIV). I related this verse to swimming, because the sport truly was suffering; that said, the sacrifices it required paled in comparison to that feeling when you get a new best time, set a record, or win. The benefits of being on a team made the grueling practices worth it. There was nothing like being surrounded with an instant sisterhood and camaraderie of skilled athletes I could learn from, rely on, and grow with. Not that the comradeship vibe was in full effect my freshman year. We had a successful team, but I saw and felt the superiority from the upperclassmen. I would often hear conversations between the seniors who were grouped together in the locker room gossiping about the underclassmen and vowed to myself that if I ever got into a position of leadership on the team, I would do my best to cultivate an environment that was both challenging and benevolent. Elite teams can't afford negativity.

Lars never eased up on his hard-driving tough-love approach, even after I proved I was at least in some way an asset to the team by scoring points throughout the dual meets earlier in my first season. One day toward the end of freshman year, I'd had enough of what felt like constant persecution. Lars had each of us race 2,000 yards, which is about 80 laps, somewhere around 1.2 miles. It was a "test set," meaning he wanted to test our fitness and use our performance as a benchmark because we would eventually do this again later in the season and throughout our time at UK in hopes to get better each time. And keep in mind that a 2,000 is not a sprint, unless you can all-out sprint while starving yourself of oxygen for somewhere around twenty minutes at minimum. I was not a long-distance swimmer, and I had no interest in proving myself to be, so I didn't care too much about how I performed. Of course, I would do my best, but I didn't feel it was very indicative of what success should look like for me. Maybe not the best mindset to have, but it made sense to me.

When we finished, Lars walked up to the huge whiteboard he would use to write out our practice, motivational quotes, or illegible symbols indicating either encouragement or critical feedback. One by one, he wrote down our names and times in the 2,000, from the fastest to the slowest. I ended up finishing somewhere in the middle of the pack on a team of about thirty-five girls. When he was done, he pulled all the girls out of the water, looked straight at me, and scoffed in front of the entire team. "Riley," he said with a smirk, "you'll never be on a relay. If this was a basketball team, you certainly wouldn't be one of the starting five. Heck, you wouldn't even be on the bench." To his point, the girls who did consistently swim on relays ranked near the top, not middle of the pack.

I saw red. Instead of saving my rage and writing down his words in a notebook later, I wanted to wring his neck now and in front of everyone. Gritting my teeth, I shot right back. "Well, if there was such thing as an eight thousand relay, then you may be right. But there isn't and you know that. This isn't an accurate indicator of anything of any relevance at all." That wasn't entirely true, swimming longer distances like that is beneficial in building endurance, but ranking in the middle didn't mean much, at least not for the events I knew I would compete for in UK. You never see four swimmers in the NCAA doing a relay of 2,000 yards each. I should have stopped there, but I could see the slight grins on the other girls' faces as I had finally said something a lot of us were feeling. I continued. "The only thing this indicates is who can get through the misery of doing a two thousand the fastest, and props to them."

I could have sworn Lars smiled after I finally got a backbone and piped up. Looking back, his attempts to make me unhinged all along was a means to an end. He *wanted* me to be assertive and stand up for myself. That day, I began to understand the fine balance of managing tough love—something I learned growing up with my dad—and not allowing myself to crumble in moments I knew the toughness crossed a line. Since that day standing in front of that whiteboard with a list of all our names and, to me, meaningless times, Lars and I began to openly build a respect for each other. A deep friendship was born.

• • •

There was an empty spot in the 800-freestyle relay, the longest (and most dreaded) relay in the sport of swimming. The relay consisted of a senior and two standout juniors, two of which were individual SEC champions and the other who was an Olympian representing New Zealand, but the fourth spot was up in the air. Eventually, I was pulled in. Me, a freshman! Three extremely strong legs and a risky one that could make or break the relay. To add to the mounting pressure of performing with seasoned athletes was the fact that Kentucky was historically known for performing well in this relay specifically.

Days before the race, the three swimmers approached me with a sobering mix of encouragement and gravity. In so many words they said, "We need you, Riley. It's up to you. If you don't perform well, you'll be letting down your team. We believe in you." My reply was quick and confident. "I got it," I promised. I showed zero sign of weakness, at least externally. On the inside, the butterflies in my stomach felt like battering rams.

With my nerves trapped in overdrive, I couldn't sleep the night before the event. Practically burned a hole through my sheet with all the tossing and turning. The words of the three team captains haunted me. It's up to you, Riley. You must do good. The message wasn't a threat, it was the truth. This SEC championships wasn't their first rodeo. As a freshman, I was the one who had everything to prove. I was almost grateful I couldn't fall asleep. God forbid I had a nightmare in which I bombed the race and was the teammate who let the rest of the team down. By the time I was in the ready room, my fear morphed into focus. It was like a flip switched. I couldn't afford to be bullied by pressure or to calculate what-if scenarios. I had to perform. And we did. We broke the school record in the process.

We finished in third with University of Tennessee winning. This one hurt considering that my siblings and I weren't allowed to even wear the color orange growing up because of my dad's career at Vanderbilt. We were only separated by a few tenths of a second. With that confidence boost under my belt, I wanted to achieve more. We qualified for NCAAs with this relay. While I was honored to have achieved my first SEC medal, I was disappointed I hadn't individually qualified for NCAAs. Only the top forty girls in the country in each event do, and while I was improving, I wasn't a standout. Well, I had three more years left.

As 2020 rolled out, my times improved, and I started making a greater impact individually. I had finally developed a sense of consistency among all aspects of training. I was having good practices every day. I brought a good attitude to each practice. I built up a proper regime in my diet, sleep schedule, and recovery methods. I even became consistent in my study habits and within my personal relationships. I made the all-SEC team again and swam my fastest 200-yard butterfly, finishing tenth in the conference. I also swam a best time in the 200-yard freestyle, coming in at eleventh, and helped bring the 800 freestyle relay team a silver medal. I was having my breakout season. This time, I qualified for the NCAA Championships individually in those events. Here was my chance.

• • •

A few days before we were to leave for the 2020 NCAA Division 1 Swimming and Diving Championships, I was sitting in class when a notification buzzed on my phone. The NCAA was canceling their basketball tournament because of the COVID-19 outbreak. March Madness had taken on a whole new meaning. I kind of knew what the virus was at this point based off what I had seen in the news and how other countries were responding, but I guess I didn't understand the severity of it and its implications. In my mind, it was a sickness contained in China that wasn't disrupting life as we knew it here in the US, at least until now. If basketball was being canceled, it seemed imminent that swimming and other sports would follow. Or maybe because swimming wasn't as mainstream and bringing in as much revenue as basketball, we would be free to compete? There was so much uncertainty at this point. The vibe at practice later that day was off. Normally at this point in the season there is so much excitement, but the mood was unusually quiet. We walked on eggshells the whole practice. We wanted to talk about the possibility of the meet not happening, the meet we worked all year for, but it felt wrong to do so. We were a team built around optimism, but were we avoiding facing reality by dismissing the different possible outcomes entirely? I remember looking at my phone after practice and reading a message that made my heart fall. The ACC had dropped out of NCAAs. Then, more messages.

Pac-12 followed suit. What kind of NCAA Championship would this be if the powerhouses like Stanford weren't even competing? As a team we weren't told anything, so, naturally, we left for dinner. There I was eating chicken fingers at Raising Canes with my roommate and my then-boyfriend-now-husband, Louis, a swimmer on the men's team, when our phones chimed at the same time. I will never forget the feeling of dread reading that message that was sent from our coaches to both the men's and women's NCAA qualifiers: return to the pool now.

When we left the pool after practice just half an hour before, it was bright and sunny. When we returned, rain was pouring down in sheets. This foreshadowing was like every predictable, somber scene in a rom-com movie. A deafening crack of lightning brightened the sky as we joined the rest of the team who had qualified for NCAAs waiting inside. We gathered in the team room silent, sopping wet on chairs with puddles forming on the floor. Lars spoke first. He had tears in his eyes. Not only was the NCAA canceling all winter and spring sports, he told us, but the university was halting all in-person classes and activities. Classes would be given online until further notice. He told us that if we lived in the dorms (which I did) we had to pack up our stuff and leave campus within the next twenty-four hours. Getting told by our coach to go home in mid-March was the most bizarre thing to comprehend. Are we excited because the season is over, something we eagerly anticipate from the minute the season starts? Are we upset because we had an entire year's, really an entire lifetime's worth of hard work stripped from us? There were more questions than answers that day. Really, there were no answers.

Admittedly, I felt a little bit of both of those feelings. Excited for some much-needed recovery and time at home. I figured this just meant a few days before we would return to campus, and remember, we never got to go home. But of course, I felt like we were robbed in a way as well. This was my chance to shine and continue the breakout season I was having. This was our chance to achieve what we'd never done before as a team. I can't even imagine how the seniors processed this devastating news. At the time, they had no idea that, eventually, Kentucky would close the campus for the rest of the semester, canceling all in-person events, including graduation. My heart broke for those girls who didn't ever get closure on their athletic careers.

On my drive home the next day, I chose to embrace going home and our season being cut short since there was really no other option and I still thought this stint would be very brief. It was a chance to spend quality time with family, something I didn't get to do much since leaving for Lexington almost two years ago. The excitement was short-lived after arriving in Nashville as I noticed a running theme. Everything was closing. Stores. Pools. Gyms. Unlike most sports, there are not a lot of substitutes for a pool. And dryland practice, while great for conditioning, doesn't quite cut it for helping you maintain your swimming edge. Swimming isn't a natural human function like running or other land sports. Unfortunately, as humans we don't have gills. How were we individually going to keep in shape? In an interview Michael Phelps gave to *Forbes*, he said, "I went five straight years without missing a single day of workout, 365 days a year. Every day I was in the water. And in the sport of swimming, when you miss one day, it takes you two days to get back."[1] Without practice, it was inevitable we'd return athletically hindered, each to a different degree but most likely for the rest of our careers.

I don't take lightly the blessing I had growing up in a house near a lake, especially when it served as a training ground from March through August of 2020. Old Hickory Lake was my saving grace. Sheathed in a wet suit, I'd warm up by swimming 400–500 meters in a little cove just off the Saundersville boat ramp, then swim about 4,000–5,000 meters out to the dock where Johnny Cash used to live, then swim back to the cove where I'd work on individual strokes and get a few more 500-meter laps in. The number of snakes and dead catfish floating on the surface I swam into wasn't very pleasant, to say the least.

Swimming in a pool versus open water is very different. In a pool, the black line is your constant companion. It keeps you straight. It reminds you that you're not alone. By now, I'd spent thousands of hours staring a black line in the pool. Of course, open water doesn't have this. And even if it did, you wouldn't be able to see it. I couldn't even see my hand stretched out in front of me when I swam freestyle. This kind of swimming requires hyper-vigilance and naturally a different type of stroke. Rather than just following a black line, keeping your head down, and breathing to the side every couple of strokes, open water requires lifting your head while looking in the straightforward direction to peek where you're going and then breathe. Once you get over the mental hurdle of not being able to see the bottom and very little in front of you, swimming is swimming. Still, they felt like two totally different sports.

Returning to campus as a junior was, to use one of the most frequently quoted words of 2020, "unprecedented." I was allowed back with a negative COVID and an antibody test. It was back when medical providers needed to shove the swab as far up your nostril as your brain, or at least it felt that way. Masks were required, even for us swimmers, which felt silly. While we swimmers didn't have to wear a mask in the pool, as soon as our feet touched dryland, out they came. All we heard all year was "Get your masks on." Covering my nose and mouth with wet, scratchy material while my lungs tried to draw in air and my body craved oxygen was unnatural. It felt like we were waterboarding ourselves every time we put the masks on straight after getting out of the water. But this was our new normal. Every few weeks, there was a new twist on the COVID rules. One week, it was okay to nix the six-feet social distancing space; another week it wasn't. One week we could all be considered close contacts if someone on the team tested positive; the next week we wouldn't be.

When the COVID vaccines started rolling out in the beginning of 2021, most swimmers got the jab out of convenience and fear of testing positive or being contact traced, which would result in more time out of the water. Let me emphasize that I'm not an anti-vaxxer. I believe in medicine, and I get my flu shot every year. I believe in science. I also believe people should be free to choose what concoctions they voluntarily put in their body. In my mind, I was young. I was healthy. I also had natural immunity from the antibodies since I had gotten COVID at home before returning to campus my junior year.

I didn't hide my lack of vaccination status from anyone on the team. I also didn't position myself on a soapbox and tell others to join or support my cause. I just trusted myself and decided I wasn't going to be coerced into doing something I didn't feel certain about. By the time there were about only four out of forty girls unvaccinated on the women's swim team, the pressure started piling. From threatening not to allow us to participate in meets, to forcing us to take weekly COVID tests unnecessarily early in the morning, sometimes multiple times a week, to hearing whispers from our athletic trainer that I was "holding back" the team because I refused to get the shot—tactic after tactic was used to change my mind, although at the same time, the athletic department and the university didn't technically require vaccines. The university liked to use the word "mandatory," but understand that that word does not equal "law." While the vaccinated were able to keep their masks off, mine had to stay on. It wasn't until the end of my senior year that I could finally workout in the weight room without wearing one. Not getting the vaccine was really the first time I learned to stand up for myself and tell authority figures "no." Even with the mental drain from all the manipulation, intimidation, and fearmongering, I'm glad I didn't get it.

• • •

Life back in school wasn't all COVID chaos. At the beginning of the season, I, along with a few other girls, including Sophie and Izzy, were chosen as captains for the women's swim team. The process was very democratic. Each swimmer received a sheet of paper with thirty or so questions. Each question asked for the name of a swimmer on the team who possessed a certain characteristic essential to captain material (examples: Who is the most selfless? Who is the most encouraging? Who can you count on under pressure?). The coaches would tally up the names and the ones who got the most votes won. It was an honor to be chosen (and to be picked again in my senior year). I didn't forget the promise I made to myself when I was a freshman.

Goal setting sat at the top of my agenda as a captain. We did this as a team at the beginning of every season. Yet I noticed, at least in my case, that I'd share some general and vague goals, but in a matter of weeks, I'd all but forget them until it was time for championship season, when it was too late to act on these goals. There are so many benefits to having a goal. For one, you can't hit a bull's-eye without a bull's-eye in sight. Psychology professor Dr. Gail Matthews conducted a study that showed people who wrote down their goals were 33 percent more successful in reaching them.[2] Not only that, but she discovered that 70 percent of people who shared their goals with others achieved what they set out to do. I wanted to be intentional in challenging each other to get better in whatever area of life we needed to improve. As captains, we sat everyone down one day at the beginning of the season, gave them each a brown paper bag and a marker, and asked them to write down their goals on the front of the bag. Goals didn't only have to be swimming oriented, but they did need to be SMART (specific, measurable, attainable, realistic, and time-bound). Mine were: 1) drink half my body weight in ounces of water each day; 2) achieve new weight room maxes in squat, bench press, and pull-ups; 3) make the A final in all three of my events as SECs; and 4) pray every day. Everyone was given permission to hold each other accountable for their goals throughout the season. At any time, any one of us could check in with a swimmer if any habits needed to change.

Next, we asked everyone to look inside the bag, where they would find thirty-nine blank note cards. "I want you to write an encouraging note to every person on the team," I said, "so when you're having a bad day or a bad practice, you can reach in and pull one note, or twenty, and remind yourself that your teammates love you, they value you, and they need you. And make these notes specific. Tell your teammates *why* they matter!" It took a while, but when we were done, we exchanged the note cards and taped the back side of the brown paper bags on the front of our lockers so we could all read each other's goals for the entirety of the season.

One of the goals we set for ourselves as a team after returning to campus following the COVID hiatus was to win an SEC championship, something our swim and dive program at UK had never done. With the title, came something else: custom-designed rings blinged out in diamonds and precious gems. Think Super Bowl rings, but ones that don't cost upwards of thirty thousand dollars.[3] My mind was made up. We were getting rings. It gave us a visual and tangible object to work toward, which kept the team focused. So, at every practice and team meeting, I'd reinforce the hard truth that we had to do what it took each day starting at the beginning of the season to get a ring come February 2021.

My junior year I was able to continue the breakout performances I was having my sophomore year before everything shut down, in large part thanks to Old Hickory Lake. The seniors were gone, and it was my time to step up and not just keep pace but set a new precedent. I continued training for the 100- and 200-yard freestyle. I wasn't a fan of the 500 because it was too long for me, and I wasn't tall enough or explosive enough to be great at the 50. My coaches would put me in the 200 fly now and again, and although I never really trained for it, I learned to power through it well. Halfway through the season in the Mizzou midseason invite, I clinched first in the 100 freestyle, 200 freestyle, and 200 butterfly, breaking my first individual Kentucky team records in the freestyle events.

When we faced Louisville, our in-state rivals, in January 2021, the Wildcats won thirteen out of sixteen events. I won the 50, 100, and 200 freestyle, resetting my 100 freestyle school record, which ranked me as the eighth fastest in the country. The SEC championship was now only a few weeks away. That goal was getting crossed off my brown paper bag.

Kentucky made history in February 2021. We scored the highest number of points in the school's history, and for the first time ever, brought back an SEC championship to campus. I was honored to be part of the 800 relay that clinched the title. I won the 200 freestyle (1:42.70) and, for the third time in the season, broke the school record in the 100 freestyle, earning sixth place in the conference. My time in the 200 butterfly was my personal best, 1:55.10, and brought me to fourth place. This meet is one of my favorite swimming memories because we saw in real time the culmination of hard work paying off. Each conference team gets to bring a combination of twenty-two swimmers and divers. Every single athlete on my team contributed points, which is a rare feat. Normally, a team has a few standout swimmers that carry the rest of the team, but not at UK. Every swimmer and diver who made the conference team scoring individual points for the team showed Lars's ability to develop all swimmers to their fullest potential, not just the ones who were already standouts when they came to college.

We went on to compete in the NCAA with an eleventh-place finish, a personal best, and, again, the most points scored at this meet in school history. I was named a first-team All-American and ultimately finished seventh in the country in the 200 freestyle, posting a 1:44.67.

And how about those championship rings? A little backstory. Because all forty girls constantly used a visual of the rings to symbolize our team's goal, we wanted the best of the best. A few days after we had submitted our custom-design ring to the assistant athletic director, he came back and told us they couldn't accommodate our request. It was "too expensive and didn't fit in the budget." Really? I've seen the men's basketball team's championship rings. And I've seen the rings our football team of more than one hundred get for winning a bowl game, not even an SEC championship. Now, I know these are the sports that bring in revenue to the university. I'm not naïve, but we made school history with this being the first in SEC championship for UK's swim and dive program. As one of the team's captains, I was determined to fix this. Bypassing the liaison who initially turned us away, I personally contacted the athletic director, Mitch Barnhart, directly. Let's just say, a few weeks later, we were all wearing the exact rings we had originally designed.

• • •

As soon as I placed seventh in the country my junior year, I immediately made it my goal to win a national title my senior year, which would mean becoming the fastest female in the country in my respective event. And it was all I could think about. Midway through the season, I was on pace to accomplish that goal. I was ranked third in the country in the 200 freestyle. I was very familiar with the swimmer who was ranked just ahead of me at second in the nation. Our times were only a couple hundredths or tenths of a second apart. I didn't, however, recognize the swimmer leading the country. I had never heard of this person before. This was the first time I became aware of a swimmer named Lia Thomas swimming for the University of Pennsylvania.

There was a lot of head scratching, for many reasons. First, top-tier athletes know of each other regardless of where they compete in the country. It didn't matter that the girl in second swam at a university in California, because we had grown up competing against each other. At that level, if we didn't know each other on a personal level, we at the very least are familiar with each other's names as we see each other at events all the time. None of my coaches or teammates had ever heard of this Lia Thomas swimmer.

Second, this swimmer was a senior. No one just appears out of nowhere their senior year of college, as girls typically peak at a younger age. Another red flag was that this person was from the University of Pennsylvania, which is not a school historically known for producing fast swimmers. This university had never produced a national champion. As a team, they had never even scored in the top 25 ranked teams. Lastly, this swimmer was ranked at the top in the 100 freestyle and all the freestyle events in between that through the mile (1,650 yards). Well-known swimming fact (really, it's a well-understood reality among any endurance sport): swimmers excel in either sprints or long distance. Of course, you can have swimmers good at both, but this sport has never seen one person be the best at both at the highest level. Think about this in terms of Olympic runners; the woman leading the nation in the 200-meter sprint isn't going to lead the nation in the marathon as well.

When I dug a little deeper, the plot thickened. Not only was Thomas virtually unknown, but this swimmer was winning races by large margins. In a meet against Columbia University on November 5, 2021, Thomas won first in the 200 freestyle by 5.4 seconds. Two weeks later, Thomas broke the school record at UPenn in the 200 freestyle, placing first by 6.1 seconds. Watch any swimming meet and pay attention to the top three swimmers. You'll rarely see a difference that wide in final times. At the same meet, Thomas won the 500 freestyle by 12.9 seconds.

Who is this person?

I couldn't figure it out. How does a phenom of a female swimmer appear out of nowhere? When I looked up Lia Thomas in the USA Swimming database, this swimmer's records only began that season. How was that possible if Thomas was obviously a seasoned athlete?

Plot twist.

A few days after these nation-leading times were posted, my coach sent me a link to an article that ended the head-scratching. It also unlocked the beginning of a future I could have never imagined. The article said:

The Penn women were led by Lia Thomas, who put up another round of record-breaking swims. Thomas, a swimmer who is a transgender woman, spent the first 3 seasons of her collegiate eligibility swimming for the Penn men's team. In prelims of the women's 500 free this morning, Thomas clocked a 4:46.42, clipping the meet record.[4]

Did I just read that Thomas swam three seasons in college for the men's team? And was that sentence just thrown into the text as if it were another stat or analysis of a time swam? I read that sentence and I read it again. And then I read it again. I was, of course, shocked, but really, I felt a sense of relief after reading and digesting this. It explained the wide margins and how this person was able to blow his competition out of the water. Lia Thomas wasn't a phenom of a swimmer; Lia Thomas was a male.

I wasn't brand-new to the transgender conversation in athletics. I knew of Schuyler Bailar, who swam for Harvard University. This was different, though, and didn't spark as much controversy because this was a female identifying as a man, therefore swimming in the men's division as a female. In 2015, Bailar was the first openly transgender swimmer in NCAA history. I hadn't given Bailar and her transition journey much thought. No one's success was being threatened by her participation with the men. It wasn't a lifestyle choice I'd make for myself, but I didn't care how Schuyler chose to live her adult life. Except, of course, when it starts affecting other people in a way that impedes common sense and fairness and our rights to privacy.

Thomas began setting school records at the University of Pennsylvania, Ivy League records, and pool records. Out of nowhere, this person took the swimming community by storm in becoming the fastest female swimmer in the nation in the 500 freestyle, 4:34:06. He also won the mile at 15:59.71, clocking in by more than 37 seconds over second place.

In December 2021, after the news had infiltrated into the swimming world, Lia Thomas, known formerly as William Thomas, stepped out of the water to talk about his journey to becoming a self-proclaimed woman. Thomas swam for the last time on the men's team during the 2018–19 season, began taking hormone replacement therapy in the spring of 2019, and spent the 2020–21 season entirely out of the water before ultimately coming back and swimming the 2021–22 season on the women's team. Before transitioning, Thomas's rankings against other males the year prior were mediocre at best. Thomas ranked 65th in the 500 freestyle, 554th in the 200 freestyle, and worse than 3,000th in the 100 freestyle. He never even qualified for NCAAs in the men's category. Among the women, he finished 1st, 5th, and 8th respectively in those same events. As of January 7, 2022, Thomas ranked first in the NCAA in the women's 200 freestyle and 500 freestyle, and 6th in the 1650 free. He was able to achieve these top times even with taking the entire previous year out of the water with "off and on" training. No girl would ever be able to take a year off and just jump right in and compete at this level again.

An anonymous swimmer from Thomas's team spoke out against what looked to be from the outside a cohesive unit in full support of this new male team member: "Pretty much everyone individually has spoken to our coaches about not liking this. Our coach [Mike Schnur] just really likes winning. He's like most coaches. I think secretly everyone just knows it's the wrong thing to do. . . . When the whole team is together, we have to be like, 'Oh my gosh, go Lia, that's great, you're amazing.' It's very fake."[5]

This anonymous swimmer wasn't alone. The majority of Kentucky's swim team, coaches and trainers included, did not support a male competing on a women's team, let alone at the NCAA Championships, which were scheduled for March 2022.

There was no way Lia Thomas would be allowed to compete. How could the NCAA see the facts presented and *not* see it how I saw it? And how my parents saw it? And how my teammates saw it? It wasn't opinionated or hateful. It was the fact that this swimmer went from being ranked 462nd among the men the year prior to now demolishing every girl in the country . . . by body lengths. Having undergone male puberty, Thomas's road to victory on the women's team was not a lateral movement. Surely the NCAA would acknowledge this obvious fact. Two months out from the championships, the organization still had not decided. As Thomas continued to demolish his competitors, I waited for someone to step up and advocate for us female athletes. No one did. Apparently, asking for equal opportunities for women in sports was way too controversial.

3.

GO TIME!

Under a 2010 NCAA rule, Thomas was eligible to participate on Penn's women's swim team because he had undergone at least twelve months of hormone therapy, which Thomas allegedly started in May 2019. According to the same policy, the organization's mandated threshold for testosterone levels in males who identified as women was 10 nmol/L.[1] For context, females produce between 0.5 to 2.4 nmol/L, meaning the minimum testosterone level enforced by the NCAA was still around ten times the average of the level females possess.[2] We will dive more deeply into what this really means regarding male advantage later. Competing in our category at our NCAA Championships, however, was an unanswered question come the start of 2022.

On January 19, rather than revisiting their policy and making their own decision, the NCAA stated this issue would be determined on a sport-by-sport basis via each governing body of that sport. If there was no policy in place, they would defer to the policy for the sport's international federation.[3] In other words, the

NCAA took a hands-off approach to this matter and left the onus in the hands of the national swimming governing bodies—USA Swimming, the International Federation of Swimming (FINA), and the International Olympic Committee (IOC). Thomas would need to comply with the decision of USA Swimming's policy makers.[4]

At the beginning of February, USA Swimming announced its new policy. In regard to male "elite athletes" identifying as women, which includes swimmers starting at age thirteen who desire to compete for American records (that is, Lia Thomas), it enacted strict rules and procedures. This national organization acknowledged competitive differences in the male and female categories that were, in their words, "supported by statistical data that shows that the top-ranked female in 2021, on average, would be ranked 536th across all short course yards (25 yards) male events in the country and 326th across all long course meters (50 meters) male events in the country, among USA Swimming members. The policy therefore supports the need for competitive equity at the most elite levels of competition."[5]

USA Swimming also demanded that males who had begun to transition provide evidence that their physical development did not present a competitive advantage over female competitors. In addition, the revised policy required that testosterone levels must be less than 5 nmol/L continuously for a minimum of thirty-six months. I thought this was a satisfactory first step in prioritizing fairness. Not perfect, but it meant USA Swimming said Thomas shouldn't be able to compete with the women based on his competitive advantage. So, the NCAA will adopt this policy, right? Wrong.

Ten days later, the NCAA retreated from their previous statement of agreeing to comply with USA Swimming's policy. The

NCAA announced that its previous policy would remain unchanged, which aligned with the approach adopted by the International Olympic Committee. It was apparent to me that the NCAA was attempting to rid themselves of any responsibility and accountability by looking to another governing body to essentially craft these guidelines for them. Looking ahead, FINA would not change their policy until June 2022, which passed with a 71 percent majority. At that time, this organization enacted one of the stricter policies concerning transgender athletes. Their current policy states that males who identify as women are only eligible to compete at the highest levels of women's international competition if they began testosterone suppression before puberty or by the age of twelve, whichever came later.[6] In addition, male athletes vying to compete in the women's category must have "continuously maintained their testosterone levels below 2.5 nmol/L."[7]

This was really the first governing body to take a bold first step in prioritizing fairness in sports. Of course, insinuating that a child should be able to and could medically transition by the age of twelve is deeply concerning—even criminal in many states with laws banning gender modification in children. Nonetheless, this was a small victory in putting facts before feelings. FINA put together these guidelines with experts that included athletes, scientists, and individuals advocating for legal and human rights. It was ultimately FINA's ruling that restricted Lia Thomas from taking an Olympic spot on the women's team, a goal he was determined to achieve, as expressed in some interviews following the NCAA Championship. By the way, we swimmers don't know what Thomas's level of testosterone was at the time of competition. Not that it matters . . . even if his testosterone levels were 0 nmol/L it would still be inherently wrong.

When I found out the NCAA wasn't changing their policy and therefore was allowing Thomas to compete in the championships, I knew it wasn't right. It didn't make any sense. I was frustrated and confused, but admittedly, I was a little intrigued. *What was this going to look like in action? Is he really as tall as the Instagram pictures of him posing next to female teammates made him appear to be? How will he place among us? Will he throw a few races to make it seem competitive? Will he use our locker rooms?* We all had a lot of questions that would soon be answered, stripping away curiosity from me and my teammates and ultimately causing us to feel ashamed forever naïvely wondering these things and feeling curious.

Thomas was scheduled to compete in the 100, 200, and 500 freestyle. Competing against the men, Thomas never swam the 100 because it was a sprint and he specialized in distance. Another thing no girl swimming at that level could ever do: totally change the events you compete in and be able to rank at or near the top of the country. Again, think of the Olympic runner analogy, a challenge that proved to be nothing for Thomas to overcome. Individually, I chose to opt out of the 100 freestyle, giving me a better chance of doing well in the 200 freestyle and 200 butterfly.

I could only imagine what a media circus this championship would be. And to actually have to compete against Thomas? I didn't know what to expect. While 95 percent of my teammates and I shared the same frustrations, we could only realistically focus on that for a short time if we were dedicated to achieving our own personal and team goals we set for ourselves, which we were. At one point, as a team captain, I tried to shut down all dialogue that obsessed over Thomas, not because I wanted to discourage independent thought (and trust me, we all knew how each other felt), but because it was hindering our focus. Was it unfair? Yes. Did it put us female swimmers at a disadvantage? Yes. But complaining and talking about this competition debacle ad nauseam wasn't going to help us swim any faster. We had to "be where are feet are," like Lars always said, and not dwell on the future. This is the moment we had been working all year, really all our lives, for. We could only control the controllables and those controllables consisted of our focus, our effort, our attitudes, and, in turn, our success. Spending any more time and energy discussing a competitor or a situation that we had no control over was pointless and would displace the drive necessary to perform how we needed to and how we knew we could.

Before the NCAA Championship, of course, we needed to tackle the SEC championships. This meet was always my favorite meet each year. The SEC was the deepest and most competitive conference, filled with the best rivalries. There was so much excitement and energy that went into this meet. And my senior year SECs in February 2022 was probably the most special meet of my collegiate career. I defended my 200 freestyle title I won the year before. I won SEC Scholar Athlete of the Year ten minutes before I broke the SEC record for the 200 butterfly at 1:51.51, the fastest time in the country and made me the tenth fastest American of all time. I was also named SEC community service leader of the year. Not even the upcoming circus of the NCAA Championship could dampen that celebration.

A week before the championships, our program's sports information director pulled the swimmers who were competing in the NCAAs into a meeting for media training. Media training for collegiate athletes wasn't necessarily anything new, particularly for highly televised sports like football and basketball, but we can all agree collegiate women's swimming doesn't fall into that category. All of that is to say that in my prior three years of collegiate swimming, we had never done media training conducted through the university. It wasn't a coincidence that our sports information director specifically addressed the freestylers. The meeting, which revolved around the elephant in the room, started with a warning. "There is going to be a ton of media at this meet. There will be journalists who will try and bait trap you into saying something you may not want to say or twist your words. I strongly recommend you not say anything. Either don't respond to questions or tell them you have no comment." Next, she told us that we were to refer to Lia Thomas using *she/her* pronouns. We went through sentences reinforcing what these *she/her* pronouns would look like. She then offered us some sample questions reporters might ask and suggested ways to deflect from giving our opinion, if and when we were asked. Even in our own personal capacity, we were told we weren't representing ourselves, but instead our words represented the university we wore on our caps and across our chests. We were reminded that we signed a scholarship indicating the relinquish of our personal rights and freedoms.

The internal battle within me raged. It was hard for me to fathom that as a twenty-one-year-old senior in college I was being instructed against something so commonsense that it's not even something you're ever taught in school. The use of pronouns is natural and something you pick up on before even forming full, coherent sentences. I didn't want to outright disrespect any individual. I certainly wasn't going to be rude or publicly ostracize Thomas on a personal level just for being trans, but I didn't understand why we had to jump through hoops to "respect" someone who clearly had zero respect for us.

When the training was over, I headed straight to see Lars. I told him that this didn't sit well with me or several of my teammates. I explained that I had done plenty of interviews before, so training at this point felt more like a way for the school to tell us what to say, how to think, and how to feel even if it went against our morals and gut instinct.

Coach nodded, then shrugged. He agreed with my point of view, but his hands were tied. Without any authority to change NCAA rules, he felt there was nothing he could do. At the time, we felt there was nothing any of us could do about this injustice. We just had to show up and swim.

The 2022 NCAA Division 1 Women's Swimming and Diving Championships took place March 16–19 at Georgia Tech in Atlanta. We arrived, as usual, to the pool a few days before the meet started to get acclimated to the environment. The first day we walked on the pool deck, we got our team registered, which consisted of getting your credentials and other logistics. Our coach was handed a big box from the official on the other side of the registration desk and our coach was instructed to pass what was inside the box out to each of his female athletes. What was inside the box? A Nike shirt that largely and proudly read "50 Years of Title IX, Creating Opportunities." Virtue signaling at its finest.

Although our curiosity was at an all-time high and we were on the lookout, neither myself nor my teammates saw Thomas during the first day of practice. It's like the powers-that-be were keeping the main attraction hidden on purpose. The next day, however, everything was exposed . . . quite literally.

No one warned us girls that we would be sharing a locker room with Thomas. This wasn't mentioned in media training. This wasn't mentioned in our meet packets. This wasn't sent to us in an email or text message on the day we arrived. Our coaches didn't even know of this arrangement. No NCAA official believed, I suppose, it was relevant or important to, at the least, give us a forewarning. None of us were prepared for the reality of undressing in front of Thomas until we were in a locker room undressing a few feet away from a 6'4" man who was simultaneously undressing with fully intact and exposed male genitalia. Wikipedia will tell you Thomas is 6'1" , , , and that is a lie (even CNN admits it!).[8] My husband (who also swam at University of Kentucky) is 6'4" and they are the same height. Swimmers are generally pretty tall, even some female swimmers are six feet tall. They paled in comparison to Thomas. He towered over every girl in that locker room and on the starting blocks next to him.

Let me first set the scene. A swimming locker room is not a place of modesty. The swimsuits we wear are skintight and paper thin. There's a reason for that. These tech suits or knee skins, as they're called, can make or break a race. They go down to midthigh or a little above your knees and can take fifteen minutes, most of the time more, to pull up all the way. And that's with much squirming, shifting, sweating, and most times an extra pair of hands from a fellow swimmer. Tucking your behind and extra skin in material that feels like it's going to rip at any second is the worst. The poking and prodding are so intense that most girls wear gloves so their nail beds don't bleed and they don't rip their suits with their nails. During this extended period of prodding, squeezing, and squishing, you're typically fully exposed. It's well understood that locker rooms in general aren't necessarily a place of comfort, but growing up a swimmer, you get accustomed to being vulnerable in this environment, meaning modesty in a swimming locker room tends to fly out the window.

At this meet in particular, you get to see friends from other universities and conferences around the country whom you only get to see this one meet each year. The locker room is typically buzzing with chatting and high-pitched laughter. Again, this is a place to be vulnerable, so there were oftentimes tears from girls who aren't pleased with how they swam or girls complaining about their coaches to anyone who would entertain it. This space was so loud, you could only make out what the people you were directly talking to were saying.

One more thing to mention that is unique to swimming locker rooms is that there is a lot of undressing, multiple times a session. We arrived in our clothes and changed into our practice suits to warm up, then we changed from our practice suits into our racing suits, then from our racing suits back into our practice suits to finish warming down, and then from our practice suits back into our clothes. So just in one session, you would undress down to nothing four times. Then we would come back for finals that same day and repeat the process all over again. Just trying to hit home the fact that there were lots of opportunities to be seen fully exposed each day.

I was getting dressed back into my clothes from my practice suit when it was like someone unplugged the sound. Dead silence. My back was turned toward the door, but before I even turned around, I knew what this silence meant. It would answer my curious question of what the locker room would look like. Upon turning around and shifting my eyes upward to the 6'4" Thomas, I immediately felt the inherent need to cover my chest, as someone with a male gaze and a male voice entered the room. Some of the girls grabbed towels, shirts, or whatever was close by and covered the exposed parts of their body. Other girls looked the other way. We were all in various stages of nakedness. None of us said a word. I can't accurately put into words the feelings of violation when hearing a man's voice in the locker room where you are fully nude. Thomas walked toward the corner of the locker room and began to change out of a women's practice suit and get naked. Right in front of us. No introduction, no "Excuse me," no explanation, no privacy for us.

My teammates and I cut wide eyes with each other, not really understanding our emotions in that moment. Of course, we felt awkward, embarrassed, and uncomfortable. I remember specifically feeling betrayed. I thought of how our privacy as females had been entirely dismissed, violated, and ignored. There was no thought to how we would respond or how uncomfortable a male sharing this changing space with us would make us feel. It felt like we were pawns in a sick game catering to the male who claimed our identity but didn't have the same physiology, anatomy, or chromosomes, to name a few . . . I desperately wanted to call my mom and dad and tell them of this situation in hopes they would reassure me that I wasn't crazy in experiencing this as a total violation of our rights to privacy as women.

Immediately, without saying a word to anyone, I walked out of the locker room and went to find an NCAA official on the pool deck. I addressed the first one I saw. He had no idea what was coming. I told him about Thomas being in our locker room. I hoped maybe he hadn't known about it and would provide a solution. I asked, "I know the guidelines of the competition that allowed Thomas to compete against us, but what are the guidelines that allows men into our locker rooms?"

"Oh, we actually got around this by making the locker rooms unisex," he explained with a concerning nonchalance.

My first thought (and the first thing I said back) was that his response implied that the NCAA acknowledged the fact that Thomas is a male because it had to change the female bathroom's status. If they wholeheartedly believed Thomas to be a woman, they wouldn't have felt the need to go out of their way to change the guidelines for the locker room. That was all the admittance I needed from the NCAA to understand they took that precaution to avoid legal action because they knew a man in a woman's locker room would be illegal on the grounds of voyeurism, sexual harassment, and indecent exposure, to name a few. My jaw tightened. "You mean to tell me any man can walk into our locker room?"

He said nothing, avoiding eye contact.

Just a few years ago, if a man walked in the women's locker room, he would be arrested and thrown in jail and thought of as a sexual predator. Never in a million years did I ever expect to attend an NCAA Championship feeling trivialized and neglected by the people who were supposed to be protecting us.

I would find out later that Kylee Alons of North Carolina State University, who is a 31x All-American, was so uncomfortable at having to share a locker room with a naked male, she changed in a storage closet.[9] Kylee, NC State's most decorated swimmer of all time, admitted to being constantly on edge whenever she had to go to the locker room. Knowing Thomas could walk in at any given moment, she always had a towel and parka nearby.[10] She expressed how grateful she was to have that storage closet to undress in. Read that sentence again.

We were asking for the bare minimum: fair competition, safety, and a private place to undress where we didn't have to worry if male eyes were watching us. Kylee is one of hundreds of female athletes at that meet who were directly impacted in the locker room by the forced presence of a male. She and I are not alone in our frustration at the violation of our privacy, but the pressures to stay silent for fear of losing the opportunity to race or our scholarships weighed heavily on us.

My first event was on the second day of competition, meaning I didn't have any events the first day. This meant I got a front-row seat on the pool deck to watch Thomas swim the 500 freestyle. For those who don't know how swimming works at this level, we must swim prelims in the morning in which the top 16 qualifiers will then come back and swim the event again in the evening at finals, where they will achieve their final and overall ranking. The top 8 make the A final/championship final, while 9–17 make the B final/ consolation finals. There were about eight or so preliminary heats of the 500 that morning, with Thomas being in the last heat and in lane four, indicating he was coming into the meet as the favorite.

Emma Weyant (Virginia), Erica Sullivan (Texas), Brooke Forde (Stanford), Evie Pfeifer (Texas), Paige McKenna (Wisconsin), Kensey McMahon (Alabama), and Morgan Tankersley (Stanford) were competing with Thomas in the finals. In the vein of being extremely transparent, not only did Thomas stick out because of a massive 6'4" height, but he also had an obvious bulge in his swimsuit where females definitely don't. It wasn't male physical features alone that made his performance distinctive from his female competitors. His body dynamics in the water were visibly different from the swimmers in the other lanes. His feet hardly kicked. He did virtually no underwater kicks off the wall after each flip turn, which was not the norm even in a longer event like the 500. Before the swimmers even touched the water, it was obvious which one was a male due to jump height, distance, and power coming off the block.

Thomas won by more than a full body length, posting an incredibly impressive time of 4:33.24. I say impressive but understand that it is far from impressive for a male. Weyant came in second place, almost two seconds later, at 4:34.99. Sullivan took home third at 4:35.92. Forde, who won a silver at the Tokyo Olympics, came in fourth. Let me put this into perspective because I know winning by almost two seconds doesn't sound like a lot. Swimming is a sport that measured down to the *hundredth* of a second. To have one person beating every girl in the entire country by nearly two full seconds is an anomaly. Instead of the expected celebratory cheers from a usually boisterous crowd, the audience's response to Thomas's win fell unusually flat. There were even audible boos from the stands. Weyant's announcement was a different story. When her second-place victory was broadcast, the aquatic center exploded in applause, whistles, and shouts of acclaim. The difference between the two swimmers couldn't have been more obvious. People were saying with applause and cheers what they couldn't or wouldn't say with their words. The collective group of parents and fans cheering created an amazing atmosphere of protection and relief for us in those brief moments.

Thomas's stolen victory from the night before left me feeling like I was going into prelims for the 200 freestyle with my hands tied behind my back. Nonetheless, I gave it my all. I was not in the same heat as Thomas that morning, but we both finished among the top eight, meaning we would be in the championship final together that evening.

I talked to my parents and my coaches about pulling out of the race at finals. I figured not swimming could be my way of taking a stand on how wrong the decision was to allow Thomas to race. They were supportive of whatever I chose to do but reminded me this was my last meet ever. When I asked an NCAA official what would happen if I didn't get on the block, the response was anticlimactic, and sobering. "This is why we have alternates," he replied. "If you don't get on the block, we would take the next swimmer up. Someone would gladly take your spot."

In thinking it over, I thought it would be foolish to give up my last race. I'd been swimming for eighteen years, fourteen of them competitively. This was my final meet that would cap off my swimming career. I deserved to race and not let Thomas stop me from doing what I loved and cared about. While I selfishly wanted to compete, I also had a team who needed points if we wanted to finish as a top 10 team, which was our team goal. It would have been impossible without those points from that event. Another idea popped into my head. I determined if I won, I would make my statement by not getting on the podium where they handed out trophies. I had made my mind up; I wasn't getting on the podium to accept my trophy no matter where Thomas or I ended up placing in an effort to make a statement that the trophy had been devalued entirely just by having him in the race.

When it came time to swim finals, I was as ready as I could have been. In standard fashion, I walked into the ready room about ten minutes before my race. Eight chairs were lined up with a number on each that corresponded to a lane. I was swimming in lane 1, so I sat in that chair. There was one other person in the room, the swimmer in lane 5, Thomas—his cap and goggles were already on when I walked in. Thomas sat with his head facing the floor. I don't remember Thomas looking up once the entire time we were in the ready room or acknowledging the other six swimmers as they eventually filed in. Other than the sound of our breath, slapping of our muscles, and solemn whispers of well-wishes, the room was quiet while the eight of us waited to be walked out to our lanes.

When eventually it was time, we walked out of the room in a single file to the pool platform, flanked on both sides by a pyrotechnic display. The crowd roared while we smiled and waved. I hate to admit it, but as much as I thrived under pressure, I lacked that adrenal feeling that normally fueled me before big races. This was a different feeling than what I was used to. It felt like despair. I felt defeated before I even got on the block, given Thomas's domination the day before. Before each of us swimmers took our stance on the block, our names were announced. Each swimmer received a robust round of applause and cheers, except for Thomas. It wasn't because no one liked him. It wasn't a personal dig. It was because a man didn't belong in the race with us and would have never received this same attention in his rightful category. And seeing it live was visibly uncomfortable to watch.

Take your mark. Beep.

I don't remember much about the specifics of my race other than the last ten meters because it felt like I was dying. In the swimming world, it's relatively rare to swim two meets well back-to-back. SECs was just a few weeks before NCAAs, where I had done incredible posting all best times, so I wasn't necessarily expecting for the race to feel painless or to perform better than the meet a few weeks prior, but this race physically *hurt*. Despite kicking as hard as I could, my legs felt like dead weight. Based off how painful the race was, I was confident I didn't go a best time which was true. I had added almost a full second from the time I had went at SECs. Right after I touched the wall, I looked at the board. My eyes weren't scanning for my name, yet. I wanted to see Thomas's results more than my own. What can I say? I told you I was curious. The number "5" blared by his name. He got fifth place. I instantly felt so proud of the girls who finished first through fourth for achieving the seemingly impossible and beating a 6'4" male. Oh yeah . . . what place did I get?! I looked for my name and, lo and behold, there was a 5 beside my name too. *What?* I looked at the board again. Thomas, 5th place. Gaines, 5th place. I shifted my eyes to my teammates, who were standing on the side of the pool, and their jaws were on the floor upon the realization that Thomas and I went the exact same time. Although I had stopped swimming, my heart rate wasn't coming down. I couldn't believe this was happening. What were the odds of us touching the wall at the exact same time down to the *hundredth* of a second? Thomas and I had tied for fifth place at 1:43.40. This was neither of our best times. We both added a decent bit, of course Thomas adding much more time than me, considering that his previous best from a few weeks prior was that much faster than my own. Shock morphed into confusion. *How was the NCAA going to address a tie with one of those swimmers being one that clearly didn't belong in this category?*

After I got out of the water, my teammates ran over to meet me behind my block and gave me big bear hugs. They knew I was likely disappointed that I didn't do as well as I hoped, so they provided reassurance they were proud of me. They whispered in my ear, "You know what you just did, right?" as if I hadn't seen the results. I could sense the atmosphere of deep unreality and shock all around us.

The swimmers who swam in the championship final walked behind the podium, where officials were distributing trophies for the awards ceremonies. Top 8 swimmers in the nation are awarded a trophy and named an All-American. Despite considering earlier not standing on the podium, thinking about it in real time, there wouldn't even be an empty spot if I wasn't up there. I was in such a moral dilemma. There would be no statement to be had if there wasn't an empty place on the podium leaving room for questions. My achievement would be wiped out, and in my place would be a smiling male who would have never finished that well competing against the men. While walking from the pool to the awards podium, I decided I would get on the podium in hopes to get a photo next to Thomas that would display the staggering physical and height differences between us.

All eight finishers were behind the podium when the trophies were being distributed. Thomas was standing next to me, towering over me, when an NCAA official approached us to let us know that we had tied. He then went on to explain how they don't account for ties in terms of trophies. He quickly and assertively informed us that Thomas would be the one to hold the trophy and subsequently take it home. Then he congratulated us on our race as he handed the trophy to Thomas, who accepted it with a smile.

What? Of course, I understood there was only one trophy, but how was it so easy for this official to decide that Thomas was to receive it? Because my heart rate was still high and my adrenaline was still pumping, I asked the official this question. It was the questions that I had been wondering all season, but no one dared ask. "Why?" I asked the official why he was adamant on giving the trophy to a *man* in the *women's* 200 freestyle. After a long pause and some stumbling on his words, he responded that the trophies were being given out in chronological order.

"Chronological order? What specifically are you being chronological about, because, well, we tied. The only thing you can be chronological about is our names, so maybe you meant alphabetical, and if that's the case, *G* comes before *T*, so what exactly *are* you being chronological about?"

The official stared at me, still fumbling for words. I watched as his brows lowered and his eyes saddened. His face and mood visibly shifted. It was obvious to me that he didn't even believe what he was about to tell me. He then proceeded to tell me that he had been advised that when photos were being taken, it was crucial that Lia be holding the trophy.

He reached for the sixth-place trophy and handed it to me. "You can pose with this trophy, but Lia will take the trophy home. You will go home empty-handed, but we can eventually mail you one."

At this point, I fully understood what was happening here. Thomas was standing inches away from me as I questioned the official for never once entertaining the idea of us both holding the trophy or offering the trophy to me (especially given the fact that Thomas just won a national title the night before).

"Riley, it's okay."

"Riley, just let it go."

"You have another event tomorrow you can finish top eight in. You can get a trophy then."

I could barely hear what were intended to be calming words from my fellow swimmers to help me calm down. Being smacked in the face with this lack of respect and consideration shredded my ability to respond to empty reassurances and polite intervention. The NCAA had just reduced everything I, really all of us, had worked our entire lives for, down to a photo opportunity to validate the feelings and the identity of a male without even a second thought to *our* feelings and *our* identity. I couldn't believe this was happening just a few months before the fiftieth anniversary of Title IX. I thought of those shirts the NCAA passed out to each female swimmer at the meet on day one. "50 Years of Title IX, Creating Opportunities" . . . How could they even pass those shirts out in good faith knowing they had been advised to give preferential treatment to the male over every female swimmer at all costs?

I want to be clear that this wasn't about the tangible object of the trophy. As a twelve-time All-American, I have plenty of those trophies at home. It was the principle behind what the NCAA had done and their reasoning behind it that threw me into a tailspin.

I remember looking over at one point and seeing the on-deck ESPN reporter Elizabeth Beisel, who is also a two-time Olympic medalist and a swimming legend, about to interview Taylor Ruck, the national champion. As I continued to express my frustration to the official, she looked over at me and mouthed, "I'm sorry."

As seven fastest females in the country and Thomas stood atop the podium, I forced myself to smile. I was aghast that no one was standing up for female swimmers in this elite competition and calling out the malfeasance of the NCAA. How could we be expected to celebrate? How could I even congratulate him? How could he be proud and accept this trophy or the one taken the night before?

In those brief moments, I waited for someone to stick up for us—a coach, a parent, someone with the NCAA, or someone with political influence and power. I thought surely someone who was supposed to be protecting us would, well, protect us. But then it hit me. We were applauding our own erasure, our own demolition. How could we expect someone else to stand up for us, if we weren't willing to stand up for ourselves? This *had* to come from us as female athletes, from us as women. This was the moment when I decided I was no longer willing to cower and lie. I felt overwhelmed by personal responsibility and conviction that I had ignored for too long. I didn't know what I was going to do, but I knew I would never again wait for someone else to call out an injustice on my behalf.

By the time I stepped off the podium, Thomas hadn't acknowledged my presence or said a word of congratulations. He hadn't said a word to any of us. In all fairness, neither did I. On the last day of the meet, Thomas ended his last race of the meet, the 100 freestyle, in eighth place at 48.18. Eighth place may not sound like domination, but it meant beating 14,000 female Division 1 swimmers.

Another interesting point about this meet was that there was *another* trans-identifying athlete at this same NCAA Championships. The notable difference was that this athlete was a female who self-identified as a man. Her name is Izzy Henig but now goes by Iszac. While we were instructed to use *she/her* pronouns when referring to Thomas, we were also told we needed to use *he/him* pronouns when referring to Henig. Henig had undergone a double mastectomy and swam only in a Speedo, with no top covering her cut-up chest. Both swimmers had written on their upper arms with a black marker, "Let trans kids play," as if they weren't *both* playing in the category that best suited them and their chances for success.

I have absolutely no problem with Henig competing in the women's category as a female (as long as she wasn't using performance-enhancing drugs like testosterone) because that's where she should compete. I bring all this up to raise the point: If we were really basing the decision to allow trans-identified males to compete in women's sports off gender identity, like the NCAA, IOC, and Biden administration claim, then why did Izzy, now Iszac, compete with the women while identifying as a man? That's a rhetorical question.

Henig ended up placing fifth in the finals of the 100 freestyle, which is an incredible achievement. The following year Henig did begin to compete on the men's team. She finished nearly dead last if not dead last every single race. To further make the point, in the one meet I watched of Henig's this year, the only male swimmer she beat was a male with one arm. If you find yourself offended by that, understand there is nothing opinionated about what was stated. Its real life and our lived experience. Henig went from top five in the country competing as a woman to the bottom of the barrel when competing against the men. I don't bring this up to mock her, but instead to highlight the concerns we have as female athletes and to show what and who is really at jeopardy.

I watched the tears fall as the girls who raced with Thomas came in 9th and 17th place, which made them ineligible for All-American honors. I saw their frustration. I shared their heartbreak and anger. They lost their spot to someone who was born a male, had gone through puberty, and had at least five times the amount of testosterone than they did. This travesty was not only encouraged but celebrated by the NCAA.

The NCAA wasn't the only organization who was applauding the rupture of women's sports. A few months later, in honor of Women's History Month, ESPN released a special on Thomas. Of all the female athletes who could have been chosen, someone who was not even born a female was handpicked. These actions are regressive and misogynistic. The special went on to tout:

> NARRATOR: . . . The Texas native competed for three seasons on the men's swim team at the University of Pennsylvania. She began her transition after her sophomore season and after a gap year due to the pandemic that forced the Ivy League to cancel fall sports, Thomas made her debut as a member of the women's team in December of 2021.
>
> THOMAS: Being trans is not a choice. I didn't have any other choice because not transitioning was not leading me anywhere.
>
> NARRATOR: She competed amidst criticism from the swimming community, competitors, and teammates. She says she hopes her persistence serves a larger purpose.

THOMAS: People will say, "Oh, she just transitioned so she
would have an advantage, so she could win." I
transitioned to be happy.[11]

No female swimmer was honored during this Women's History Month special by ESPN. Only Thomas.

My original plan after graduating from the University of Kentucky was to go to dental school. I had graduated with my degree in human health sciences and minor in health advocacy. I had taken the Dental Admissions Test (the miserable four-hour test required to get into dental school), scored in the top percentile, and was mentally prepared to work in people's mouths for the rest of my life. I had been awarded more than $25,000 in scholarship money for various achievements like my academics and community service involvement. Weirdly enough, I had hoped to specialize in endodontics, which is essentially a concentration in root canals. I had already put my deposit down and accepted my seat. But I could so clearly see what's at stake if someone doesn't pursue this fight. I knew this was only the beginning of a polarizing issue that would affect girls and women across the globe. I felt like I could look into the future and see the trajectory of where this issue was headed. I prayed for direction, wisdom, and strength daily. I still do. God reinforced that the quickest way to make Him laugh in my face was by making plans for myself and my future. He clearly has a sense of humor. If He brings us to it, He will bring us through it.

As I recount the events that transpired in that pool that day, I wholeheartedly believe God had his hand on all of this and still does. It has become apparent to me that God doesn't call the equipped, he equips the called.

When deciding what to do with my future, I was experiencing a pretty hefty internal conflict. As an athlete, you set goals and you work to achieve those goals. I felt like if I were to defer dental school, I would be abandoning the goal I once set for myself. After lots of prayer, God had made it clear that dental school would have to wait. To appease that internal conflict, I justify God's calling by telling myself I am still working on the root of the problem coming out of people's mouths—just a moral and ethical problem rather than a physical one. This kind might even be more painful.

4.

———

A CLEAR AND UNFAIR ADVANTAGE

Though I hadn't completely removed myself from the circus at the time, at prelims the morning before Thomas and I raced, I witnessed firsthand what it looks like when women are robbed of something they earned.

My team sat next to Virginia Tech. Reka Gyorgy, a VT swimmer, had just gotten out of the water after racing in one of the earlier heats of the 500 to stand beside her coach as they watched the final heat conclude. This was the heat that Thomas was swimming in, really the heat he was dominating. I knew of Reka, but I didn't know her that well. I knew she was a fifth year from Hungary. If you were a student-athlete who had been affected by the COVID shutdowns, you got an extra year of eligibility if you wanted it.

I was standing next to Reka and her coach, and I could hear their conversation. As a Rio 2016 Olympian, Reka knew she was going to be right on the cusp of making top sixteen, which would secure her spot at finals. When the heat finished with Thomas winning, Reka looked to the board at the final morning rankings.

When the names and places pulled up, her coach hugged her immediately. It wasn't a congratulatory embrace. Reka came in at 17th place. After he consoled her, she grabbed my hand, tears dripping down her cheeks as she turned to me and said, "I just got beat by someone who didn't even have to try."

By this point, I hadn't yet raced against Thomas, but the injustice of what was transpiring was clear as day. As was the lack of advocacy on behalf of us female athletes.

A few days later, Reka, devastated and refusing to stay silent, wrote an open letter to the NCAA from her Instagram account. She has stated that anyone who publishes her statement does so at its full length to protect her words from getting twisted or misinterpreted. Respecting her wish, here is what she wrote:

Dear NCAA,

I would like to address this past week's events and express my thoughts. First, I would like to remind everyone that I am a human being and that as a human being I experience feelings and emotions.

My name is Reka Gyorgy from Hungary. I am a 2016 Rio Olympian, represented Virginia Tech for the past 5 years, a 2 time ACC Champion, 2 time All-American and 3 time Honorable Mention All-American.

With all due respect, I would like to address something that is a problem in our sport right now and hurting athletes, especially female swimmers. Everyone has heard and known about transgender, Lia Thomas, and her case including all the issues and concerns that her situation brought into our sport. I'd like to point out that I respect and fully stand with Lia Thomas; I am convinced that she is no different than me or any other D1 swimmer who has woken up at 5am her entire life for morning practice. She has sacrificed family vacations and holidays for a competition. She has pushed herself to the limit to be the best athlete she could be. She is doing what she is passionate about and deserves that right. On the other hand, I would like to critique the NCAA rules that allow her to compete against us, who are biologically women.

I'm writing this letter right now in hopes that the NCAA will open their eyes and change these rules in the future. It doesn't promote our sport in a good way and I think it is disrespectful against the biologically female swimmers who are competing in the NCAA.

I swam the 500 free at NCAA's on March 17th, 2022 where I got 17th which means I didn't make it back to the finals and was first alternate. I'm a 5th year senior, I have been top 16 and top 8 before and I know how much of a privilege it is to make finals at a meet this big. This is my last college meet ever and I feel frustrated. It feels like that final spot was taken away from me because of the NCAA's decision to let someone who is not a biological female compete. I know you could say I had the opportunity to swim faster and make the top 16, but this situation makes it a bit different and I can't help but be angry or sad. It hurts me, my team and other women in the pool. One spot was taken away from the girl who got 9th in the 500 free and didn't make it back to the A final preventing her from being an All-American. Every event that transgender athletes competed in was one spot taken away from biological females throughout the meet.

The NCAA knew what was coming this past week. They knew opinions and minds will be divided and chose to do nothing. This week has been more about reporters, media

and division in our sport than things like two women going
under 21 seconds in the 50 freestyle, 3 women going under
50 seconds in the 100 butterfly and the first woman IN HIS-
TORY to go under 48 seconds in the 100 backstroke. Thurs-
day was not a specific athlete's fault. It is the result of the
NCAA and their lack of interest in protecting their athletes.
I ask that the NCAA takes time to think about all the other
biological women in swimming, try to think how they would
feel if they would be in our shoes. Make the right changes for
our sport and for a better future in swimming.
 Thank you for reading,
 Reka Gyorgy, Virginia Tech swimmer

Reka was the first female swimmer to publicly express her displeasure in allowing Thomas to compete against the women. To my knowledge, the NCAA never responded to Reka's concern.

• • •

Before I delve into the biological differences between men and women, let's get back to the basics. There's an official diagnosis for people who feel that they were born in the wrong biological body. Gender dysphoria is a clinical medical condition included in the *Diagnostic and Statistical Manual of Mental Disorders, Fifth Edition, Text Revision (DSM-5-TR). It is diagnosed in adults and children if they display at least two or more of the following as well as distress and negative impairment in life function:*

- A marked incongruence between one's experienced/ expressed gender and primary and/or secondary sex characteristics (or in young adolescents, the anticipated secondary sex characteristics)

- A strong desire to be rid of one's primary and/or secondary sex characteristics because of a marked incongruence with one's experienced/expressed gender (or in young adolescents, a desire to prevent the development of the anticipated secondary sex characteristics)
- A strong desire for the primary and/or secondary sex characteristics of the other gender
- A strong desire to be of the other gender (or some alternative gender different from one's assigned gender)
- A strong desire to be treated as the other gender (or some alternative gender different from one's assigned gender)
- A strong conviction that one has the typical feelings and reactions of the other gender (or some alternative gender different from one's assigned gender).[1]

What we're seeing today is an increase in rapid hormonal and surgical intervention rather than emotional and psychological treatment by practitioners, particularly when other factors, like a history of depression, trauma, or autism, contribute to a minor's well-being. There is a surge in adolescents, ages six to seventeen, who claim to struggle with some of or all the symptoms of gender dysphoria. According to a study conducted for Reuters, from 2017 to 2021 the number of kids who received the diagnosis almost tripled. In 2017, there were a little upward of 15,000 adolescents and just four years later, the number jumped to little over 42,000.

One of the most famous transgender individuals who suffer from gender dysphoria is Caitlyn Jenner, formerly known as Bruce Jenner. An Olympic gold medalist and former world-record holder in the decathlon, he became a beloved icon after his win in Montreal in 1976. Men wanted to be him, and women wanted to be with him. He was an American hero who displayed patriotism, masculinity, and the idea that if you work hard enough, anything was possible. What Americans around the country didn't know was that, deep down, Jenner had struggled with gender dysphoria since he was young. He had been dressing as a woman in secrecy years before his Olympic success. Jenner had been married three times, with his most recent bride being Kris Kardashian in 1991, but the couple officially divorced in March 2015 after twenty-three years together. In April 2015, after privately wearing women's clothing and taking hormone replacement therapy (HRT) for many years, Jenner publicly announced plans to live life identifying as a woman.

Jenner and I may disagree on lifestyle choices, but we are allies when it comes to protecting women's sports and spaces. In fact, he publicly made clear it was unfair for Lia Thomas to participate on the women's swim team. Right before the NCAA was due to release their updated policy in including trans-identifying males in women's sports, Jenner recommended they "make the right decision . . . to stop this right now." Jenner's perspective is especially credible on the issue of allowing trans-identifying males into women's sports due to his transgender status and his incredible athletic achievements in being one of the United States' most decorated athletes of all time.

In a recent interview, Jenner said that transgenderism is "oversaturated due to indoctrination and is the latest way the left is destroying the family unit—growing government, the indoctrination in the classroom, and the subsequent drastic increase in children being transitioned is a huge problem. We won't see the true impact for years to come."

Jenner has claimed to have "gotten more flack for being a conservative Republican than I have for being trans." It's comical yet ironic when I see accusations being hurled at Jenner for being transphobic. Based on the structure of the word "transphobic," wouldn't that mean that Jenner has an irrational fear of, well, himself? I consider him a great friend and an ally with whom I'm so grateful to share a mission. Even though I don't understand what it is like to experience gender dysphoria, we agree on the topics that make sense. Like keeping women's sports for women.

Jenner is not the only LGBTQ ally in this fight to defend sanity. Martina Navratilova, one of the all-time greats of tennis, fully supports not allowing males to play in women's sports. In an op-ed, she explained her support of a separate category for participants who are not females. "Once somebody has gone through male puberty, there is no way to erase that physical advantage. You cannot simply turn back the clock, for instance by trying to lower testosterone levels." When Megan Rapinoe said she approved replacing a female soccer player with someone who merely claimed to be a woman, Martina had one thing to say: "Yikes!"

To pretend that male athletes do not have a physical advantage over female athletes defies logic, science, and, quite frankly, common sense. But hey, what do I know? I'm just a collegiate swimmer with a bachelor's degree in human health science.

To provide more clarity on the science behind the differences between the sexes, I want to introduce Dr. Carole Hooven to this conversation. Dr. Hooven got her PhD at Harvard and went on to teach there for twenty years in behavioral endocrinology, becoming codirector of undergraduate studies in human evolutionary biology. She's studied the subject of sex and gender within humans and primates for twenty-five years. Dr. Hooven is also the author of the critically acclaimed book *T: The Story of Testosterone, the Hormone That Dominates and Divides Us.*

But before I get into Dr. Hooven's extensive research on the biology of the two sexes, I must first tell you how she earned a spot among the "canceled" in a university that ironically boasts the motto *Veritas* (Latin for truth).

Right after her book was released, Dr. Hooven was asked to appear on the television show *Fox & Friends* to discuss an article about the pressure academic professors felt using words like "male" and "female" in teaching. Although Dr. Hooven didn't necessarily share the same ideologies or worldview as the Fox News network, she agreed to appear on the show for several reasons. As an author who was passionate about her subject, she desired for her book to have a broad reach. She also wanted to make clear to the public that language should be respectful but also true to itself. Finally, Dr. Hooven hoped to explain on-air that the two sex categories of male and female are "clear, indispensable scientific terms" and therefore are not words that present a threat or infringement on any individual's rights or value.[2] She wasn't going to get the opportunity to talk about this for the *Harvard Crimson*, never mind CNN.

What Dr. Hooven said on *Fox & Friends* on July 28, 2021, shown below, sent Harvard University into a tailspin.

*The facts are that **there are . . . two sexes . . . there are male and female**,[3] and those sexes are designated by the kinds of gametes we produce . . . The ideology seems to be that biology really isn't as important as how somebody feels about themselves or feels their sex to be, but we can treat people with respect and respect their gender identities and use their preferred pronouns, so understanding the facts about biology doesn't prevent us from treating people with respect.[4]*

Enter the swift backlash Dr. Hooven never could have imagined coming. Laura Simone Lewis, the director of the Diversity and Inclusion Task Force at Harvard's Department of Human Evolutionary Biology, ignited the fire that eventually influenced Dr. Hooven to take a permanent leave of absence. Without even discussing the interview privately with her colleague, Lewis tweeted to Harvard University, and the public, that she was "appalled and frustrated by the transphobic and harmful remarks"[5] of Dr. Hooven. According to this task force director, the mere admission that sex is binary and biological instantly made this beloved professor a danger to her students. She claimed it hindered efforts to make the department a "safe space" for "all gender identities and sexes."[6] In the coming weeks and months, Dr. Hooven was socially ostracized on campus by the school administration and ultimately retired from her position. So much for Veritas.

Before she left Ivy League academia, Dr. Hooven emailed a statement to the university's paper, the *Crimson*, in response to the vitriol being hurled her way. She also wanted to make clear she wasn't going to be bullied and would continue to stand for what was right. Dr. Hooven wrote:

> *... What I teach about has special appeal for students who are in the minority in terms of gender expression, identification, and sexual orientation, and the facts can feel quite personal. I do my best to set a tone of trust and respect. I expect my students to sometimes disagree with me, and I expect that some people will feel offended or even hurt as they encounter and struggle with new ideas and information. I do not patronize my students or tell them what to think about controversial social issues. Instead, I try to create an environment in which students are motivated to seriously engage with the evidence and arguments I*

present. . . . This is why I have strong feelings about teach-
ing practices and the value of clear language. And I see that
more and more educators are changing language and even
backing off of controversial topics not because they think
it's the right thing to do as educators, but out of fear. This is
not the right way forward. We can be caring and sensitive
to the needs and identities of everyone, while also sticking
to biological reality.[7]

Dr. Hooven will be the first to tell you from experience that
distorting science doesn't help anybody. In her words, "Nobody's
rights should hang on myths and untruths . . . you should support
everyone's right to tell the truth."[8] To reiterate, the truth is that
there are only two sexes, male and female.

• • •

"But what about intersex individuals?" I knew you were going to
ask. People disagree about the terms that should be used to
describe conditions in which one's sexed anatomy or physiology is
different from what's typical for their sex, but the most common
terms are "intersex" and "DSD," which stands for either "disorder
(or difference)" of sexual development. These terms are used to
describe situations in which sexed traits, like external genitalia
(that is, vagina or penis), sex chromosomes, hormones, or secondary sex characteristics like voice, body hair, or breasts, differ from
what would be expected based on one's sex. Think of a person who
has ovaries and female (XX) sex chromosomes, but who has what
looks like a penis.[9] The existence of these conditions in which
people have some unusual differences in sex-related traits doesn't
undermine the fact that there are two distinct sexes; it underscores that they are the standard, since the nature of these

conditions is that they differentially affect males and females, impacting their health, physical features, and behaviors in specific, sex-related ways.

In 2009, Caster Semenya from South Africa dominated the 800 meters at the World Track and Field Championships. Semenya won by more than two seconds.[10] Rumors, from competitors and others, began to spread about her male-like features, including an unusually muscular frame, a deep voice, and a lack of breast tissue.[11] Even Pierre Weiss, the general secretary of the International Association of Athletics Federations (IAAF), questioned her sex: "She is a woman, but maybe not 100 percent."[12]

While Semenya was classified as female at birth based on external genitalia, genetically, he is a male with a genetic condition called 5-alpha-reductase deficiency (5-ARD). Here's a little on how this works. In the womb, we all start out with something that looks something like an undeveloped clitoris, and inside of our abdomen, we all have either testes or ovaries. In male fetuses, those testes produce high levels of the androgen testosterone, and that's what causes that clitoris-like structure to grow into a penis. The key to understanding this condition is that to grow a penis, testosterone must be high, and also must be converted into a more potent androgen called dihydrotestosterone (DHT). It is DHT, essentially, that grows the penis.

But in people with 5-ARD, which has important effects on males only, the body can't produce the enzyme needed to convert testosterone into DHT—5-alpha-reductase. So without DHT, even though testosterone levels are normal for a boy, these individuals will be born with what looks like a clitoris and a vagina (that doesn't connect to a cervix or uterus), and may be incorrectly sexed as females. And since DHT is also required for the testes to descend from the abdomen into the scrotal sac toward the end of pregnancy, people with 5-ARD are also born without visible testes. But they still produce plenty of testosterone that helps the male body to grow big and strong during puberty, just like any other male.

Semenya has XY (male) chromosomes, undescended internal testes, which produce testosterone, and no womb or ovaries.[13] Semenya does have high testosterone levels *for a woman* but has testosterone levels inside the typical range for that of an adult male. The only potential sports-relevant difference between Semenya and other males is that his DHT levels are low. But there is no evidence that this is, in fact, relevant for sports. There appears to be no effect of DHT on muscle mass, strength, power, or speed. His male-typical testosterone levels promoted all of that during and after puberty, like any other male. Even blocking testosterone in adulthood doesn't remove all the physical benefits provided by high testosterone in puberty.

After the 2009 race, Semenya couldn't compete until the governing bodies of track and field, World Athletics and the IAAF, determined how to proceed in light of what they described as "her unusually high testosterone levels" (for a woman). In 2011, World Athletics, with the IAAF joining the ruling later, decided that "all female athletes with hyperandrogenism" (a medical condition that produces high level of androgens, or testosterone) and XY chromosomes had to medically lower their testosterone.[14] Semenya complied, and his race times slowed. But with his greater muscle mass, and other traits like lower body fat, and larger heart and lungs, even lowering his testosterone didn't prevent him from winning a silver medal in the 800m in 2012 (this was upgraded to a gold when former Olympian Mariya Savinova got her medal taken away for doping).[15] In 2015, IAAF changed the rules and Semenya was able to compete without having to reduce his testosterone levels. He (easily) won gold in both the 2016 Olympics and the 2017 World Championships. Speaking of the 2016 Olympics, the top three winners in the women's 800m—Semenya, Francine Niyonsaba (Burundi), and Margaret Wambui (Kenya)—all had male (XY) sex chromosomes and were widely suspected of having the same condition as Semenya.[16] In 2018, the rules changed again. World Athletics introduced new regulations affecting athletes competing in the women's category in middle distance races, who also had high testosterone, XY sex chromosomes, and internal testes (male DSDs). They were now required to lower their testosterone levels to those of "a healthy woman with ovaries," below 5 nmol/L.[17] But even these levels were well above those of a typical "healthy woman."

These athletes with male DSD, almost all of whom, as far as we know, had the same condition as Semenya, were given several options to lower their testosterone levels. They could take a contraceptive pill, have a monthly injection of a testosterone blocker, or have surgery to remove their testes. Semenya refused all of these options and has been unable to compete since then. He challenged the decision before the Court of Arbitration for Sport in Switzerland, but in 2019, the court ruled the regulations would remain in place as they "were necessary to ensure fairness in track and field."[18] In July 2023, however, the European Court of Human Rights ruled it was discriminatory for Semenya to have to lower natural amounts of testosterone produced to compete.[19] As of the time of this writing, World Athletics have stated the rules they established in 2018 would remain in place.[20]

Without fairness, what are sports? Every sport is inherently dependent on rules that define the boundaries of the competition.

• • •

Why does the biological fact of the two sexes really matter in the arena of sports? It's the same reason why we have any category. The 12&U (twelve-and-under) group doesn't compete with eighteen-year-olds. Able-bodied athletes don't compete in the Paralympics. Is it fatphobic that we don't allow heavyweight boxers to compete against featherweights? Obviously, that's a rhetorical question because everyone knows that's not why these categories were created. It would put the featherweights at risk if we didn't implement this system. It gives each weight class a chance to show their capabilities based on their own physical ceilings and limitations. It's the exact same thing when it comes to the sexes. Not only can we see obvious physical differences between males and females, but researchers from the Molecular Genetics Department at the Weizmann Institute of Science identified about 6,500 genetic differences between the two sexes. Dr. Moran Gershoni explained, "The basic genome is nearly the same in all of us, but it is utilized differently across the body and among individuals. Thus, when it comes to the differences between the sexes, we see that evolution often works on the level of gene expression."[21]

I'm going to talk about how Title IX came into being and its significance later, but I want to emphasize here that women fought to create their place in athletics to showcase their abilities and strengths within their own uniqueness.

Centuries ago, it was once believed that women were not able to play sports because they lacked the energy it required and such activities would injure their reproductive organs, putting their fertility at risk.[22] Over time, these myths, of course, were debunked and female sports were born. What was not questioned or discredited was the scientific fact that once boys hit puberty and testosterone levels sharply rise, thirty times higher in fact than prepuberty levels,[23] in contrast to girls, boys begin to outperform girls in sports.[24][25] I saw this clearly in my own experience of swimming. Around ages 11–12, the girls and boys were relatively comparable. Because girls went through puberty before boys did, I would go as far to say the top-end girls were even faster than the boys most of the time at this age. But this all changed in the 13–14 age group. Boys started to turn into young men. They got taller, more defined, more explosive off the blocks and walls. Those boys I would always beat in practice started outperforming me. There was nothing I could do about it, which irritated 13-year-old me beyond belief.

Dr. Hooven explains that once a male goes through puberty, he experiences changes in bone mineral density, height, muscle mass, limb length, hand span, and hemoglobin. All of these changes translate to natural advantages over females in speed, strength, and power, most of which are not removed even after the use of testosterone blockers.[26][27]

Puberty is a game-changer. In the words of Dr. Hooven, "A male level of T [testosterone] in puberty and adulthood (with possible contributions from prenatal T), is the master key for superior performance in most sports."[28] Consider that male athletes have around 4–12 percent body fat and female athletes, 12–23 percent. This is not a fatphobic opinion or a statement intended to offend or harm a woman; it is a fact.[29] This amount of body fat in women is necessary to bear children as it protects the uterus.

As is another fact that elite male athletes have an average of 10–50 percent performance advantage over female athletes.[30][31][32] The difference is higher in activities that are more explosive. For instance, in weight lifting, the difference can be as high as 37 percent. In long and high jump, it's around 18 percent; gaps between fastest tennis serves and baseball pitches range from 20 to in excess of 5-.[33][34] Performance differences larger than 20 percent are generally present when considering sports and activities that involve extensive upper-body contributions. The gap between fastest recorded tennis serve is 20 percent, while the gaps between fastest recorded baseball pitches and field hockey drag flicks exceed 50 percent.

Sports scientist Ross Tucker argues, "Male attributes are such powerful contributors to performance that, if you didn't control them, they would dominate and drown out all the other performance contributors."[35] In an interview with Medscape he said, "Women's sports exist because we recognize that male physiology has biological differences that create performance advantages. Women's sports exist to ensure that male advantages are excluded. If you allow male advantage in, you're allowing something to cross into a category that specifically tries to exclude it. . . . If someone wants to allow natural advantages to be celebrated in sports, they're arguing against the existence of any categories, because every single category in sports is trying to filter out certain advantages."[36]

Look at Tori Bowie, an Olympic, world, and US champion in track and field. Her 100-meter lifetime best of 10.78 was beaten 15,000 times by adult and young males in 2017. Allyson Felix, another Olympic, world, and US champion, is a similar example. Her 400-meters lifetime best of 49.26 was beaten over 15,000 by men and boys in the year 2017 alone.[37] These comparisons do not evidence the superiority of male athletes over female athletes; they are intended to evidence the basics of physiology. We can't hide from the truth, even if it might make someone, or a group of people, uncomfortable or offended.

Biology is not bigotry.

Just take that low end of performance advantage that male athletes have over female athletes, 10 percent. It sounds small, but according to Tucker, the gap is actually so large that if we didn't have a category for female athletes, we wouldn't see any on an elite level.[38] As Tucker puts it, "Many women outperform many men, but at any matched level, many men outperform all women."[39]

The Soccer Tournament (TST) is a seven-a-side event that includes thirty-two teams made up of famous international former soccer players who play to win one million dollars. At the time I was working on this book, the US women's players, who were coached by soccer legend Mia Hamm and included World Cup winner Heather O'Reilly, competed against Wrexham AFC, an all-male professional soccer club in Wales. The women's team was defeated by 12–0 but took the loss well. O'Reilly was quoted as saying, "We're super proud. Hopefully we've proved to anybody, just go for it, just live. What's the worst that could happen? We lose 16–0 to Wrexham?"[40] Both teams were made up of soccer superstars. The men beat the women. It's not because these women didn't try hard enough or were less skilled. It's because the male team had advantages the female team didn't and could never have. There's a reason there's a Men's World Cup and a Women's World Cup.

Even tennis phenoms Venus and Serena Williams have experienced losing to a male with not nearly as much notoriety as they have . . . in a blowout. In 1998, in a matchup against Karsten Braasch, the 203rd ranked male tennis player from Germany, Serena lost 6–1 and Venus lost 6–2. Keep in mind Serena is a 23-time Grand Champion and her sister a 7-time Grand Champion. Serena herself said, "I hit shots that would have been winners on the women's Tour, and he got to them easily."[41]

Is it a good time to mention at the time Braasch was smoking a pack of cigarettes a day, and smoked during changeovers the day of the match? He also admitted to playing a round of golf and drinking a few cocktails before facing the Williams sisters as well as performing like "a guy ranked 600th."[42] Thirteen years later, in an interview with David Letterman, Serena noted she would lose to Andy Murray 6–0 in just a matter of minutes. She went as far to say men and women's tennis is a totally different sport.[43] Serena told Letterman, "I love to play women's tennis. I only want to play girls because I don't want to be embarrassed." I bet she never thought that glaringly obvious statement would be deemed controversial and get her immediately canceled, but here we are.

This was even a point I had to make testifying in front of the Senate Judiciary Committee in June 2023. I was one of two witnesses chosen by the GOP of five in total on a hearing surrounding the broader picture of the gender ideology movement. I was sat next to the president of the Human Rights Campaign, Kelley Robinson. Senator John Kennedy from Louisiana had already asked Robinson how many genders she thought there were, to which she responded that there is essentially an infinite number of genders, before he asked her, "You don't believe that a biological male has a physical advantage in sports over a biological female?"

Confidently, she responded, "Not as a definitive statement."

"How many female members of the NBA do you see?" Good point, Senator Kennedy. None.

"Well, I can say that there has been this news article about men that think that they could beat Serena Williams in tennis, right? That they think they could actually score a point on her, um, and it's just not the case. She is stronger than them."

Senator Kennedy cut her off to quickly turn to me and ask, "Ms. Gaines, what has your experience been? Male, female."

Without hesitation, I calmly said, "Both Serena and Venus lost to the 203rd ranked male tennis player, which they're phenoms for women. My experience, my husband swam for the University of

Kentucky as well. In terms of accolades, in terms of national ranking, I was a much better swimmer than him. He could kick my butt
any day of the week . . . without trying."[44]

I figured that point was enough to prove the point of my argument: a male switching to the women's team to compete against
the women is never going to be a lateral movement. I didn't even
have to get into the specifics of the fact they lost in a blowout to a
man who had just finished a round of golf and was drinking and
smoking in between sets and who also admitted he played like a
"guy ranked 600th." But sure, Mrs. Robinson, if your argument
was that Serena Williams could beat Senator Kennedy in tennis,
you would be correct. But that's disingenuous. Sorry, Senator Kennedy, I think there are a lot of women who could beat you in a tennis match. Myself included, I'd like to think.

I trust you get the point that men and women are, in fact, different in a way that, on average, gives males advantages when it
comes to sheer strength or athleticism. I can't help but reiterate
that just because most men are longer, stronger, faster, and have
better endurance than women, thanks to testosterone, it does not
make the female sex inferior. Rather, the differences between the
two sexes are something that should be recognized and celebrated.

Allowing males to compete in women's sports on an elite level
is not something to be lauded for inclusivity. It is something that
must be stopped based on unfairness. Fair competition is not about
allowing competitors into the race or the game because they identify a certain way. Like Sebastian Coe, president of World Athletics,
said, "Gender cannot trump biology."[45] Facts over feelings, always.

• • •

You're probably wondering, but what about hormone replacement
therapy (HRT)? If a male takes hormone suppressants and female

hormones, which will reduce his level of testosterone and increase his level of estrogen, wouldn't that give him an equal playing field to compete against female athletes? Short answer, not in the slightest. Sharron Davies uses the analogy of a boiled egg, which I find to be brilliant.[46] Once an egg has been boiled, it can never be unboiled or returned to its natural state. While testosterone blockers will cause muscle loss in a male, even with taking estrogen, he will not reach the hormone levels of a female.[47] And even if he could, there are other advantages outside of factors affected by testosterone that will never be mitigated, like height, heart size, lung volume, bone structure and strength, etc. Women are more than a testosterone level.

A study published in the *British Journal of Sports Medicine* in 2020 observed forty-six males who identified as women in the US Air Force from 2013 to 2018.[48] For two years since starting testosterone, the males participating in the study who were on HRT successfully completed 10 percent more push-ups and 6 percent more sit-ups than their female counterparts. After two years, though the males appeared to level off, they were still 12 percent faster on the 1.5-mile run compared to their female peers. This study alone shows that males retain strength and endurance advantages even after hormone suppressants.

Another study, published in *Sports Medicine*, examined the old criteria currently determined by the IOC (similar to the NCAA policy) that require males who are transitioning to have less than 10 nmol/L for at least twelve months prior to and during competition and deemed it insufficient.[49] Considering the average level of testosterone for females is 0.5 to 2.4 nmol/L,[50] this policy is an absolute joke. Researchers Emma Hilton and Tommy Lundberg reported that "the performance gap between males and females becomes significant at puberty and often amounts to

10–50% depending on sport. . . . Current evidence shows the biological advantage, most notably in terms of muscle mass and strength, conferred by male puberty and thus enjoyed by most transgender women is only minimally reduced when testosterone is suppressed as per current sporting guidelines for transgender athletes."[51]

In March 2013, Fallon Fox came out as the first male MMA fighter to identify as a woman and compete in the women's category. Fox underwent HRT, breast augmentation, and hair transplant surgeries in 2006 and afterward entered the MMA arena. Now a transgender rights advocate (TRA), Fox has five wins on his record, including three TKOs and two submissions. In 2014, he fought Tamikka Brents. Although Brents did not believe fighting a male was fair, she still got in the ring. "If I'm slated," Tamika said, "I'm going to fight. I'm not going to back down from a fight."[52] Shocker, the fight was over in the first round by TKO. Suffering from a concussion and orbital bone fractures, Brents required staples in her skull and head. In an interview after the fight, she admitted to being overcome by Fox's strength.

> I've fought a lot of women and have never felt the strength that I felt in a fight as I did that night. I can't answer whether it's because she was born a man or not because I'm not a doctor. I can only say, I've never felt so overpowered ever in my life and I am an abnormally strong female in my own right. Her grip was different, I could usually move around in the clinch against other females but couldn't move at all in Fox's clinch.[53]

Fox took to Twitter a few years after the fight to respond to a user who criticized him for his participation in the women's division. He proudly tweeted in 2020, "For the record, I knocked two out. One woman's skull was fractured, the other not. And just so you know, I enjoyed it. See, I love smacking up TEFS [*sic*] in the cage who talk transphobic nonsense. It's bliss!"[54] TERF stands for trans-exclusionary radical feminist. A male openly glorifying and boasting in the brutal injuries he inflicted on a woman while also threatening to do the same to any other woman who dares to oppose or even question his participation in the women's category? How tolerant, kind, and inclusive.

If there's one sport where you would think sex-based categories would be necessary, it's probably boxing, but nonetheless, USA Boxing has now implemented guidelines that would allow males who have gone through reassignment surgery and hormone testing to compete in the category consistent with their gender identity. Think about what this means. In the name of inclusion, men are being allowed to punch women in the face with no consequences. Not only with no consequences, but these men will be glorified for such actions by being awarded prize money, championship belts, and titles. This is what we're calling "progress"?

Unfortunately, male-female injuries aren't limited to sports that involve punching and kicking. In September 2022 during a high school volleyball game, a male self-identifying as a woman spiked a ball that hit female player Payton McNabb in the face.[55] She was immediately knocked unconscious and left in a fencing position on the ground until she came back around. A full year since the incident and Payton is still partially paralyzed on her right side, her vision and memory are impaired, she has to have special accommodations for testing at school because she can't retain information like she could before the hit, and she wasn't able to play college sports as she had hoped. How many more stories of injustice against women and girls before we learn our lesson?

• • •

Unfortunately, there's a long history of injustice in female sports. In today's world, we are giving permission for female athletes to compete against people who have a proven unfair advantage. Sharron Davies, as well as many other world-class athletes in the 1970s, knows what this is like all too well. At just thirteen years old, Davies represented Great Britain at the 1976 Montreal Olympics and was the youngest competitor. This woman is no stranger to mental and physical toughness. As an athlete for most of her life, she's had to contend with some harsh realities. Sharron broke both of her forearms when she was eleven. Her father, who was also her swimming coach, didn't press pause on the practice. It almost reminds me of my dad, except this made throwing me in a cold pool in the middle of winter seem mild. Her dad wrapped both casts with plastic bags and said, "There's no reason why you can't just kick."[56] Sharron tore the ligaments in her knee the next year. You can imagine what her dad did. That's right. He tied her legs together and she swam only with her arms until she could kick again.[57]

Despite continuing to set records and win titles in global championship events, including the Commonwealth Games, European Championships, and World Olympics through 1992, no amount of mental toughness, hours in the pool, or strength training sessions could prepare her to compete against the artificially induced testosterone-fueled power, endurance, and speed of the East German phenom female athletes.

The early 1970s was the start of East Germany's journey of becoming an Olympic powerhouse. In 1968, this tiny country took home 25 Olympic medals, 9 of which were gold. Suddenly their triumph trajectory took a major upswing. East Germany dominated at the 1972 Montreal Games and shocked the globe by winning 66 medals; 20 were gold. They continued to excel. In 1976, this tiny country began to mirror the victories of Olympic dynamos like the United States and Russia, which boasted populations 18 times their size,[58] and won 90 medals, 40 of which were gold. The East German female swimmers alone won 11 out of 13 swim events, a historic feat that had never been done before.

US Olympian Shirley Babashoff, who set 11 world records and 39 US records, questioned the meteoric rise of the East German swimmers. She knew something dubious was in force. In an interview, she said, "It was pretty obvious that something happened.... I thought the East Germans had replaced the women's team with men in women's swimsuits."[59] During the Olympics, when she made comments about her competitors having deep voices and mustaches, which they did, Shirley became a scapegoat for a sore loser. What she said in an interview rings true with what is happening in the female sports arena today: "It was just the oddest thing that this country was doing this in front of the whole world and no one blinked. To be absolutely shut down by this little tiny country where apparently all the best women swimmers came from . . . and if you said anything bad about them you were a poor sport."[60]

The media started calling her "Surly Shirley," but Shirley wasn't surly at all. She would turn out to be right. Wendy Boglioli, Shirley's teammate, said this about her East German competitors: "They were very strong women; they were very fast; we thought they were machines. Here (we) were, four of America's best athletes ever put together on a team, and every single day the East German women were winning every, every event."[61]

In 1980, East Germany's achievements toppled everyone's expectations. They won 126 medals, 47 gold. But here's the twist Shirley had anticipated. Because East Germany was a communist country separated from the West and much of the world, they were able to tailor a custom experience for their athletes to ensure top athletic performance and global glory. They didn't do it through strict training, nutrition, sleep, or stretching routines. They did it via doping.

The strategy was a state-sponsored drug program called *State Plan 14-25*. Over ten thousand athletes,[62] including girls as young as ten years old, were recruited and given male hormones, Oral Turinabol, an anabolic steroid that came from testosterone. But here's the thing. These females had no idea they were being given untested drugs that would forever change their physiology and biological chemistry. They were told they were taking vitamins.[63] If they refused, the girls would be kicked off the team.[64] It's reported that female athletes not only were given Oral Turinabol until competition time but they were also given testosterone injections while they were competing.[65] According to Dr. Werner Franke, a molecular biologist and his wife, Brigitte Franke-Berendonk, a former Olympian, both of whom exposed State Plan 14-25 in the 1990s after the fall of the Berlin Wall, "Special emphasis was placed on administering androgens to women and adolescent girls because this practice proved to be particularly effective for sports performance."[66]

The medals came with a devastating price, paid dearly by the athletes. These young women suffered from a number of physical side effects during the process, including facial acne, deepened voices, and excessive hair growth in their pubic area and on their legs.[67] Far more serious were the high incidences of heart, liver, and kidney damage[68] including calcified hearts, the need for long-term dialysis, and tumors that led to death; ovarian and breast cancer, and gynecological problems.[69] [70] Not to mention infertility problems, miscarriages, and pregnancies that resulted in a higher rate of babies with disabilities like club feet and chronic disease.[71] One report showed that athletes who were found to be pregnant during the doping scandal were ordered to have abortions.[72] Many of the athletes also suffered from mental issues, including depression and eating disorders.[73]

In 1986, Heidi Krieger was Europe's shot-put champion. Krieger experienced so many physical changes from the steroids, she lost her identity as a female. In 1997 she underwent a sex change operation. According to Heidi, who now goes by Andreas, the East Germany state doping program "killed Heidi."[74] Krieger's life today is unfortunately filled with physical pain and fatigue.

Fourteen-year-old Rica Reinisch had been given her "little blue pills in a chocolate box."[75] When she was fifteen, she won triple gold and set four world records in swimming at the 1980 Olympic Games in Moscow. Two years later, she collapsed at a training session due to inflamed ovaries. She was forced to retire from swimming at the age of sixteen. More health problems ensued. She suffered from two stillbirths and a serious heart condition.[76] Rica says, "What makes me sad is that I will never know how good I could have been."[77]

In the 1980 Moscow Olympics, Davies had a shot at the gold for the 400 individual medley, which consisted of 100 meters of each stroke in the order of butterfly, backstroke, breaststroke, then freestyle. She was in the best shape of her life. While strong and confident, the British young woman couldn't help but be skeptical of the three East German women in the pool with her. By then, rumors were flying about how East Germany rose to meteoric athletic power. Olympic athletes who competed against these female powerhouses knew their performance was boosted by some type of unfair advantage. Still, the Olympic Committee never demanded a full investigation. In her book, Davies writes:

These girls had an artificial winning edge. That's what the rest of us faced. It was unsporting and unfair, and, of course, it broke the rules, but the rule-makers failed to hold inquiries into dubious results after questionable dominance at every passing international competition. Actually, it was worse than that, because that second group of men responsible, Olympic bosses, put some of the GDR doping masterminds on the IOC's medical, scientific and anti-doping committees tasked with staying one step ahead of cheats. In fact, those GDR officials were there to make sure they stayed three steps ahead of the anti-doping police to avoid detection.[78]

Davies never got her gold. East German Petra Schneider won first at 4:46 by a full ten seconds over Sharron, who came in at 4:56 and clinched silver. Petra would end up testifying against the doctors and trainers who injected her with testosterone when the doping scandal finally went to trial from 1998 to 2000 once the men were impacted.

Davies sees similar parallels between how international sports authorities handled the doping scandal fifty-plus years ago and how organizations are allowing males to compete in women's sports today. She writes in her book *Unfair Play*:

I feel a deep sense of despair that we don't learn from history. Having failed female athletes for half a century by refusing to take action when a whole nation doped its females with a decisive dose of male advantage, Olympic authorities have watched the transgender crisis unfold and responded in exactly the same way. They've let it go. Yet again, it's female athletes who will pay the price.[79]

Davies has experienced what I now see happening all too often to girls and women across the world—women having records, titles, sponsorships, podium spots, and prize money being robbed from them because of men who demand inclusion into our sports and our locker rooms. Prior to 2015, the IOC required those men who self-identified as women to undergo sex reassignment surgery in addition to having at least two years of hormone replacement therapy.[80] Today, the IOC's policy is significantly more lax, despite growing scientific evidence for male athletes' unfair advantage. Even back when East Germany was doping their athletes, scientists concluded that "androgenic initiation has permanent effects in girls and women, where increases in strength and performance do not return to pretreatment values after the drug is withdrawn."[81]

Because of the relentless work of Sharron Davies and others who saw the harm in allowing both men and women to cheat by using performance-enhancing drugs, most sport-specific governing bodies like the IOC and the NCAA have strict guidelines against these now-banned substances. The NCAA even banned Celsius, a popular energy drink, for having too much caffeine.[82] Here reads an insert from the NCAA's website highlighting the immorality of using banned substances:

The NCAA bans the use of performance-enhancing and recreational drugs to protect the health of college athletes and ensure fair play. The risks for student-athletes using these drugs are high; a positive drug test will result in the loss of eligibility and suspension from sport, could negatively impact health, and in some cases, is just plain cheating.[83]

On the banned substance list is none other than the anabolic agent testosterone.[84] While the NCAA considers the use of testosterone cheating, it can also earn you a nomination for NCAA Woman of the Year. But I'm getting ahead of myself.

Though it's not a communist doping scandal that today's female athletes must contend with, it's the battle between gender identity ideology and reality. The Tokyo Olympic Games in 2021 welcomed three openly transgender athletes: Quinn, a Canadian soccer player; Chelsea Wolfe, an alternate on the US women's BMX freestyle team; and Laurel Hubbard, a weight lifter from New Zealand. All of these athletes played for the women's team. Quinn, who was born female and identifies as a male, still competes with the women. I think we all know why Quinn didn't play with the men's Canadian Olympic soccer team.

Hannah Arensman, a national cyclocross champion, retired at the end of 2022. She didn't want to end a successful career of thirty-five wins, coming in the top five in her last seven races,[85] but because she was repeatedly forced to race against many males with androgenized bodies in the women's category, she was consistently put at a disadvantage, causing her to love her love for the sport entirely. In her words:

> *I have decided to end my cycling career. At my last race at the recent UCI Cyclocross National Championships in the elite women's category in December 2022, I came in 4th place, flanked on either side by male riders awarded 3rd and 5th places. My sister and family sobbed as they watched a man finish in front of me, having witnessed several physical interactions with him throughout the race. Additionally, it is difficult for me to think about the very real*

*possibility I was overlooked for an international selection
on the US team at Cyclocross Worlds in February 2023
because of a male competitor. Moving forward, I feel for
young girls learning to compete and who are growing up in
a day when they no longer have a fair chance at being the
new record holders and champions in cycling because men
want to compete in our division.*[86]

*Thankfully, Union Cycliste Internationale (UCI) has
now followed the likes of FINA (the international governing body of swimming) and World Athletics (the international governing body of track and field) have created
guidelines that prevent any individual who has gone
through male puberty from competing in the category that
does not match their sex. The policy is by no means perfect
(actually pretty far from it as it insinuates if you've transitioned by the age of 12, then you can compete in the category matching your gender identity), but it is a bold first
step in prioritizing fairness over inclusion. I wish more spe
cific sport governing bodies would take notice of FINA,
World Athletics, and UCI. Even the International Chess
Federation (FIDE) instituted a new policy banning males
from competing in women's only chess tournaments and
vice versa. They didn't do this to make the point women are
less intellectually capable than men, but rather to enforce
women's opportunities are strictly for women.*[87] *Another
unusual but needed governing body to stand with women
is the International Angling Sport Federation.*

At the 2023 Angling World Championships in Sicily, a male
identifying as a woman was set to compete in the women's category. For this reason, the England angling squad refused to

compete in the tournament, which, in turn, resulted in the new rule preventing this scenario from occurring again.[88]

My grandmother's generation fought so this wouldn't happen. We deserve to have equal opportunity to compete and succeed. We deserve to be champions.

5.

MAKING WAVES

The first media interview I ever gave after the NCAA Championships almost didn't happen. During the media training for the NCAA qualifiers at the University of Kentucky, we were told to forward all media requests at the meet to our sports information director (SID), who was also the one conducting the media training. We were told to do this since she was the one trained and qualified to coordinate requests for us. That made sense because, after all, it was within her job description.

Before Thomas and I even competed against each other, a slew of reporters tried to bait me into sharing my thoughts on the upcoming race. They would find your name on the heat sheet, then search for you on social media. They even found my parents' email somehow. My teammates' inboxes were full as well, indicating these reporters were desperately trying to get someone to bite the hook and give them a quote or story they could take back to their publishers. I held off on responding to any requests before we raced because I felt like I needed to be directly impacted before being qualified to talk, which, looking back, was not true at all. After we raced and the trophy fiasco, I decided I would take a public stand acknowledging how we faced harmful and blatant discrimination on the basis of our sex. Although I had a sea of reporters and journalists to choose from, I knew I only needed to respond to one to get the story out. After vetting them, I chose to talk to Mary Margaret Olohan, who was working with the Daily Wire at the time. After I forwarded our SID's contact information to the reporter with the hopes she would coordinate a time for us to talk, our SID swiftly texted me, "I declined the interview request. . . . You did the right thing by giving her my number!"

> ME: Wait, but I do have some things I would like to say, and I do want to make a statement in some way. Both the girls who will probably get second and third tonight are publicly supportive of Thomas, but I don't think that represents the rest of us female athletes. I want to say something about it if no one else will speak up for us.
>
> HER: I will remind you of our conversation a couple of weeks ago. But you know we'll support you and stand behind you no matter what!

I couldn't help but catch the feeling that this woman's response was based on a script she was forced to follow. While she continued to relay her support and encouragement through words like "support" and "encourage," something in her tone seemed to express passiveness and apprehension.

Before I called Mary Margaret, I called Mitch Barnhart, the athletic director at the University of Kentucky. I briefly explained to him what had happened and how we felt about it. When I say "we," I meant 95 percent of us on UK's swim and dive team. My phone call to him was an act of respect; I felt he needed to know, and I truly valued his opinion and advice. Barnhart and I had maintained a great relationship all four years of my collegiate career. He is a great Christian example and was someone who always just exhumed leadership in the best and most effective way by always leading by example. As the AD at UK for over twenty years, he was well respected and influential in the world of athletic directors. When I decided to call him, I was genuinely debating whether taking a public stance was a good idea and if it was worth the risk of damaging my future based on what they told us would happen if we spoke out. The last thing I wanted to do was portray my school poorly, given everything they had poured into me. I truly loved my university. Mitch's response overwhelmed me: "Riley . . . I love *you*. I support *you*. I would support whatever stance you took since it's my job, but I'm so proud of you for doing what's right." I will never forget what he said next. "Speak your heart, stay true to your convictions, and don't worry about painting this university in a bad light because we're behind you."

While I was grateful for his encouragement, at the time, I didn't think too much of it. I figured this would be his response and I thought this is how any athletic director would treat their student-athlete. But, boy, I would soon learn how naïve I was to think that. To my knowledge and based off the conversations I have had with girls across the NCAA at all divisions, no athletic director at any public university has backed their female athletes in a similar situation with such unparalleled support. I don't believe it was a coincidence I ended up at Kentucky. I learned after the fact that right after I had reached out to Mitch, he called every other athletic director in the SEC and told them that they had "better stand behind my swimmer." It was highly unusual for someone of his caliber to be so forthright and bold in a climate where advocating for female athletes is considered transphobic and hateful. Mitch knew the truth and he knew my heart. What was happening was wrong and unfair, and he wasn't willing to throw his moral compass out the window in order to conform or be "politically correct."

And neither was I.

• • •

My objective in talking to Mary Margaret was to voice the message that we, female athletes, were wronged in this NCAA competition. At the same time, I didn't want to hurt anyone's feelings. I think this is largely from how my teammates, my competitors, the coaches, and I had been conditioned. While there was a lot of external pressure to stay quiet, we also put a lot of internal pressure on ourselves and overanalyzed what our future might look like if we didn't conform. My language and tone were on high alert. I was so concerned with getting the message out the "right" way—and by right, I mean what I thought to be loving, kind, and not offensive—that, looking back, I made slight compromises. For example, I struggled with the pronoun situation initially. In the vein of being transparent and with the hope of being relatable, I didn't see the harm in using the preferred pronouns at first. I knew it contradicted both biology and common sense, but I wanted to be what I was told was respectful and not come across as transphobic. I'm no psychologist, but I'm sure this has to do with the characteristic of agreeableness, one of the Big Five core personality traits. Agreeableness is about wanting social harmony and being seen as giving, empathetic, cooperative, and kind.[1] On average, women tend to be more agreeable than men.[2] This doesn't mean there aren't any agreeable men or disagreeable women; it just means you are more apt to find women who want to be "nice" than men who have that same bent. I've since discovered that sometimes wanting to be seen as "kind and inclusive" can detract us from speaking how we really feel in the manner that we really mean.

Contrary to the seemingly popular opinion among the LGTBQ community and of most progressives, I believe being forced to use preferred pronouns promotes reality distortion and a lack of basic respect for biology. Since I started advocating for women's sex-based rights, I began to realize that even when I tried to be what I thought was kind and inclusive and used preferred pronouns, it wasn't enough. Unless we undoubtedly believed men could turn into women and experience all the same things women do while not daring to question it, then you were showcasing transphobia. I was fully embracing fiction in the guise of showing respect.

Looking back, this struggle was in action when I first started speaking to reporters and anyone who would listen about wanting to maintain female-only spaces. Turns out, no matter how "nice" one tries to be, advocating for female rights is simply unacceptable to some people. These are the kind of men and women who are not going to listen to your message or the words coming out of your mouth. Instead, they are going to hear what they want to hear and then vilify *you* for it.

It finally occurred to me that I was bending over backward and compromising on what I knew to be right in hopes of appearing respectful to someone who had no respect for us as women. While Thomas was technically following the rules in place, there was no consideration for the feelings, privacy, equal opportunities, or dignity of me or the other female competitors. In sports at this level, male inclusion demands female exclusion. It's not trans-phobic to see the desire and need for equal opportunities, privacy, and safety.

I no longer feel like I must defend the derogatory labels or com-promise to convince people my argument isn't rooted in hate. Who I am and what I stand for is based on common sense and morality. The language I speak and write must reflect that. There is an enor-mous difference between "he was exposing male genitalia" and "she was exposing male genitalia" and even just using "Thomas was exposing male genitalia." This is gaslighting and hurting women in the name of not wanting to offend the male. I guess I needed to discover on my own terms what it truly means to be unapologetic in standing firm for what you believe and for what's right. Along with pronouns, I have now realized there are other ways I was compromising the truth. When you think about it, the term "biological female" or "biological male" is nonsensical. Why do I have to describe myself as a biological female when the word "female" already implies what I am, since it's an immutable sex based term rooted in science? When we use this language, we are compromising and catering to the delusions that a man can ever be a woman. Language matters. If thoughts can corrupt language, then language can corrupt thoughts. The mission is far more important to me than denying biological realities in the name of inclusion.

> The Party told you to reject the evidence of your eyes
> and ears. It was their final, most essential command.[3]
> —GEORGE ORWELL, 1984

In my first experience with a journalist post-NCAA champi-onship, I made it clear to Mary Margaret that I was appalled at the

NCAA and the way the organization was treating the athletes they supposedly supported. I told her that the sports organization just turned "their backs on all of the females, not even just in swimming, but in all NCAA sports, just to appease a small minority. . . . Title IX has been around for 50 years. The NCAA was even passing around Title IX shirts and on the back of the shirts it said equity, fairness. And I just thought it was a bit ironic that you preach one thing but do another."[4]

I believe this Daily Wire interview gained national attention for a couple of reasons. First and foremost, sports are something that resonates with everyone and reaches across party lines. Who doesn't love sports? Second, I think people finally saw the severity of what we collegiate athletes had experienced. I think when you initially hear the term "transwoman," you think of someone who is fully committed to the transitioning process and has had the reassignment surgeries and has computable testosterone levels to that of a female, when in reality, that wasn't what we saw with Lia Thomas at all.

This Daily Wire exchange quickly sparked a barrage of media interviews and requests for appearances at national events. My phone had never engaged in this much action. One minute I was trying to figure out my life postcollege like a typical grad; the next minute I was trying to finesse my organizational skills to better manage my packed calendar so I didn't miss a phone interview or forget to call someone back. My biggest fear was missing an opportunity to share my story. Never did I ever imagine sharing a platform with former president Donald Trump. But in August 2022, after accepting an invitation from the Conservative Political Action Conference (CPAC), I sat in the audience nodding my head as President Trump introduced the issue of men infiltrating women's sports. Of course, he had a hilarious, charismatic way of telling our story as female swimmers at that meet. He even exaggerated it by saying, "Some women are being badly injured by the windburn that's caused by the man going so much faster. The wind is blowing. It's just terrible. It's so unfair." I froze when he called my name in front of tens of thousands of people around me. His Secret Service detail looked surprised. Shell-shocked, I walked onstage and stood beside him. Imagine that, a college swimmer preparing to be a dentist being summoned by the forty-fifth president of the United States to communicate the message that women's sports should only be for women? Surreal and something I never could have foreseen.

I was done swimming, my school load was light, and I was in my last few months before dental school (or so I thought), so I figured I would take these few months to fully pursue this fight before moving on with my life. I was thrust into a position of giving truth a voice on podcasts, through op-eds, and in the media. Impassioned by my mission, I didn't say no to anyone who wanted to talk to me. *You want me to come and talk on your podcast that gets a total of six listeners? Absolutely!* I probably should have vetted the people sending me these requests, but hey, there's always a lesson to learn.

About a week or two after my first interview, I was beginning to feel more confident not just in sharing the truth, but in expressing myself. I was trying to ignore the pressure to stick with certain pronouns or stay away from certain words. All I wanted to do was tell the truth and not cower from the reality of what I was feeling and what happened. For instance, I shouldn't have to apologize for feeling uncomfortable in a locker room when a 6'4" man comes in and starts undressing and exposing very male parts next to us females. It took time to stand up without apology. I remember the first time I fumbled my words out of insecurity.

When a random woman (or what I thought to be a woman at the time) reached out to me on Instagram and asked me for my perspective on a book she was writing about transgender participation in sports, I didn't hesitate to say yes. The second Kristina said, "Hello," and began introducing himself at the start of our telephone interview, I knew it was a male posing as a woman. His voice was a dead giveaway. While I wasn't expecting to be asked questions by a trans-identifying individual, I wasn't necessarily opposed to it. Yet the surprise threw me entirely off guard. The burgeoning confidence I had been building up took a nosedive.

When he specifically asked about the locker room piece, I said something to the effect of, "Well, we weren't *that* uncomfortable." To be clear, that wasn't true. That statement flew out of my mouth because I didn't want to ruffle feathers. I regret it to this day. I wish I had expressed myself with more clarity, but by the time we hung up the phone, I vowed never to water down the truth again. The locker room *was* that uncomfortable. Like every journey in life, I chose to grow from the moment.

I remember the exact moment I vowed once and for all to stop adhering specifically to the usage of preferred pronouns. I was speaking on the University of North Carolina Wilmington campus, and when I told the story of racing against Lia Thomas, I referred to Thomas as a "he." I was going to tell my story through the lens of a scientific truth: sex is binary, not ideological.

Halfway through my talk, a group of transgender activists, many men who had beards and were wearing dresses, came into the room in which I was speaking. They walked to the back of the large room, turned their phone ringers on, and started texting each other. The chorus of "dings" from the notifications popping off on each of their phones wildly interrupted my train of thought, although I didn't skip a beat. More than being bothered by obnoxious behavior, I was horrified when I caught myself listening to what I was saying. I had stopped using pronouns that match Thomas's sex and had started referring to Lia Thomas as a "she." I don't even know if anyone noticed, but I did. And I didn't like that. That was the last time I ever made that mistake.

• • •

Two things happened the more vocal I became about my story and when I publicly questioned the NCAA's transgender policy. One, it stirred up a salty hornet's nest. Two, it cracked open a door for public-yet-private support.

I wasn't surprised when the hate started piling on. I didn't *not* expect it. Hate mail. Death threats. Nobody wants to receive that. But I support the constitutional right of all Americans to speak freely. Even if it is to send a message like this to a woman who is standing up for other women:

Transphobic b****.

Just admit you f***ing suck at swimming and need something else to blame it on besides the fact that you're just bad. And by the way if you even bothered to read a book or educate yourself mildly you'd know she* has no advantage because the hormones she's taking actually decrease her levels all around and put her at an overall disadvantage compared to imbeciles like you who aren't taking hormones and still can't beat her.

You also look like more of a man than she ever did.

---

* Lia Thomas.

I could write a whole book just from the almost comical hate comments I've received for the stance I've taken. At first, these negative comments weighed heavy on me, but then I began to see some patterns in the hate I was getting and who it was coming from. It came from people with no profile pictures. Troll accounts. It was coming from people who had clearly never played a sport in their life and didn't understand the value of hard work and fair competition. They didn't understand the adrenaline rush you get when you achieve the goals you've worked toward your whole life.

And the comments were extremely personal, essentially clustering around three accusations:

1. You're transphobic.
2. You're ugly.
3. You're not a good swimmer and you probably should have tried harder, sore loser!

These were petty personal attacks rather than thoughtful counterarguments. They backfired because, ultimately, they made me feel reassured and like I was doing something right. You don't waste ammunition on targets you don't want to hit, and I was certainly right over the target. The vile name-calling and threats spoke more about their insecurities than it did about me.

I hear the word "transphobic" so often the power of what it really means is getting choked by rhetoric. It's become nothing more a label slapped on a person with an opposing view. This happens online and in person. In December 2023, I testified before a subcommittee of the House Oversight Committee. The title of the hearing was "The Importance of Protecting Female Athletics and Title IX," which was ultimately intended to urge the Biden administration to halt on their illegal, administrative rewrite of Title IX, which would deem it discriminatory to prevent trans-identifying students from playing sports aligning with their gender identity. These new changes propose that women's sports aren't just for women, but for anyone who says they are a woman.

Representative Summer Lee (D-PA) began her opening remarks with, "It's disappointing to me that although the title of this hearing implies a much-needed discussion, we're likely going to be forced to listen to transphobic bigotry." There's the word again. Upon reading this, I felt heartbroken. Not defensive or frustrated but disheartened. Congress is the beating heart of the American republic, and a sitting member resorts to childish name-calling rather than making her points with logic, fact, science, or lived experience.

When it was time to read my testimony, I shared the growing number of concerns and experiences of women losing out on opportunities and being injured in their sport. I explained how there is a place for everyone, regardless of gender identity, sexual orientation, or race, to play sports, but we must stop unsafe, unfair, and discriminatory practices toward women in the name of inclusion. I concluded my testimony with an ad lib in response to Representative Lee. I couldn't help myself. "Ranking Member Lee, if my testimony makes me transphobic, then I believe your opening monologue makes you a misogynist."

The hearing went into a tailspin. I had just used her own language against her. My line of thinking was that if being pro-woman is deemed anti-trans, then wouldn't, by her own logic, being pro-trans inherently be anti-woman? And what do we call someone who is anti-woman? A misogynist. In an attempt to erase history, Lee moved to have my words taken down on the grounds of "engaging in personalities." Let it be known that congressional record still stands: Representative Lee is a misogynist.

Alongside the unavoidable and inevitable backlash, something else happened. I started getting a lot of support. The positive feedback I was receiving was tenfold the amount of negative. But the issue was in the first few weeks, much of the support was given through the privacy of a direct message. Some of these secret thanks came in the form of whispers or a quick wink from someone across the room when I was out in public. I'm talking about people who locked arms with my viewpoint of supporting female athletes and female-only spaces, but at the same time, refused to budge from the sidelines, or from behind private screens and personal social media accounts. At first I was so excited despite whether it was private or public because this meant we were garnering support in some capacity, but soon these feelings of excitement began to turn into frustration.

The messages I received roughly translated to, "Let me know if there is anything I can do to help you out anonymously." While I couldn't believe many people (athletes, coaches, parents) weren't willing to take a stand for common sense and the importance of single sex-spaces, over time I understood the weight of the pressure these people felt. One coach told me he had to stay silent because if he didn't, the administration would gladly replace him with someone else who would publicly advocate for males to compete in women's sports, and he couldn't bear knowing his athletes weren't at least somewhat protected. Athletes I knew personally were afraid to speak up because they could potentially lose their scholarship, their roster spot on the conference team, playing time, and more. Parents explained to me that standing up for the truth in their circles could warrant them being fired from their jobs.

So, while anyone could (and did) tell me things like

- "Take a forever nap"
- "Kill yourself"
- "I hope your husband cheats on you"
- "The world would be a better place without you in it"
- "I pray infertility on you"

and less "mild" versions of the above, few were willing to publicly stand alongside me at first because there was so much at stake for them. They risked everything from being able to provide for their families to losing the very thing they had been toiling toward for decades. I see that a lot more clearly now when the repercussions of people speaking out have been laid public. By no means is this justification for remaining silent. I just began to understand that the threats and risks people feared were legitimate. I now don't have much sympathy for people who know what's happening is wrong yet choose to say nothing. At this point, I believe those who remain silent are just as responsible as those who created the guidelines.

Just look what happened to Travis Allen and his daughter, Blake, in the Vermont town of Randolph. In 2022, fourteen-year-old Blake, a freshman and member of her high school volleyball team, voiced concern because a male who began to identify as a female was allowed to join the girls' team as well as change in their locker room. One day before leaving for an away game, the transgender player entered the locker room. Blake and other girls felt extremely vulnerable and uncomfortable and asked this athlete to leave, but this person refused. These girls and their parents complained to the school, but their complaints were dismissed. Blake's high school ultimately ended up opening a harassment, hazing, and bullying investigation on Blake for "misgendering" the male student when she referred to him as a "dude" who does not belong in the women's locker room.

The school charged Blake with harassment and bullying, which included a two-day suspension and required her involvement in a "restorative justice circle," in which the school would determine if Blake's apology was sincere. Blake's dad, Travis, took to Facebook to stand up for his daughter and responded to the male player's mother's claim that Blake had "made up this story for attention." Travis wrote, "The truth is your son watched my daughter and multiple other girls change in the locker room. While he got a free show, they got violated." The school responded with suspending Travis from his job as the middle school girls' soccer coach without pay. Travis was asked to give a public apology. But he refused and decided to pursue legal action. He prevailed. The school district agreed to a settlement of $125,000 and Travis was reinstated to his coaching position.[5] Travis stood up for his daughter the way all fathers should.

One of my dear friends, Paula Scanlan, a former swimmer at the University of Pennsylvania and ex-teammate of Thomas when he went by both Will and Lia, knows firsthand the pressure behind publicly standing up for female athletes. In 2022, Paula appeared in the documentary *What Is a Woman?* She chose to be featured anonymously as a blacked-out silhouette. This was filmed before the drama surrounding the NCAA Championships, where Thomas and I tied. When I began to speak out, Paula connected with me. We spoke privately for about a year. Since then, she has come out publicly to fight for women's rights.

When Paula and her teammates first learned that Thomas would be joining the female swim team at the university, there was zero space for dissent. They weren't even allowed to question the arrangement. The female swimmers were forced to undress in front of a man with male genitalia eighteen times per week.[6] When they voiced their concern, the female athletes were told that Thomas's place on the team was "nonnegotiable," and if anyone shared views to the contrary with the media, they would "regret it."[7] For the swimmers who felt uncomfortable with the scenario, the university would provide them with counseling services in an "attempt to re-educate us to become comfortable with the idea of undressing in front of a male."[8]

Paula said this in an interview:

> It worked. The university wanted us to be quiet, and they did it in a very effective way. They continued to tell us that our opinions were wrong and that if we had an issue with it, we were the problem. And it's frightening, and your future job is on the line. And after that point, no one would talk about it anymore. They effectively silenced us even within talking to each other.[9]

Paula told me that her and her teammates were forced to go to weekly LGBTQ education meetings in which they learned how by being "cisgender," they were oppressing their teammate, Thomas. The parents of about ten UPenn swimmers wrote a letter to the NCAA early in the season expressing their discomfort. Part of the letter read:

> At stake here is the integrity of women's sports. The precedent being set—one in which women do not have a protected and equitable space to compete—is a direct threat to female athletes in every sport. What are the boundaries? How is this in line with the NCAA's commitment to providing a fair environment for student-athletes?[10]

The administration responded with:

Please know that we fully support all of our swimming student-athletes and want to help our community navigate Lia's success in the pool this winter.

   Penn Athletics is committed to being a welcoming and inclusive environment for all of our student athletes, coaches, and staff and we hold true to that commitment today and in the future.

   We've encouraged our student-athletes to utilize the robust resources available to them at Penn, and I'd like to share them with you as well. These include Counseling and Psychological Services, the LGBT Center, Restorative Practices, and our Center for Student Athlete Success staff.[11]

Here is what I believe this email was actually communicating:

Please know that we fully support all of our swimming student-athletes and want to help our community navigate Lia's success in the pool this winter because that is the priority here, not your mental health, well-being, or questions you may have about this arrangement.

   Penn Athletics is committed to being a welcoming and inclusive environment for all of our student athletes except those who are females and express concerns of losing scholarships, playing time, or a spot on the roster to a male claiming the identity of a woman. We hold true to that commitment today and in the future.

   If you don't feel comfortable seeing male genitalia, here are some resources you should seek in an effort to make yourself okay with it. These resources include reeducation

services where we will tell you how you're the problem and
work on ways to alter your perspective to see Lia as the vic-
tim and yourselves as the perpetrator.

The few teammates, including Paula, who continued to object
to Thomas's participation were warned that any public outbursts
or unveiling of their opinions could result in losing a future job
opportunity, a space in graduate school, and a spot on the team.
They were told their actions would follow them forever and they
would be forever known as a transphobe.

That's effective in keeping 18–22-year-old girls quiet. Imagine the pressure these young women must have felt, who already
had so much on their plate being student-athletes trying to balance school, athletics, personal relationships, and their own
well-being. In the eyes of the University of Pennsylvania, allowing a male to play on a female team was a matter of life or death,
and the female swimmers held the power of both entities in their
hands. Simply put, the university demanded compliance of its
swimmers. A male would be joining the girls in the pool and in
the locker room. Hopefully this highlights why so few female
athletes felt confident and secure enough to stand up for themselves by voicing their concerns. The treatment UPenn's women's
swim and dive team received was way more common than the
response I got from Barnhart.

Paula was asked to write an anonymous article for the school
newspaper on why she didn't agree with Thomas joining forces
with the female swim team. She told me the staff working for the
school's paper had a list of rules she had to follow for her opinion
to be published. Paula was specifically not allowed to refer to
Thomas as a male or use anything other than *she/her* pronouns
when referring to him. She could not even use the words

"biological female" in her writing. Paula submitted the article. When it was published, the paper had watered it down even more, almost to the point where one wouldn't be able to tell which side of the issue the anonymous author fell on. The article was up on the school paper's website for only a few minutes before it was taken down without any advance warning to Paula.[12] From my understanding, university staff members threatened to quit if the article remained on the website.

Paula is passionate about advocating for female-only spaces for a few reasons. In her own words at a congressional hearing surrounding the issue:

> One may ask, why do I speak so passionately about issues that seem hypothetical or that some may perceive as impacting only a small number of women? This is not hypothetical, this is real. I know women who have lost roster spots and spots on the podium. I know of women with sexual trauma who are adversely impacted by having biological males in their locker room without their consent.
>
> And I am one of these women. I was sexually assaulted on June 3, 2016, in a bathroom.[13]

Remember the #MeToo movement and how it advocated for female victims and their truths to be told? Well, know the people who supported that movement are the same people accusing these very victims of being the problem.

• • •

A swimmer from Harvard shared this message that was sent to their entire women's team in 2022 surrounding the Lia Thomas controversy:

The conversations and controversy surrounding Lia have been challenging to read. In particular, they focus or [sic] what is fair and what is ethical. Regardless of your personal stance, Lia has been incredibly transparent and is abiding by all NCAA rules. That is a fact. Having watched [Schuyler Bailar]'s transition first hand, I can tell you that if it wasn't for the support of the teams, he may not be here today. Life is more important than politics.

While we will never tell you what to do or what to believe, it doesn't benefit our team from winning a championship if we spend our collective energy getting annoyed or frustrated. Let the NCAA figure out their next steps. Let us focus on our team. And if any press reaches out, then please direct them to our Sports Media Office and ideally, refrain from comment.[14]

On the surface, this statement may seem benign. It definitely shows Harvard University's support of athletes competing in the category that matches their gender identity rather than sex in their circuit, right? Knowing the nuances of language and the relationships between academic institutions and athletes, again, here's what I believe the statement really meant:

Let [me] divert your attention from inherently feeling like something is wrong, by asking you to focus on how great Lia has been. Let me emotionally blackmail you into accepting mistreatment because otherwise you are complicit in a potential death. Exchanging your fair treatment for someone else's benefit (a male in this case) is a justifiable cause. And the fair treatment of women is "just politics" anyway.

While we won't tell you what to do, we're telling you it is a bad choice to fight this. Let the men in charge at the NCAA decide your fate. Immerse your thoughts and feelings into something else to ignore the obvious injustice you face. Let other people decide if you are worthy of fair competition without your input or voice. Oh, and finally don't talk.

Aren't colleges supposed to be places where free expression, intellectual honesty, and civil discourse are encouraged?

Make no mistake, this issue is much bigger than just fairness in women's sports. The higher-ups in academia, the media, corporate America, and more want to control how you think, how you feel, and what you say. When people gain the courage to voice the truth or simply recite a known and proven fact, the threat of censorship is a real possibility. Journalist Meghan Murphy took to Twitter in 2018 and referred to a transgender individual—in this case, a man who self-identifies as a woman before filing over a dozen lawsuits against female estheticians for refusing to wax male genital parts—by his sex.[15] Murphy was banned from the social media platform indefinitely. In separate tweets, Murphy opined that "women aren't men," and "How are transwomen not men? What is the difference between a man and a transwoman?"[16] Based on these words, Twitter accused the journalist of hate speech and being in violation of their policy. In her words:

What is insane to me . . . is that while Twitter knowingly permits graphic pornography and death threats on the platform (I have reported countless violent threats, the vast majority of which have gone unaddressed), they won't allow me to state very basic facts, such as "men aren't women."[17]

Murphy sued Twitter but the courts subsequently dismissed the lawsuit.

In 2019, when Maya Forstater, a researcher at the Centre for Global Development, tweeted that biological sex was unchangeable, she lost her job.[18] Global best-selling author J. K. Rowling responded to Maya's tweet in support and received a backlash of harassment.[19] The author's name was removed from a school building, and she has been derided by critics as a "witch."[20] Four years since she took a public and unquestionable stand for women, she has come out and said she would "happily do two years [in jail] if the alternative is compelled speech and forced denial of the reality and importance of sex." In her tweet, she further went on to say, "Bring on the court case, I say. It'll be more fun than I've ever had on a red carpet."[21] Mic drop.

Olivia Krolczyk, twenty, received a grade of "zero" from her professor in women's gender studies in pop culture at the University of Cincinnati for using the terms "biological women" in a proposal about males who self-identified as women in sports. The professor told Olivia, "Please reassess your topic and edit it to focus on women's rights (not just 'females') and I'll regrade." Olivia was told the phrase "biological woman" reinforced "heteronormativity, what she later referred to as "cisheteronormativity."[22] What does that word even mean?

The head coach of a Vermont snowboarding high school team lost his job the day after a three-minute talk with some of his players in which he mentioned that males have a physical advantage over females.[23]

At a 2023–24 Pennsylvania House appropriations budget hearing, State Representative La'Tasha D. Mayes asked University of Pittsburgh chancellor Patrick Gallagher to cancel three incoming speakers at the university, Mayes's alma matter, one of which was yours truly, because we had "crossed the line of free speech over into hate speech targeting transgender students and the transgender community."[24] Thankfully, Gallagher valued the virtue of free speech over lies and emotional rhetoric. That felt like a win since it's not uncommon today for speakers with views like mine to be censored on college campuses.

In November 2023, I was set to speak at the University of California, Davis. Now, this is a school with a long history of shutting down conservative speakers and events. Milo Yiannopoulos, a right-wing commentator for Breitbart, went to UC Davis to speak in 2017, but the event was not even able to take place due to the number of protestors who rallied at the event. Milo isn't the only one who had their First Amendment rights violated while being on UC Davis's campus. The same scenario happened in 2022 with Turning Point USA contributor Stephen Davis. At a Charlie Kirk event at UC Davis in March 2023, the protestors broke through barricades, windows were shattered, and multiple arrests were made. You may be wondering "Riley, why would you go into the belly of the beast?!" Easy answer: because that's who needs to hear my message the most.

To promote the event and to administer the free tickets, I used a ticketing platform called Eventbrite. The event was listed under the title "Protecting Women's Sports." The event didn't last long on the platform before I received an email from Eventbrite alerting me that my event was no longer able to be permitted on their marketplace as it "discriminate(d) against, harass(ed), disparage(d), threaten(ed), incite(d) violence against or otherwise target(ed) individuals or groups based on their actual or perceived race, ethnicity, religion, national origin, immigration status, gender identity, sexual orientation, veteran statues, age, or disability."

I was baffled, but not surprised, as I was used to censorship for advocating for women's sex-based rights (as you probably noticed, nowhere in that email did they list "sex" as a category worthy of being protected from discrimination). I started having some thoughts pop into my head, so I began doing some research. What events did they leave up while finding it necessary to remove mine? Of course, all events pertaining to the LGBTQ+ community remained, but that's not the kicker. You know what types of events were also still up? Several "Palestinian resistance fighter" events that appeared to be in support of Hamas, the terrorist group that launched an attack on Israel and its people that resulted in the beheadings, murders, rapes, kidnappings, and torture of innocent Israeli citizens.[25]

I took to X to publicly ask Eventbrite why they were anti-woman but evidently pro-terrorism, and this is the response received from the cofounder and chairman of the platform:

> I am the Co-Founder and Chairman of Eventbrite and to accuse Eventbrite of being Pro-Hamas is egregious and moronic. How could you make an unsubstantiated slander that I support these genocidal maniacs? Please go f*** yourself! (The last comment represents the individual views of Kevin and not that of Eventbrite, etc, etc).

How mature and respectful for a founder of a company to tell a twenty-three-year-old girl and those in alignment with her mission to keep males out of women's sports and locker rooms including Clay Travis and Outkick to go "f*** ourselves." Also, notice how quick Kevin Hartz was to defend himself to the pro-Hamas accusation, but crickets in response to the anti-woman accusation. Not a good look. When someone reveals themselves to you, believe them.

As you can imagine, the public was outraged by the actions of Eventbrite and its founder, so much so that the ticketing platform received a milder version of the Bud Light treatment. Thousands of users canceled their accounts and deleted the app entirely. Even Governor Glenn Youngkin of Virginia announced that the state of Virginia, his political committee, and his official office would no longer be using Eventbrite. His reasoning was simple: the platforms refusal to allow events like my Protecting Women's Sports event and because "there's no place to sit on the fence when it comes to the barbaric attack by the Hamas terrorists on Israel."

Needless to say, Eventbrite turned their comments off on all their social media platforms and removed the Hamas events. My event was never restored and no apology or justification was ever given by Hartz.

In the few weeks leading up the event at Davis, I started getting tagged on social media posts of students there. They were posting digital fliers of the counterprotests planned. One read:

TRANSPHOBIA ISNT WELCOME IN DAVIS
ON NOVEMBER 3RD, DAVIS COLLEGE REPUBLICANS
WILL BE BRINGING NOTORIOUS TRANSPHOBIC
SPEAKER RILEY GAINES TO UC DAVIS
WE WILL NOT STAND FOR THAT BULLSHIT
RALLY AT 5:30PM, NOVEMBER 3RD AT VANDERGOEF QUAD
BRING SIGNS
BRING FRIENDS
BE READY TO MAKE NOISE

An email sent to students said:

Attention Davis Community! Another Transphobic Speaker is coming to our campus.

Last time a transphobic speaker was brought to this venue, Proud Boys attacked our students. Now this event is being promoted by Moms for Liberty, an SPLC-designated hate group that's incited SIX bomb threats at our schools!!

These events put our youth and our community at risk by inviting violent transphobes into our town to wreak havoc!

For the phrase "Davis is for Everyone" to have any meaning, we must show up to support trans youth and kick out this transphobic speaker!!

I hope you'll join the community on Nov 3rd at 5:30pm on the Vanderhoef Quad (near the Mondavi center) to show that transphobia isn't welcome in Davis and we will XXXXX hate.[26]

Oh, the irony of saying "for the phrase 'Davis is for Everyone' to have any meaning, we must kick out Riley Gaines."

To the protestors' dismay, I was able to give my speech on the UC Davis campus thanks to the diligence of law enforcement officers who showed up in full riot gear, the FBI, and the bomb squad. Barricades were broken through, doors were busted in, windows were shattered, walls were graffitied wishing death upon me, Antifa showed up and again chanted, "Riley can't swim."

While females and our supporters are facing more and more opposition for voicing scientific facts or merely their opinions, actual hate-filled diatribes and public outbursts that not only promote but encourage violence are applauded.

Sarah Jane Baker is a male from England who now claims to be a woman and, at twenty-one, was convicted and imprisoned for kidnapping and torturing his stepmother's brother and spent the next thirty years in prison.[27] In 2017, Baker cut off his own testicles while in jail to be more comfortable identifying as a woman. Two years later, Baker was released from prison and is now a trans rights activist (TRA). In 2023, the "self-declared transanarchist" was speaking at a pride rally in London when his talk took a disturbing turn.

Speaking to a crowd of fifty thousand, Baker pridefully declared, "If you see a TERF, punch 'em in the f***ing face."[28] The audience roared in support of Baker's incitement to violence.

A spokesperson for the London Trans Pride said this in response: "Sarah and many others in our community hold a lot of rage and anger and they have the right to express that anger through their words."[29] Other common phrases used verbally or touted on shirts and signs by TRAs include "decapitate TERFs" and "Kill the TERFs."[30][31] The Trans Radical Activist Network organized a "Trans Day of Vengeance" following the mass shooting by an openly trans shooter in March 2023 at the Covenant School in Nashville, where six lives were taken, including three nine-year-olds. The organizers say the word "vengeance" was used because it means fighting back with vehemence.[32]

If you advocate for female-only spaces and competition in sports, you could lose your job and/or friends and family, be labeled as transphobic and a slew of other defamatory terms, and suffer the consequences of what gender ideologists would consider hate speech. If you hold an opposing viewpoint, however, feel free to share your message loud and proud.

Hate speech is not just speech you hate.

When a former journalist at the *Economist* and Irish bestselling author Helen Joyce was asked to speak at Caius College at Cambridge University, fellows and students received an email from the college master that described her as "offensive, insulting and hateful."[33] She wrote a book titled *Trans: Gender Identity and the New Battle for Women's Rights*, about the idea of gender self-identification, "the idea . . . that people should count as men or women according to how they feel and what they declare, instead of their biology."[34] When the hardback version of her book was published, Helen was demonized. She was accused of wanting to kill trans people, being a racist and homophobe, and having the opinion that men are better than women.[35] None of which was true. What this woman did say, however, was that "humans cannot change sex; that males are on average much stronger than females and commit nearly all violent and sexual crime."[36]

In her book, Helen makes a great point about how a liberal, secular society can embrace different belief systems. Whether you believe you will one day be reincarnated into a worm or be welcomed into eternity in heaven with Jesus Christ, we should be able to at the least recognize and tolerate different worldviews. Gender identity ideology, however, suffocates all other beliefs. Helen says, "Gender self-identification . . . is a demand for validation by others. The label is a misnomer. It is actually about requiring others to identify you as a member of the sex you proclaim."[37]

In September 2021, the British medical journal the *Lancet* published a cover that highlighted a certain phrase—"bodies with vaginas," from a pull quote in one of the journal's articles.[38] Uh, did the author mean women? Is it too hopeful to think he was just trying to reach a target word count? This wasn't an error or a misprint. It was an intentional wording, or lack thereof to be more specific, that became an exploding trend that continues to this day. Simply put, society is erasing women so it can include men.

At the cost of being inclusive to all who simply feel like a woman, female-related terms are becoming obsolete or at the least, offensive. Words like "mother" and "woman" are apparently so concerning and offensive, we are being told to use more gender-inclusive and friendly terms like "birthing person," "birth giver," "uterus owner," "cervix haver," "menstruator," "bleeder," "chest feeder." The list goes on.[39] Most recently (and most offensively yet comical) is what a cervical cancer charity is calling a vagina: a "bonus hole." In defense of this transgender-inclusive language that Jo's Cervical Cancer Trust recommends practitioners use, this is what they say:

> Our mission at Jo's is to prevent as many cervical cancers as possible, and a big part of that is increasing uptake of cervical screening. Women are our main audience at Jo's, however some trans men and/or non-binary people have cervixes and to reduce as many cervical cancers as possible it is important that we also provide information for this group and the health professionals who support them.[40]

By "trans men" they mean females. And those "non-binary people" they're referring to would also be females. Notice how they didn't say some trans women have cervixes . . . because they cannot. That is physically impossible. If you are as confused as I am by Jo's response, welcome to the club. This language is being pushed upon by the very practitioners we visit when getting a pap smear, or delivering a child, or getting prescribed birth control or when our lives are on the line.

A paper published in the *Frontier of Global Women's Health Journal* and authored by nine medical professionals highlights the implications of desexing language of female reproduction. What does it do? It dehumanizes, diminishes overall inclusivity, and reduces recognition and the rights of the mother/baby relationship.[41] The fight for women's rights advocated that language centered around "he" and "him" ignored females. By eliminating female-centric language like mother, breastfeeding, vagina, uterus, and woman, we are doing the same thing. In October 2023, the Michigan legislature voted to change the word "woman" to "individual" in their breastfeeding antidiscrimination legislation.[42] Even some Republicans voted for Senator Jeff Irwin's (D) bill too. In what world can anyone *but* a woman breastfeed?

Changing language and opening the female spot to all persons makes for a strong sense of belonging and kindness, or so we're told. I'm all for inclusivity, just not at the expense of more than half of the population of the world (51 percent) and our sex-based rights as females.

We are allowing ourselves to get trampled on, and we're smiling in the process. Yes, many women have locked arms and stepped up to preserve women's rights and reality. At the same time, many have not. It's easier to comply with the masses and promote inclusivity. After all, doesn't inclusivity make one virtuous? Sure, but what we're seeing is not inclusion. It's exclusion. And what we're seeing is not "progressive," taking us forward in a positive direction. It's regressive, taking us back more than half a century in time. What happens when it's your scholarship on the line? Or a male who has a history of domestic violence or sexual abuse is allowed at your local rape crisis center? Or your daughter who gets no say in whether a man can undress right next to her in the locker room?

It's worth noting that, typically, when men feel threatened, they stand up and say something. The minute there was a picture of Dylan Mulvaney on a Bud Light can, buyers of Anheuser Busch, mostly men, called for a boycott and the beverage brand tanked, losing roughly $27 billion in stock.[43] Could you imagine if suddenly male-specific terms such as "father" or "erection" were deemed not "gender inclusive" enough? I can say with absolute confidence that if a female claiming the identity of a man started making demands of males like we're seeing happen to women, most men wouldn't stand it for a second. Do you ever see men referred to as ejaculators? Or persons with vas deferens? Or prostate-havers? Or persons with erection capabilities? No. I mean think about it and ask yourselves why. I believe it's because reasonable men would not tolerate that behavior. Again, look at how men responded to the Bud Light controversy. Bud Light's market is typically men, so you can imagine the blunder the marketing director had when she decided that a man dressed as Audrey Hepburn sipping on a beer was a good idea. Their typical consumers, men, quickly let the beer company know they would not stand the mockery. As women, we tend to be more likely to smile while were discriminated against based on our sex or any time we're wrongfully slighted. We clap as a male stands atop the podium and gets a medal placed around his neck. Make no mistake, it's not because we are ecstatic to give up our awards or because we think this is fair. It's because females tend to desire more innately (and through enculturation) to be more agreeable, conciliatory, altruistic, and emotionally involved, which are all great qualities, especially as it pertains to motherhood. While the fairness-in-sports argument showcases our biological differences, it's clear that men and women differ in more than just strength and physical attributes. Our personality traits differ. While identifying as women, the men entering women's spaces are assertive, aggressive, and demanding the language and words which we refer to them by.

Now, that's not very ladylike, is it?

6.

———

IN IT TOGETHER

O n July 12, 2022, I received an email from my university alerting me that I had been nominated for "NCAA Woman of the Year." This is the most prestigious award for collegiate female athletes. It was more than just honoring athletic achievement. It was the culmination of everything I had worked hard for in the past four years. Really, my whole life. Besides just athletic achievements, this award considered academic success, dedication to community service, and one's overall ability to be an effective leader with exceptional character. Each university got a single nomination among all their women's sports teams on campus. At the University of Kentucky, we had the No. 1 WNBA draft pick, Rhyne Howard; Abby Steiner, who was breaking world records in track and field; a national championship volleyball team; as well as a rifle team that achieved the same accomplishment as the volleyball team. But they chose *me*. I was so honored when I received this email. I, along with 576 other female college athletes across the country, had been nominated. Five hundred seventy-seven total nominations may not sound like an exclusive group, but this was out of a pool of 229,000[1] female athletes. The nominees were in the top 0.25 percent of the most well-rounded elite female athletes in the country across all sports.

The problem was, "NCAA Woman of the Year" was not exclusive to just women. Lia Thomas was also included in that list of nominees.[2]

Thomas.

A mediocre male athlete who spent three years of his collegiate career competing against the men.

For "*Woman* of the Year."

• • •

Thomas's nomination felt like a slap in the face. *That* was who the University of Pennsylvania thought made the most admirable, accomplished, and well-rounded "woman" out of all their sports teams on campus? Thomas was born in 1999. If he began hormone replacement therapy in 2019, some might make the argument that he had spent about 13 percent of life living as a woman by the time he was up for NCAA Woman of the Year. Of course, I know he spent 0 percent of life as a woman and that will always remain true. What does Thomas's nomination say to the 576 female athletes who received letters for this award that said the organization wanted to "honor incredible women and reflect on the impact of women in intercollegiate sports"? And what does this nomination say to every female athlete at UPenn?

I wasn't alone in seeing the duplicity in this. Months earlier, a former Olympian and NCAA champion, Nancy Hogshead-Makar, wrote a letter to NCAA president Mark Emmert expressing her concern in allowing transgender males who now identify as women to compete in female collegiate sports.[3] Here is Emmert's response:

> *As the top governing board of the NCAA, the Board of Governors firmly and unequivocally supports the opportunity for transgender student-athletes to compete in college sports.*
>
> *We understand there are differing views on transgender student-athlete participation in sport. The NCAA's current policy is anchored in the evolving science on this issue and in the sport-specific policies of the US Olympic and Paralympic Committee's national governing bodies, of international federations and of the International Olympic Committee when relevant. Further, the policy provides the Board of Governors and the Committee on Competitive Safeguards and Medical Aspects of Sports the opportunity to review and approve each policy to ensure it aligns with the core values of the NCAA. The resulting sport-by-sport approach preserves opportunities for transgender student-athletes while balancing fairness, inclusion and safety for all who compete.[4]*

Did he really use the verbiage of "evolving science" to justify allowing men to compete with women? I love Nancy's take on Emmert's response. This Olympic gold medalist and civil rights attorney who is fighting for women's rights and combatting LGBT discrimination said,

> *This statement from Emmert might be the most insulting out of several asinine and offensive comments. If the NCAA*

indeed treated its athletes with dignity and respect, it would not have forced biological-female athletes to compete against an athlete with obvious advantages. In each of the three events in which [Lia] Thomas advanced to the final, the meet was not fully open to the ninth-place and 17th-place finishers in those events. Because Thomas was allowed to compete, those athletes were denied true opportunities.[5]

Nancy is also the president and founder of Champion Women, an organization that advocates for access and equality in sports participation and provides legal advocacy for girls and women. Through extensive research, this organization has determined that despite the strides Title IX has made in the last fifty years, inequalities between male and female opportunities in collegiate sports continue to widen. For example, almost 93 percent of universities and colleges are not meeting any of the standards Title IX sets to demand equality between men and women in sports.[6] In addition, women miss out on over $1.1 billion in athletic scholarships every year.[7]

An example of this gender inequality was recorded live in 2021 by Oregon University's basketball forward Sedona Prince. Sedona posted a video on TikTok, which went viral, that compared the workout rooms between the women's and the men's NCAA tournaments. The men's boasted state-of-the-art facilities, while the women's consisted of a thigh-high rack of dumbbells and a few yoga mats. The glaring disparity was shocking and garnered so much national outrage that an external investigation into NCAA practices was launched. That review concluded damning findings into how the organization "normalizes" and "perpetuates gender inequalities" and has zero practices in place to remedy those inequalities.[8]

Fast-forward to a year later. Males merely saying they are women—with absolutely no changes to their body chemistry—are allowed to compete with and against females—yet another direct violation of Title IX.

• • •

Let's go back to the beginning. What exactly is Title IX?

Title IX is a federal civil rights law that was signed by President Richard Nixon on June 23, 1972. Made up of only thirty-seven words, none of which is "sports" or "athletics," the legislation reads:

No person in the United States shall, on the basis of sex, be excluded from participation in, be denied the benefits of, or be subjected to discrimination under any education program or activity receiving Federal financial assistance.[9]

Short, but powerful and effective. Notice that sex is not defined because no one at the time or prior saw it as necessary. Though Title IX is fundamentally about discrimination in the educational arena, this law is commonly recognized most notably about the opportunities it created for women in athletics. According to sports historian Victoria Jackson, this landmark legislation was crucial "even just for legitimizing the idea that women could play."[10]

Title IX is a powerhouse within the female sports arena thanks to the word "activity." As female athletes, we owe our gratitude to Democratic senator Birch Bayh of Indiana, who ushered the law through the Senate, and Representative Patsy Mink of Hawaii, who sponsored it in the House. According to tennis legend Billie Jean King, whose testimony "all but guaranteed the passage of Title IX,"[11] Senator Bayh almost didn't include the word "activity." At the last minute, he and fellow lawmakers decided to leave it in.[12] The inclusion of that four-syllable word has changed and continues to change the futures of millions of females in the United States. To continue to protect the provisions of Title IX, King created the Women's Sports Foundation in 1974 (of which Nancy Hogshead-Makar served as president from 1991 to 1993).

Before Title IX, about 30,000 women played college sports (compared to more than 229,000 in 2022), and 294,000 girls in high school played sports[13] (compared to 3.24 million girls in the 2021–22 school year).[14] Female athletes pre–Title IX had to sew their own uniforms, had little reason to dream about athletic opportunities beyond college, and frankly, weren't taken seriously.[15]

Without the women's sporting category that resulted from Title IX, I would not have been afforded the chance to swim at the University of Kentucky on a full scholarship, I would not be a Southeastern Conference record holder. I would not be a twelve-time All-American. I would not have developed lifelong friendships with my teammates. I would not have the leadership skills and confidence that I have now. Men received all these things without a change in the law. It wasn't too long ago that women were a historically oppressed group (yes, I'm strategically using the language that those who oppose the protection of women's sex-based rights use now).

But now the Biden administration is helping to erode these opportunities for women and girls nationwide. As of the time of this writing, the government is actively working to rewrite Title IX. These changes are on track to supposedly be implemented in spring of 2024 and will require schools to allow transgender athletes to compete on teams that align with their gender identity, except where it would undermine "fairness in competition" or safety.[16] Keep in mind, the new policy doesn't define fairness. It doesn't define transgender. It doesn't define gender identity. Nor does it define women. It's all subjective and comparative, meaning unelected bureaucrats and officials can interpret these terms to mean what they want. The proposed rule places the burden of Title IX squarely on the shoulders of women. Under the new rewrite of Title IX, it's up to the female athletes themselves to prove with specific evidence that any male they would be subjected to competing against has an unfair competitive advantage. The framework claims the idea of men possessing athletic advantages is perceived, unverified, and alleged. It says sex-based criteria stronger than self-ID policies may not be considered if it proves to be physically or emotionally harmful to transgender athletes. But what about the harm amending Title IX would do to women?

How can we defend what we cannot define? A lifelong liberal woman once asked me this poignant question; it has stuck because it's so provocative and rings so true.

The same elected officials and figures who once took pride in celebrating women by implementing Title IX are the same people now working to undermine these benefits in the name of "inclusion." The irony is painfully obvious.

But this rewrite affects much more than just collegiate sports and athletics. Equating sex to gender identity as it pertains to educational programs means males identifying as women could and would be randomly assigned to live in and share a dormitory room with 17–18-year-old girls. It means males could and would have full access to all bathrooms, locker rooms, changing spaces, and once sex-separated private spaces on college campuses. It means males could and would take academic and athletic scholarships away from women. It means transgender males who perceive themselves as women could and would join sororities, which we're already seeing happening at the University of Wyoming among the Kappa Kappa Gamma sorority. Members of the sorority sued, arguing that membership should be limited to women, or adult human females, while a man who had not transitioned other than wearing women's clothes demanded to be a part of their sorority. A judge threw out the lawsuit saying, "The Court will not define 'woman' today."[17] The six plaintiffs involved in the case are restrategizing their lawsuit and will continue pushing forward to fight for the sanctity of protecting women's spaces. These girls were promised sisterhood, but instead got the brother they never wanted.

The worst part is that we, as women, are being silenced. Our universities and institutions are gaslighting and emotionally blackmailing us into feeling like we are in the wrong. They want us to feel guilty for demanding fairness. There are so many frustrated women in sports right now. Too many are not visible. We know rules like these aren't fair, but we are effectively coerced into submission. Our colleges and their administrations have taken a page out of the *Communist Manifesto* playbook and are running with it.

MOFA. Make Orwell Fiction Again.

It shouldn't take bravery to demand the bare minimum, which is equal treatment and opportunities to compete and succeed. There is a place for everyone to compete, but women should not have to compromise their well-being, safety, privacy, and opportunities for these places to be made available to them. Such an approach is regressive and deeply misogynistic. How many girls must be hurt, lose opportunities, or feel exploited in a locker room before people in power realize this?

Remember I mentioned how we have Billie Jean King and her trailblazing efforts to thank for Title IX? That same woman who fought so strenuously to uphold the rights of female athletes is now actively fighting for males to be included in female sports and spaces. "Feminists" like King are undermining everything they once fought relentlessly and unapologetically to implement and protect.

What's becoming clearer as time passes is that gender identity ideology is becoming more important to Title IX than the reason (or the people) for which Title IX was created in the first place. This critical thirty-seven-word legislation is not about women anymore. Nor is it about the merits of facts, science, or biology. It's about feelings and catering to self-expression and self-identity.

Candice Jackson is an attorney who served as the acting assistant secretary for civil rights and deputy general counsel in the US Department of Education from 2017 to 2021. She currently fights for the sex-based rights and interests of incarcerated women. She describes the hijacking of Title IX like this:

The Biden administration now interprets Title IX to cover "gender identity discrimination" side by side with sex discrimination. And because a "gender identity" means anyone's personal, subjective view of themselves as "male, female, both, or neither," a law cannot protect both gender identity and sex. When a law gives equal footing to a purely subjective characteristic that can "determine" an objective characteristic, it is the objective characteristic that falls by the wayside. . . . What does it mean for every aspect of an educational environment to treat everyone according to their individual gender identity? It means compelling students, teachers, and staff to use every student's chosen pronouns. It means denying girls and women the privacy and dignity of using the restroom out of the presence of boys and men. It means assigning college freshmen dorm roommates who are of the opposite sex. It means girls and women not making a sports team, or losing out on sports records or scholarships, because boys and men are allowed to compete "as women." It means school and college health centers jumping onto the "affirmation only" model and providing mental health and even medical interventions like cross-sex hormones, to college students who are barely of age. It means campus groups for women or for lesbians are deemed "discriminatory" unless they include men who identify as women in their events. It means a sexual assault victim on campus has to refer to her rapist as "she" during a Title IX proceeding.[18]

Those legislators and policy makers who support this rewrite are asking women to retreat from the strides they have made to make males feel more comfortable. Women are being asked to deny their legitimate existence and uniqueness to cater to males who infringe upon our opportunities and spaces. Let me be clear. Women are not the problem. Women are not doing anything wrong by advocating for our biology, our rights, and the spaces that were created specifically for us. Title IX was enacted and enforced to protect girls and women, not men who want to be like us, so it's us who need to fight to reclaim it.

It's mind-boggling to me that in 2023 we need to define what sex is within the law. Thanks to gender identity ideology, it's *so* hard to define what a woman is that not even a sitting Supreme

Court justice can do it. During a hearing, Senator Marsha Black-burn asked Judge Ketanji Brown Jackson if she could provide a definition for the word "woman." Jackson stated, "No, I can't."[19] As to why she couldn't define a simple word, Jackson stated she wasn't a biologist.[20] What an embarrassing and indefensible excuse. In the wise words of activist Kellie-Jay Keen, "I'm not a veterinarian, but I know what a dog is."

So back to the question of how can anyone defend what they cannot define. Simple, you can't.

• • •

Pretty quickly after I took a public stance acknowledging how men competing in women's sports was harmful to its existence, I began to feel as if I was complaining. I was shedding light on the topic, and people were beginning to understand the severity of what we were up against, but I didn't feel like changes were being made to prevent other girls from being impacted in the same way that we were as NCAA swimmers. Growing up, my dad always told me, "Put up or shut up." He would go on to say, "You can com-plain all you want, Riley, but unless you're willing to do some-thing to change what it is you're whining about, then you're merely just complaining. And no one likes to be around a complainer."

My dad was right. I couldn't stand to surround myself with people who hosted pity parties for themselves but weren't willing to fix the very fixable issues they had. That's when I decided that just highlighting the injustice we faced as females wasn't enough; I had to do something about it. I started to involve myself in the oh-so-confusing legislative process. I took it upon myself to start learning about what laws were in place to protect women in sports at all levels. At the time, just a handful of weeks after my race with Thomas, I had no idea what I was doing. Keep in mind, I didn't have a degree in politics, nor had I taken a college course relating to government or the civil process. I knew the three branches of government and that was about the extent of my knowledge in this sphere. I by no means felt prepared or equipped to do what I am now doing. My face would turn the color of a tomato while presenting to the class in my public speaking courses in college. I now fully understand that God does not call the equipped; he equips the called. Think about Moses who led the Israelites out with Aaron and his staff, or Joshua in his defeat over the Canaanites, or Esther's triumph over Haman that ultimately led to the deliverance of His people. Esther 4:14 says, *"For if you remain silent at this time, relief and deliverance will arise for the Jews from another place, but you and your father's house will perish. Yet who knows whether you have come to the kingdom for such a time as this?"* Most people know the ending of that verse in Esther, but I think fail to remember the first part, *"For if you remain silent at this time."*

Now, I believe civil courses should be a requirement for people of voting age and anything less is a disservice to this country and the people who reside here.

I discovered that different states across the country were trying to introduce and pass some version of the Fairness in Women's Sports Act. Every state has its own title and unique specifications. For example, in Mississippi it is termed the "Mississippi Fairness Act," and in Texas it's known as the "Save Women's Sports Act." Also, each state applies the law to different grade levels. The gist of this legislation is that everyone competes in the category that matches their sex at birth.

In 2020, Idaho was the first state to get this amendment passed into law. I would be remiss if I didn't mention the sponsor of this bill and the first representative to put this commonsense legislation forward, state representative Barbara Ehardt. She and I travel often to different states to testify in support of this act. Barbara is a force of nature. She's played and coached Division 1 basketball for fifteen years. I always refer to her as our "coach" in this fight. She calls me the "team captain." She's one of the best and most selfless allies in this fight and I'm proud to stand with her. She saw the trajectory of this issue and tried to get other states to follow suit before girls like me went through what we did.

According to Idaho's Fairness in Women's Sports Act, "having separate sex specific teams furthers efforts to promote sex equality. Sex-specific teams accomplish this by providing opportunities for female athletes to demonstrate their skill, strength, and athletic abilities while also providing them with opportunities to obtain recognition and accolades, college scholarships, and the numerous other long-term benefits that flow from success in athletic endeavors."[21] Makes sense, right? Unfortunately, because "females" do not include males who simply identify as female, bills like the Fairness in Women's Sports Act have unsurprisingly been deemed anti-trans, hateful, and discriminatory.

Like I mentioned, it's with all humility I admit I had no idea what I was doing at first as I started traveling from state to state advocating for those who didn't have the same testimony or platform that I had. I was doing this entirely out of my own pocket. In the spring of 2022, I started working with the Independent Women's Forum (IWF), a national organization that serves to enact policies that enhance people's freedom, opportunities, and well-being.[22] IWF works to protect women through actively creating and helping pass legislation that would, for instance, make daycare more affordable, protect independent contractors from being unfairly taxed, and reform licensing laws so women can flourish in their work.[23] This group has been foundational in providing me with resources to understand the logistics of the political sphere as well as tools to increase my effectiveness in spreading the message. IWF proclaims that *every* issue is a women's issue.

• • •

The first time I involved myself in the passage of this bill was in April 2022 in Kentucky's General Assembly session, in the state's capital only a month or so after the whole NCAA experience. Senate Bill 83, also known as the Fairness in Women's Sports Act, was sponsored by Senator Robbie Mills and ensured that girls and women would compete with and against girls and women (what a novel thought) from sixth grade through college. No one knew I was going to be there. Imagine the Democrats on the Senate floor when they saw me sitting upstairs in the Senate chamber. There was an immediate visible panic when I was introduced, and they realized who I was and why I was there. My presence dismantled their narrative that this topic was a "nonissue." As I would eventually continue testifying in different states, the following interjections came up ad nauseum:

"Why are we creating a solution to a problem that doesn't exist?"

"There are only four transgender athletes in the entire state!"

"It's only high school girls' basketball. It's not *that* competitive anyways. Who cares?"

I don't think the politicians realized that with these arguments they admit this is a problem or at least a potential one. Do they have a specific number of girls who have to lose out on athletic opportunities in mind before they find it worthwhile to protect women's sports? Twenty? A hundred? One woman? Is one girl not enough?

This is the statement I read standing alongside Kentucky senator Mills:

> *I want to explicitly say there are no hateful feelings or ill will towards Lia Thomas or any transgender athlete for that matter. That's not the issue. The issue is the rules that have been set in place. Those are the problem, not her. We, and when I say we I mean majority of female athletes, want all people to live as they choose and be treated with respect, but we cannot ignore the biological and anatomical differences between males and females that are blatantly obvious and scientifically proven. . . .*

I was so apologetic for feeling the way I did. I felt it necessary and urgent to proclaim that I was not against trans individuals. I agree with the things I said in terms of having no animosity toward Thomas and the fact that every single person should be treated with respect, but I wouldn't say this unprovoked now because I realize defending women is not inherently anti-trans. That verbiage and defense shifts the message of the argument from pro-woman to potentially being seen as anti-trans.

During the session at the capitol building in Frankfort, Kentucky, I noticed for the first time how this issue fell almost entirely on party lines. Most Republicans were in favor and most Democrats against. But wasn't it the left who claimed to be champions for women's rights? I was perturbed because this really wasn't a political issue, or at least it shouldn't have been. Sports are the one thing that should never get political, although we've seen that shift over recent years as players have begun kneeling for our national anthem and ESPN reporters frame every postgame interview they can around skin color.

Another common theme I noticed with politicians is how they would cite the untruth that this "anti-trans legislation *bans* trans athletes from competing in sports *entirely*." I remember speaking in Virginia in January 2023 on behalf of HB-1387. Here is what the bill says:

> *Requires each interscholastic, intercollegiate, intramural, or club athletic team or sport sponsored by a public elementary or secondary school or by a public institution of higher education to be expressly designated as one of the following based on biological sex: (i) males, men, or boys; (ii) females, women, or girls; or (iii) coed or mixed if participation on such team or sport is open to both (a) males, men, or boys and (b) females, women, or girls. The bill requires identification of the student's biological sex on an athletics eligibility form signed by a licensed physician, nurse practitioner, or physician assistant to be submitted by any such student who desires to try out for or participate in an interscholastic, intercollegiate, intramural, or club athletic team or sport. The bill prohibits any such team or sport that is expressly designated for females, women, or girls from being open to students whose biological sex is male.[24]*

I shared my lived experience and testified in support of this bill. Delegate Jeff Bourne objected to this bill and looked me in the eyes as he said, "I grow really tired, as a lot of us do, coming here and have to fight over and over again because a certain small percentage portion of very small-minded people need a group or a person to hate. And that's all this bill is."[25] He later tweeted that he "testified against legislation that would have prevented Virginia's transgender kids from playing in school sports. We have to make sure that ALL of our kids know that they belong."[26]

I agree with Delegate Bourne about making sure our children know they belong, but I don't think it makes me small-minded to ask for fair competition. Making this bill about bigotry and anti-trans sounds great for sound bites and pulls beautifully on heartstrings, but doing so only perpetuates misinterpretations of what the argument is and further divides us. All kids can play sports, just play in a category that's fair and safe for everyone.

When I read Delegate Bourne's tweet, my brain instantly went to the thought of him potentially having a daughter. I took to his Instagram to curb my curiosity. It broke my heart to realize that he did. And to make matters worse, almost all the pictures of her on his profile were of her competing or training. Bourne was willing to throw away his own young daughter's chances to participate in sports at a higher level to publicly appear virtuous. I responded to Bourne's tweet by reposting a picture of his daughter who was working out on a squat machine and wrote, "I was curious and looked up your Instagram and saw this. Would you be okay with a biological male taking your daughter's roster spot? Her chance of collegiate success? Her national championship title? Her privacy in a locker room?"[27] Bourne never responded, but he did happen to turn off the replies under his post once I brought attention to it and people began to call him out on it.

Kansas state representative Marvin Robinson was the lone Democrat representative in Kansas who found it important and urgent to vote in support of what he thought was the fair and moral thing. As you can imagine, Robinson's vote sparked outrage and the feeling of betrayal among his party.

On a radio talk show Marvin appeared on to defend his vote in support of this bill, Marvin shared how another Democrat colleague told him trans teens would kill themselves if the legislation were to become law. This colleague then asked Robinson if he would feel blame and guilt for their death knowing it's at his hands? When asked that he said he gasped and thought how cruel a question to ask someone. State party officials even issued a statement calling for him to resign. The chair of the Kansas Democratic Party's LGBTQ+ Caucus, Brandie Armstrong, said, "If Rep. Robinson is going to allow hate to overrule his commitment to Democratic values, he needs to step aside and let a real Democrat represent his district. Democrats barely have representation in Kansas as it is. The least someone who claims to be part of our party can do is represent our ideals."[28] Now, do you see why Democrats don't tend to stray from party lines?

As of the time of this writing, twenty-three states have passed some version of a bill that says you compete with the category that aligns with your biological sex. As I write this, I'm actually sitting in the airport after an exciting day standing alongside Governor Greg Abbott of Texas at a ceremonial signing of S.B. 15, the Save Women's Sports Act, which ensures collegiate athletics are protected from members of the opposite sex intruding. This bill signing took place at the Texas Women's Hall of Fame at Texas Women's University, which could not have been any more appropriate for the matter. At the signing today, we were spit on, had glass bottles thrown at our feet, liquids were dumped on us, and we were shouted down by the hundreds of protestors who showed up to intimidate us. They jeered at me, the other female athletes involved in the passage who came, the legislators, and Governor Abbott, shouting:

Racist, sexist, anti-trans!
You have blood on your hands!

Eventually, similar legislation was taken up to a federal level to combat the Biden administration's proposed Title IX rewrite. Representative Greg Steube (R-FL) introduced the bill on the House side while senator and coach Tommy Tuberville (R-AL) put it forward in the US Senate. The Protection of Women and Girls in Sports Act of 2023, which "generally prohibits school athletic programs from allowing individuals whose biological sex at birth was male to participate in programs that are for women or girls,"[29] passed in the House of Representatives on April 20, 2023, but is not expected to pass in the Senate, where, at the time of this writing, it sits waiting to be heard. It:

> *provides that it is a violation of Title IX of the Education Amendments of 1972 for federally funded education programs or activities to operate, sponsor, or facilitate athletic programs or activities that allow individuals of the male sex to participate in programs or activities that are designated for women or girls. (Title IX prohibits discrimination on the basis of sex in federally funded education programs or activities, including in public elementary and secondary schools and in colleges and universities.) Under the bill, sex is based on an individual's reproductive biology and genetics at birth.*[30]

This bill fell *entirely* on party lines. This means that *all* 203 Democrat representatives voted in opposition of maintaining the integrity of women's sports. Every single one of them. The most disturbing part is that most of the Democrats who voted in opposition of protecting girls and women are mothers and fathers to daughters of their own. Not a single Democrat voted against the grain. You really mean to tell me that every single person who voted "Nay" *really* believed what they were voting for? Every single one of them would be okay with their daughters undressing inches away from a fully grown and intact male? I hold on to this hope in my heart that they don't actually think that. If they do, I think there is a separate conversation that needs to be had involving Child Protective Services because that is perverse, disturbing, and would make them a sellout to their own children.

This polarization was eye-opening for me; it was the moment I realized legislation wasn't the most effective or quickest way to make sure no girl or woman had to share a podium or locker room with someone born a man. Up until this point, I rejected the notion of women boycotting their games, races, or matches. I didn't think girls should have to make that compromise. I sure as heck didn't want to sacrifice my last meet that rounded off eighteen years of hard work because of some selfish male, but after seeing the way this bill fell on party lines, I again came to the realization that this must come from us. We can't expect others to make the sacrifice of going against the grain when we as female athletes weren't willing to make sacrifices ourselves. It's incredibly unfortunate this issue has reached the point where we're suggesting girls as young as ten or twelve don't compete in the sport that they love to make a point, but we've seen boycotts be an effective way to communicate a broader message throughout history. It would only take one time meaning in the long run, fewer girls would be injured in their sports, be exploited in areas of undressing, and lose out on opportunities. A necessary and worthwhile trade-off.

As if voting "no" wasn't enough, most of these representatives had seething words to say in response. Representative Mark Takano, a Democrat from California, called the debate "traumatizing" and said it would make school sports "less safe for women and girls."[31] I'm not following that one. Representative Robert Garcia claimed that through this bill, "House Republicans are choosing to bully and belittle trans children."[32] Wisconsin state representative Dave Considine, who happens to be bald (I know what you're thinking, just keep reading), said, "Some parents are concerned that their daughter might miss out on a scholarship. They might miss out on playing for this team or that team. Boy, that doesn't sound like a community. That sounds like selfishness. I'm sorry to label it that way, but that sounds like what it is to me." He continued to say we needed to just "work harder."[33]

Ah, the classic "train harder" argument. That's like me telling Representative Considine that if he really wanted to grow hair on that bald head of his, then he should just grow hair.

Representative Glenn Ivey from Maryland took to Twitter to say "[this bill] does NOT put children first. Sports should be safe, accessible, & fair for everyone. [This bill] would mean the forced inspection of student-athletes, which is an egregious violation of a student's personal dignity. This would impact ALL student-athletes across this nation."[34]

So let's get this straight: Checking the birth certificate and/or ensuring that every athlete has a routine physical exam before competing equals egregious violation of personal dignity. Forcing girls to undress in front of an intact and exposed male genitalia does *not* equal an egregious violation of a woman's personal dignity, but rather a kind and inclusive gesture. Please, make it make sense!

• • •

In January 2023, the NCAA was set to have a large conference in San Antonio where they were going to announce the winner of NCAA Woman of the Year. Being a nominee for this award, I decided I would go, but I wasn't going in support of the NCAA and the actions that pursued my senior year. I wanted to be part of advocating for female athletes on the ground. In addition to working with IWF, I had closely worked with a coalition of organizations like the Independent Council on Women's Sports (ICONS), Concerned Women for America (CWA), International Consortium on Female Sport (ICFS), Women's Liberation Front (WoLF), Women's Declaration International (WDI), LGB Alliance, Alliance Defending Freedom, Texas Values, and more. The amazing part about this coalition was that it wasn't just composed of conservative organizations; There were several left-leaning feminist groups whom we linked arms with. They were the kind of radical feminists that stood by the feminist movement original intent. This shows how this issue extends far beyond party lines in the real world. Joining forces with ICONS and others, we had a few things planned. One of the first things I did in conjunction with others was write a letter to the incoming NCAA president, former governor of Massachusetts Charlie Baker. Before attending the rally, we sent a copy of a letter to the NCAA headquarters in Indianapolis, Indiana, as well as to Baker's home. In the four-page letter, I wrote about my experience racing against Thomas and included a few other facts like scientific literature and stories of other female athletes in similar positions as I was. Here are some tidbits:

> *Although I can't speak for everyone who competed against Lia Thomas, I can attest to the tears that I witnessed from finishers who missed being named an All-American by one*

place. I can attest to the extreme discomfort in the locker room from 18-year-old girls exposed to male genitalia in our changing spaces. I can attest to the anger and frustration expressed by girls who had worked so hard and sacrificed so much to get to this moment only to have to compete in a farce. And I can attest to the fact that, around the country, female athletes who protested the inclusion of Lia Thomas in the women's division were threatened, intimidated, and emotionally blackmailed into silence and submission. I can attest to the fact that female athletes in the Ivy League were told that if they are uncomfortable seeing male genitalia in the locker room, then they should seek counseling from university resources including the LGBTQ+ education center.

Let me be clear, I am not against providing trans-athletes a space to compete. I fully believe there is a solution that can accommodate trans-identifying individuals without compromising equal opportunity or privacy for female athletes. I have recently started working with Independent Women's Forum to actively work towards pushing legislature at the state and federal level that enforces an appropriate solution prioritizing fairness in women's sports all while being inclusive.[35]

In this letter, I requested a face-to-face meeting to share more about my experience and scientific evidence pointing to the fact men and women are different in ways that typically makes males advantageous in something that requires sheer strength or athleticism, so adequate policies can be put in place preventing males from competing against females. I sent this letter on January 5, 2023. I sent it by email. I sent it to the NCAA headquarters. I even sent it to President Baker's house as priority mail, meaning he had to sign off on it. He testified in front of the same Senate Judiciary Committee that I sat in front of a few months prior, and when asked the question by Senator Mike Lee if he had "apologized to those female athletes and any others similarly situated for the trauma inflicted as a result of those decisions by NCAA," Baker responded with "I don't know the answer to that question."[36] How disingenuous. Allow me to answer Senator Lee's question for him: No. No, he has not. It's been ten months since that letter was sent in January. Crickets.

Understand that I don't see myself as some victim wanting to throw a pity party for myself. I just want to ensure what happened to myself, my teammates, my competitors doesn't happen to girls like my younger sister. It's about turning an unfortunate circumstance into something positive. Lemons to lemonade.

Earlier that day at that NCAA conference, Marcie Smith and Kim Jones, cofounders of ICONS, as well as other policy makers, athletes (including myself), parents, and spokespersons from the groups mentioned above, organized a rally right outside the convention hall. Our goal was to be a collective voice and demand that the NCAA stop discriminating against female athletes. ICONS had delivered a legal demand letter to put the NCAA "on official notice that your practice of allowing male athletes on women's teams constitutes illegal discrimination against women on the basis of sex."[37] During the rally, Marshi Smith, former NCAA champion swimmer from the University of Arizona, gave a statement:

We hereby demand that you take direct and immediate action to establish rules to keep women's collegiate sports female. In the world of college sports, it is impossible to

*provide equal opportunities for both sexes (as required by
Title IX) without female-only teams. Yet the NCAA imple-
ments and perpetuates a policy of allowing male athletes on
women's teams, even as sports governing bodies and federal
courts increasingly reject these unjust and inequitable policies that exclude young women from their own teams.*[38]

This letter was endorsed and supported by the entirety of the
coalition. I spoke at the rally, as did Nancy Hogshead-Makar; Lin-
nea Saltz, former NCAA track-and-field athlete who competed
against the first male athlete identifying as female in Division 1
cross-country; Patricia Etem, former Olympic rower, one of only
two African American women to ever compete on the US national
and Olympic rowing teams; and many others.

We had a permit to conduct our rally and we did it peacefully. At one point, a representative of the NCAA came outside
and asked us to leave, but because we were legally allowed to be
there as it was public property and we had gone through the
hoops and hurdles of maintaining a permit, we refused. We were
informed that a mass text was sent to the attendees of the convention to not be alarmed by the "protestors" who are outside and to
"stay safe," as if we were dangerous. When the rally was over, I
marched right to the front of the building, where two NCAA representatives reluctantly met me. I handed the legal demand letter
over to someone from the NCAA, which included a petition
signed by tens of thousands of concerned citizens, and explained
to them what it was. To this day, this is still the most personal and
forward-facing anyone has come to addressing this issue with the
NCAA directly.

At this same conference where the NCAA would announce
their NCAA Woman of the Year, they also had a big convention

hall where companies and organizations could buy a booth and sell their products/services. All the athletic directors, chancellors, and presidents of universities walked around this convention hall during the free time they had at the multiple-day-long conference. I figured what better way to be in a position where we couldn't be ignored than renting a booth and putting myself in front of these authority figures. I applied for a booth under my name of Riley Gaines and was denied. I thought to myself, that's weird . . . I'm trying to give the NCAA $2,000. I applied again using my name and was denied a second time. Keep in mind I had been outspoken for nearly nine months at this point. I applied again under an alias, and of course they accepted my money. The founders of ICONS and I passed out pamphlets talking about the importance of Title IX and stopped every single athletic director who walked by and shared our experience at the 2022 NCAA Division I Swimming and Diving Championships. I shared the details of the unfair competition, the trophy fiasco, the locker room, the silencing. I told them how what we went through wasn't unique by any means, as it continues to happen at the hands of the NCAA across the country. Every one of them listened with respect and kindness and said the same thing in response: "Thank you for what you are doing. Keep fighting and pushing forward!" Hearing things like this the first ten or twenty times was really encouraging. But after the fortieth or so athletic director who verbally high-fived our efforts, I started wondering: If these men and women truly agreed with our efforts, then why was it continuing to happen? If we were all on the same page, then what was the discrepancy? Why were we catering to the minority?

I began to press. "That's great you feel that way! Would you be willing to put your name to it?" I would ask.

The almost unanimous response was "Ohhhhh, no. You see, our university really can't risk having a lawsuit or losing federal funding. I can't risk losing my job. I have a family to feed." Then they quickly turned away and removed themselves from the conversation entirely.

In the days following the 2022 NCAA Championships, Mark Emmert, the president of the NCAA, released a statement doubling down on their decision. The statement was that he unequivocally stood in his decision to allow Lia Thomas to swim with the women because it was based in "evolving science." At this same conference, we saw Emmert and he had the nerve to tell us to keep fighting, privately of course. The audacity for him to tell us to "keep fighting" when he was quite literally the one we were fighting.

As mentioned but now proven, it wasn't just the female athletes who felt an immense pressure to stay quiet. If our leaders can't find it in themselves to defend girls and women, then we need new leaders.

• • •

Protecting women's sports was considered an important stance to take until the definition of a woman was hijacked by gender identity politics, which is where we are today. In 2022, the Independent Women's Law Center, the Women's Liberation Front, and the Independent Women's Voice joined forces to stand up for common sense and created the Women's Bill of Rights (WBOR) to help people like Supreme Court justice Ketanji Brown Jackson, who struggle with defining these commonsense terms.[39] This legislation is meant to provide concrete clarity to the long-established understanding of terms such as "woman," "man," "girl," "boy," "mother," "father," "male," and "female." I know what you're thinking . . . We *have* to have a law that defines these words? Yes. Unfortunately, in 2023, we do.

The WBOR states:

> *For purposes of state/federal law, a person's "sex" is defined as his or her biological sex (either male or female) at birth;*
>
> *For purposes of state/federal law, a "female" is an individual whose biological reproductive system is developed to produce ova; a "male" is an individual whose biological reproductive system is developed to fertilize the ova of a female;*
>
> *For purposes of state/federal law, "woman" and "girl" refer to human females, and the terms "man" and "boy" refer to human males;*
>
> *For purposes of state/federal law, the word "mother" is defined as a parent of the female sex and "father" is defined as a parent of the male sex;*
>
> *When it comes to sex, "equal" does not mean "same" or "identical";*
>
> *When it comes to sex, separate is not inherently unequal.*[40]

This bill is crucial because it prevents unelected bureaucrats and officials from redefining these words to fit their narrative or the radical agenda that they're pushing, which has become common practice from large governing bodies and corporations. The NCAA did this and hoped no one would notice that they explicitly violated the federal civil rights law of Title IX. It's important to understand that the WBOR does not establish new legal rights for women or any new laws in general. It also doesn't prevent any new laws from being implemented that would protect the rights of trans-identifying individuals. The bill never even mentions the word "transgender." Without even using that word, it's deemed anti-trans just for vowing to protect women. Think about that and ask yourself, "Why?" If being pro-women is deemed anti-trans, wouldn't pro-trans inherently be anti-women?

The sole purpose of the WBOR is to give longevity to bills that use these terms. For example, the Fairness in *Women's* Sports Act. What good is legislation if we can't agree on what a woman is and therefore who this bill applies to? But WBOR extends far beyond just sports. The bill will also help to preserve single-sex spaces in which privacy and safety are needed, including locker rooms, domestic violence shelters, sororities, and rape crisis centers.[41] It also is necessary for statistical purposes. Before our very eyes, we're seeing data surrounding women be misconstrued to include the results of males claiming the identity of women. Women's sexual crime rate is being altered as male rapists identify as women. Women's health statistics as it pertains to cervical/prostate cancer and pregnancy are being amended to include the statistics of men. Ultimately, this new data negatively impacts the outcome and treatment of women, giving all the more reason to define that word and other sex-based terms in law.

According to Jennifer C. Braceras, director of the Independent Women's Law Center, and Lauren Adams, legal director of the Women's Liberation Front:

> *Although we call the model legislation the Women's Bill of Rights in order to call attention to the many ways in which redefining sex disproportionately harms women, it is not just women's rights and equal opportunity that are at stake: The legal redefinition of basic sex-based terms also*

threatens freedom of speech, accurate data collection, parental rights and scientific integrity.

Recognizing these threats, a group of federal legislators has introduced a version of our Women's Bill of Rights as a bicameral congressional resolution. Were it to pass, the congressional Women's Bill of Rights would not prevent Congress or the states from enacting legislation to protect people based on characteristics such as "gender identity." But it would prevent unelected bureaucrats or judges from twisting current law to accomplish through the back door what Congress lacks the political support to do via the democratic process.[42]

In April 2023, Kansas became the first state to sign into law the WBOR, or Senate Bill 180, when the state's House of Representatives overrode the governor's veto, 84–40. Kansas's Senate previously overrode the veto of the bill 28–12 with bipartisan support.[43]

Next, I worked to help get WBOR passed in my home state of Tennessee—the second state to pass this legislation. Its passage shows how the entire feminist movement has been flipped on its head. Tennessee was the thirty-sixth state to implement voting rights for women, but now the second state to be able to accurately define what a woman is in order to protect our sex-based rights. The juxtaposition is almost comical but certainly ironic and worth highlighting to see how this movement is now contradicting everything it once worked hard to ensure.

Oklahoma became the third state to put into effect the WBOR. This state differed from the rest because Governor Kevin Stitt became the first governor to use his statutory power to sign an executive order on this bill. The word "woman" is used in Oklahoma statute approximately 584 times, meaning there would be just as many opportunities for the word to be reinterpreted in a backdoor way leaving women at jeopardy. Because Stitt acted, that can't legally happen anymore.

On August 27, 2023, I met with Governor Jim Pillen of Nebraska and asked him to mirror what Governor Stitt did. Three days later, Pillen signed an executive order. That is leadership. The most special and coolest part about it all was that Pillen signed WBOR on the same day that the state of Nebraska set a world record for women's sports attendance at the Nebraska volleyball game. Just over 92,000 fans packed in Memorial Stadium to watch the University of Nebraska play Omaha's women's volleyball team, which ended in the Huskers winning 3–0. Exactly 92,003 people gathered in one spot to cheer on incredible women as they showcased their athletic abilities. That should encourage all of us. There is no doubt in my mind that the signing of this bill on August 30, 2023, was strategic. That day, Governor Pillen sent a message to nearly one million Nebraskan women as well as girls across the country—a message that says we are *worthy* and that we *matter*.

While it's not WBOR, Governor Sarah Huckabee Sanders of Arkansas took the initiative to sign an executive order that removes "woke, anti-woman" language from state documents in October 2023. What's woke language? Pregnant people, birth giver, laboring person, chestfeeding, etc. Could you concur what words they really meant? Of course, you could. In the press conference following her executive order, Huckabee Sanders stated that the left is "using nonsense words to erase women and girls and, more importantly, to erase our voices and our experiences." Referring to the birth of her three children, she went on to say, "That experience underscored to me that a woman's perspective is important and fundamentally different from a man's. Nowadays though, only conservatives seem to be making that point. On the left, women have taken a backseat to political correctness." I wish she would have shouted her final point from the rooftops so all could hear. She wrapped up by saying, "How many times should a woman have to be insulted before we stand up and say 'We've had it'? It shouldn't even take one time, but one instance for me is enough for us to stand up for women and say that we can do better. And we will."[44] A woman standing up for women. More than what most who would have previously been referred to as "feminists" are doing for women.

At the federal level, Representatives Diana Harshbarger of Tennessee, Mary Miller of Illinois, Debbie Lesko of Arizona, and Jim Banks of Indiana are among twenty-one other representatives leading the charge in the House. Senators Cindy Hyde-Smith of Mississippi and Cynthia Lummis of Wyoming and others are sponsoring it in the Senate.[45]

Representative Doug LaMalfa of California said this of the bill: "This is all of our fight. This really is a struggle of good versus evil. If we can't defend our girls, our women, for their ability to associate—whether it's in athletics or even in the workforce—then we're really messed up in this country."[46] And yet, this bill is deemed controversial. Not that long ago, feminists and progressives would have entirely agreed. Representative Claudia Tenney of New York stated, "We are so pleased that Representative Lesko has put this bill in. It's an honor to be a co-sponsor, along with everyone else on this bill, to protect women, protect women's sports, protect their daughters, and protect their grandchildren of the future."[47] If we don't codify the definition of sex-based terms, laws that prohibit sex discrimination will cease to mean anything at all, and single-sex spaces will no longer exist.

I didn't end up winning NCAA Woman of the Year. Lia Thomas didn't either. While it doesn't take away from the principle of Thomas being nominated for this award, All-American soccer player Karenna Groff of the Massachusetts Institute of Technology took it home. At least for 2023, an award for a woman is still in its rightful hands.

7.

BLOOD IN THE WATER

O n April 6, 2023, White House Press Secretary Karine Jean-Pierre used an interesting choice of words to discuss legislation promoting fairness in sports and parental control in education and health care. She said:

> *This has been one of the worst weeks for—of 2023 so far in terms of anti-LGBTQ bills becoming law in states across America. Three anti-LGBTQ laws have been enacted so far this week in Kansas, Indiana, and Idaho. Just yesterday, the North Dakota Senate passed ten anti-LGBTQ bills in just one day, a single-day record. . . . Look, this is awful news, let's be very clear about that.*
>
> *LGBTQI+ kids are resilient. They are fierce, they fight back. They're not going anywhere and we have their back. This administration has their back.*[1]

Note and remember the phrase: *They fight back.*

When I watched Ms. Jean-Pierre's press conference, I didn't think too much of these three words. But less than twenty-four hours later, after I'd returned home from being held for ransom and kidnapped, I finally realized the significance of what it meant for the trans community and its allies to "fight back."

• • •

Because I had recently graduated from college, I felt like I had a pretty good idea of how much emphasis these institutions were putting on diversity, equity, and inclusion (DEI) in the classroom—even if it meant lowering their standards. Education had turned into indoctrination. Many Christians and/or conservatives in my generation were thought of as equivalent to criminals, even in certain departments in schools in the South like University of Kentucky. Being a conservative is akin to being a white supremacist, and holding Christian beliefs has become synonymous to an intolerant homophobe. One study found that 7 out of 10 conservative academics in US university/college social science or humanity courses admit to self-censoring themselves out of fear of being punished.[2]

The fall and spring semester following the 2022 NCAA Championships, I felt it was important for me to get back on college campuses to share my experience with students of my generation across the country. I want to help my generation understand the consequences for us and for those who come after us if we don't return to common sense in our policies and practices around gender identity. By April, I must have spoken on nearly a dozen college campuses.

Turning Point, a non-for-profit organization that promotes conservative values and the importance of creating conservative activists, had invited me to speak at an event called "Saving

Women's Sports" at San Francisco State University (SFSU) in California on April 6, 2023. I planned on sharing what it takes to be an elite athlete, what the unfair competition at the NCAA tournament felt like, what the locker room scene looked like, how we female athletes were silenced, and what I had been doing since that time to enact change. I wasn't naïve enough to think I would be welcomed with open arms and a bouquet of flowers. I knew saying yes meant entering the belly of the beast, but I was actually excited for the event. Not because I was desperately seeking out controversy or hostility, but because this opportunity would most likely give me the chance to be in front of a group of people where I could change hearts and minds. That's why I started my activism in the first place. I *thought* I knew what I was getting myself into when I agreed to set foot on SFSU's campus.

Before arriving in San Francisco, I publicly announced the event and what I would be speaking to. I was very clear that everyone was welcome.

> *I encourage everyone to come. I encourage people with differing views than myself to come because I think it's important that these people who don't agree with me, at least are willing to hear my perspective being someone who was directly impacted by this.*[3]

Some members from SFSU's Turning Point chapter had been tabling in the days leading up to the event to spread awareness and buzz. They had captured a video of a blue-haired student walking up to the table where they passed out fliers and she dumped her entire drink all over their property.[4] She broke one of their iPads in the process. I was told Turning Point filed a police report for destruction of property, but the campus police did absolutely nothing. This same blue-haired girl had been spamming my Instagram with hateful comments and threatening messages. Looking back, I guess she was warning me not to come and what I could expect if I did.

Before I get into what the event looked like, let me paint a picture of what the city of San Francisco looked like. I arrived in the city earlier in the day, which left me a few hours to spare before I needed to be on campus. I decided to visit a nearby mall. In the one hour I was at the mall, I watched cars get their windows smashed in by carjackers. I watched as people filled backpacks with unpaid merchandise and confidently walked out of the store without paying for it. I watched security officers who were posted at the entrance of these stores witness the theft and do absolutely nothing about it. I went to the bathroom inside the mall and was followed in by a homeless lady without shoes. I washed my hands as she injected heroin in her arm. I certainly didn't see anyone hold a door open for another person. Nor did I see anyone flash a friendly smile to another person as they walked by. I did see piles of feces littering the ground right outside the entrance doors to the mall. The San Francisco I saw was a dystopia and most everyone I encountered there looked miserable. I immediately craved the Southern hospitality I was used to.

Navid Mehdipour and David Llamas, the field representatives from Turning Point, informed me of the plan to arrive at a particular parking garage on campus an hour and a half before the event. There we would meet with campus police. The police were supposed to escort me as well as review security precautions and exit strategies just in case things took an ugly turn at any point before, during, or after the event.

I showed up to the parking garage at the set time, but campus police were not there. I ultimately concluded they weren't coming, after I had waited for about fifteen minutes or so. I didn't think much of it and figured I would be just fine handling some docile heckling on my own if it came to it. Navid, David, and I walked over to the HSS Building, where the talk was being held in a classroom on the third floor that holds a maximum of about seventy-five people. I assumed the police would show up as promised at some point, but less than an hour before the event began, they were nowhere to be found.

Through social media I had become aware of a counterevent being held challenging my presence. It was a sign-making event where those who opposed my message and presence could gather, create posters, and march over to the event together. At 6:15 (forty-five minutes before I was set to talk) I could hear chanting from outside the room. I looked out the window and saw protestors marching over. Naturally, I felt unnerved, but still not too worried. This was what I had anticipated. The doors opened at 6:30 and the protestors coming from the counterevent made sure they were first in line to secure front-row seats. The room quickly filled to full capacity with the majority in the room there in opposition. One source documented at least two protestors of the event for every one supporter.[5] Still, no police.

The protestors had been warned they could not bring their beautifully crafted signs into the room. With black Sharpies, they had acted fast to copy and paste what their signs said onto their bodies. Written on their faces, palms of their hands, or forearms were statements like "You have blood on your hands" or "Sore loser! You lost to four cis women!" plus an array of other colorful commentary. I'll let you use your imagination. That didn't bother me. These people had a right to their opinions just as I had a right to free speech. My purpose that evening was to share my story and genuinely engage in a peaceful discussion with college students about fairness in women's collegiate sports. Looking back, it's amazing the amount of naïveté I still held on to.

Sitting front and center was the blue-haired girl from the Turning Point video I mentioned earlier. She scooched her desk as close as she could to me in an effort to intimidate me. I just smiled at her and told her I saw the video of her dumping her drink on the iPad as well as the comments she left on my social media, but I was still glad she was there.

There were two doors in the classroom. One led to an adjoining classroom in the back of the room and was closed during my talk. The other door was the entrance and exit to the classroom and was open until I began sharing my story. Navid and David had told me they had been in contact with the police in the days leading up to the event, and the police reassured them all doors to the building would be locked to prevent gathering outside the room once the room reached capacity.

• • •

As seven o'clock approached, I looked around the room, saw most of the crowd in front of me marked up with Sharpies, and began my speech. Without a police presence in the room, I felt nervous looking in their eyes and seeing only vitriol, but I did it without the external appearance of fear. Those who came to listen in support looked more nervous than I did but managed to give me a reassuring look.

About halfway through my talk of forty-five minutes or so, I could hear a large crowd chanting outside the building. "Trans rights are human rights!" "Trans rights are human rights!" I tried to ignore the chorus, but it gradually grew louder and louder. The voices were moving closer. The crowd was clearly making their way into the building. I continued talking and tried my best to drown out the voices of what sounded like a few hundred people at least. By the time the mob surged through the hallway outside the classroom, their voices reached full-on fury. One end of the hallway would yell: "*Trans rights are under attack!*" And the other side of the hallway would yell back: "*What do we do? We fight back!*" The coordinated shouting match continued for several minutes.

"*Trans rights are under attack!*"

"*What do we do? We fight back!*"

Obviously, hearing these chants was unsettling, but I continued my speech. I still trusted that, despite their absence from our original planned meeting, the campus police officers would be present somewhere outside the room to prevent an escalated or overcrowded situation, as they had promised.

Keep in mind, as disruptive as the screaming had become, it was still the right of every person who was protesting. I'm proud to live in a country where people can disagree and speak their beliefs openly. At this point, I was certainly being disrupted, but no one was being harmed. I felt it important to open the floor for questions, specifically ones in opposition, so I could rebut any claims those with dissenting viewpoints had and reiterate why fairness and upholding our rights as women trump inclusion.

Here's a sample of some of the questions and comments that were posed that evening:

"If you're uncomfortable seeing a man in the locker room, why were you looking to begin with? Doesn't that make *you* the pervert?"

"Since you're transphobic, does that mean you're homophobic too? Since you have such a problem with women attracted to women seeing you naked, you clearly don't think lesbians should use the women's locker room either, do you?"

"If you want to ban a genetic advantage, shouldn't a taller than average basketball player be banned for his natural height? I mean, since you preach about fairness, you would clearly support that, right?" Although they were not asked in good faith, all of these questions and comments were relatively easy to rebut.

During the time of the Q&A, the ruckus just outside the classroom had stopped and chanting ceased. I imagined that meant those who were protesting felt like they had done the job they came to do and went home. I felt a sense of relief.

• • •

Right after Navid announced the end of the event and thanked everyone for coming, the audience got up to leave. As soon as the classroom door opened for the people in the room to exit, a surge of protestors rushed into the room. At the same time, the lights in the classroom flickered as I watched the angry mob make their way toward me at the front of the room. Then the room went dark. I remember feeling disoriented. Fists were waving and punching the air as protestors rushed me. Phone lights flashed in my face. I looked to my left and right but couldn't see anything. I didn't know where Navid, David, or the other Turning Point people were. Angry screams of "we fight back" were hurled at me. The same words Karine Jean-Pierre used the day before leaving the invitation to violence unfulfilled when she spoke those words but warranted and encouraged. I was jostled and hit multiple times. I couldn't make out if I was getting hit with closed fists or open hands. *What* was happening? And *how* did it happen so quicky? Upon looking at the hatred in this mob's eyes, I began to pray. I didn't pray for myself. It was involuntary and instinctual to pray for those as they ambushed me and assaulted me.

No one was there to protect me, and I was unable to defend myself, so I knew I should try to document the chaos. The mob had pushed me up against the whiteboard at the front of the class-room. The voices raged, a repeated mantra erupting at rising decibels:

"We fight back!"

Everything happened so fast. As I was trying to get my phone out, a woman wearing all black clothes and a face mask grabbed me by the arm and ordered, "Come with me!"

I had no idea who she was. For all I knew, she was a protestor with the intention of holding me hostage. I snapped my elbow out of her grasp.

"I'm with the police," she assured me, her tone softening. "Riley, you need to come with me now."

Knowing the police hadn't shown up in the first place and amid a hundred-plus people screaming expletives in my face in a dark room, you can imagine my hesitation to go anywhere with her. But really, I had no other choice. It was either go with her to potential safety or stay where there was certain violence. While protestors continued to lunge toward me, fists flying, she grabbed my arm and guided me through the packed room. We couldn't get out the main door of the classroom because it was filled with pro-testors who were still flooding into the room. We managed to escape through the door to the adjoining classroom where other police officers were waiting for us in the small hallway that con-nected the rooms.

Campus officers formed a tight circle around me and together we made our way down the hallway. As soon as someone on the opposite side of the hallway glimpsed my blond hair peeking through the sea of uniforms, a barrage of footsteps and cries sounded from both directions of the hallway. A few of the ring-leaders stood out. As they called me names and shouted expletives at me, the other students cheered on in harmony through loud shrieks and coordinated chants. It was a bad combination, because they were clearly all feeding off one another. Just as happiness is contagious, so are fits of mob rage.

The unruly mob had blocked all the exits, so we couldn't safely exit the building. Unless they were willing to exert force and get physical, it was impossible for the officers to shield me and get down from the third floor, let alone out of the building. The officers pulled me into another classroom along that same hallway to wait. For how long and for what, no one seemed to know, not even the officers, who by this point seemed to be more frazzled than I was. The prisoners were running the asylum.

More expletives and threats ensued. The voices blurred into one guttural sound. I truly felt a presence of evil that evening. I felt like I could hear the voices of the protestors morphing into something inhuman. It wasn't just a protest by college students against a swimmer with opinions they didn't like. When I looked into the eyes of these protestors, I saw vengeance. I saw vitriol. I saw violence. This chaos felt spiritual in nature.

• • •

Had the event transpired as planned, I would have been on the way back to the airport for my flight home. Instead, I was barricaded in an empty classroom with a handful of campus police. They had locked the door to the room, which was located along that same hallway as the room where I had spoken. On the other side of the door, the mass of protestors stood steady, battering the door with their fists and demanding I come out. Even though I recorded bits and pieces of the anarchy on my phone, there was so much screaming and repeated statements of "f**king b**ch," it was hard to catch every word the protestors were screaming. Some of the statements that I was able to decipher from what I was able to record on my phone included:

> *If she didn't want the smoke she shouldn't have came here . . . Tell her to come talk her s**t and then we'll let that b**ch leave . . . .You just look like a racist. I could see it in your eyes . . . you and your ancestors . . . racist b**ch . . . transphobe b**ch! F**k you! All that training was for f**king nothing . . . You come on this campus and think we not goin' start a f**king riot?!*

It all happened so quickly. I was being held in that classroom against my will. The organizers of the event were nowhere to be found, and I later learned that a campus reporter was live-tweeting the whole situation, releasing minute-by-minute information of what was happening and where I was. This encouraged even more protestors to the area and amped up what was already a tumultuous scene.

Immediately after getting to the room where I would be trapped for the next four hours or so, I tried to get the officers to help me understand what had just happened. I was incredibly confused, shaken, and discombobulated. I asked outright for reassurance that I hadn't done something to provoke this. I was looking for them to tell me that never should have happened and was completely unwarranted. Instead, the officers responded with "we can't reassure you right now as to what was deserved in that scenario. We must remain neutral and without comment." I recall that they never asked me if I was injured or okay or needed medical attention.

I called my husband. Of course Louis felt shock, rage, and helplessness when I reiterated what had just happened, what was *currently* happening. After calling my husband, I called my dad. He had an even more concerned reaction. He made me put him on speakerphone with the officers. I'll let you use your imagination as to how that went and what was said. The officers didn't say much except "Yes, sir" and "No, sir."

A few officers were in the room with me at that point, and each of their walkie-talkies seemed to be going off every two minutes. Someone was either listening to a voice buzzing into the speaker or talking to someone on the other end. I couldn't understand much of what any of the officers were saying to one another. It sounded like cryptic codes and numbers.

"What's going on? Why can't we just leave?" I asked the officers. "I'm pretty sure I'm being held against my will, and I'm pretty sure we call that kidnapping. Isn't it your job to get me out of here?"

"I'm sorry, but for your own safety, you can't leave, Ms. Gaines," one of them responded. More buzzing from a walkie-talkie. I glanced at my phone and panicked. I had a 5 percent charge left on the phone.

Outside the door, protestors continued to chant, "No justice. No peace. No justice. No peace." I remember thinking that statement did not make any sense given the context of the event. Who exactly was not given justice? Despite the nonsensical aspect of the chanting, the mantra did wonders to keep the emotions of the crowd elevated to a level of frenzy. It's kind of impressive that this mob did not lighten up for the nearly four hours they were there.

While I sat at a student desk, I took the opportunity to talk to the officers and try to make sense of a few things.

"So, I was told police was going to meet me in the parking garage at five thirty but no one showed up. Why was that?" I asked one of the officers.

One of them shrugged and replied, "There must have been a miscommunication. I don't know."

"And what about the doors?" I continued. "I was told the doors to the building were supposed to be locked right when the event started so no one would be allowed in. Why didn't anyone lock the doors?"

One of the officers looked at me and said, "Well, uh, there are a lot of doors."

Their answers were either embarrassingly pathetic or completely nonexistent.

When I continued pressing, one of the officers was honest with me and said something to the effect that they couldn't do anything in this moment because they couldn't be seen as anything other than an ally to the LGBTQ+ community. The same community on the outside of those doors calling these officers "racist pigs for protecting a white girl like her [me]."

I looked at my watch. A knot tightened in my stomach when I realized I was certainly going to miss my flight home. I started tearing up at the thought of having to spend the night in San Francisco. "I just want to go home," I said aloud.

A campus lieutenant looked at me and without missing a beat said, "That's a pretty selfish thing for you to say. Don't you think *we* want to go home too?"

And that's when I lost hope and stopped holding out for these officers to do the job they were paid and sworn in to do. It's also when I lost it and began to cry. I was scared for my safety, and I felt abandoned on the wrong side of a one-sided justice system. And I was simply exhausted. Because of the time change, at this point I had been awake for nearly twenty-four hours straight.

"Do you guys even have a plan? Can't you just kick these people out so I can get out of this building?" I asked with desperation.

"There's nothing we can do until the SFPD shows up," the officer replied.

About two hours into being locked in this room, I remember looking outside the window and seeing local police cars drive up to the front of the building. Officers got out of their vehicles but stayed out front. "Why aren't they coming up?" I asked.

One of the campus officers said something about the local officers having to get permission from their bosses. They tried to explain the hierarchy of how there is a system in place they must follow, but they couldn't even accurately describe what it was. "So they have to ask permission to do their jobs when someone is in danger . . ." I said out loud.

No one responded.

Finally, an hour later, about ten or fifteen city of San Francisco police officers swarmed the room. I could sense an immediate shift of energy. These officers were visibly larger, taller, stronger, and immediately assured me that what I had endured was nothing short of crazy, something no one should have to go through. These officers formed a plan and sprang into action. One of them told me they were going to form a tight circle around me, and we were all going to leave together after they delivered several warnings over about twenty minutes for the protestors to disperse. We waited, but the protestors didn't listen.

"We're going to stick by you real close, Ms. Gaines," he assured me. "No one will be able to get through, I promise."

"Okay, I'm just ready to get out of here," I replied. Just before the door opened, officers hemmed me, in forming a diamond around me. They were so close I could feel the mass of bulletproof vests, metal buttons, and weapons hanging on thick belts.

It was midnight by the time we shot through the hallway like a rocket as protestors tried their hardest to charge toward us, continuing to fire a barrage of insults and expletives at the top of their lungs.

"You f**king b**ch! Transphobe! Sore loser! Stupid a** b**ch!"

"Let us at her!"

We flew down the staircase, out the lobby, and out through the front doors of the building, while protestors outside caught wind of our movement and started chasing us down the street. We were met with even more vitriol outside, as additional protestors had gathered in response to the reporters who were there delivering real-time updates. The people from Turning Point were waiting for me in their car, and I had only a few seconds to leave the safety of my police officer huddle and jump into the passenger seat. I literally had to run from the middle of the diamond formed around me and into the car to avoid being slammed to the ground by protestors. It was like a scene from *Black Ops–Zombies*. As I hopped in through the open door, I thanked the officers over my shoulders and quickly slammed the door shut. There was no police escort off campus or any sort of follow-up ensuring I got to where I needed to get safely.

On April 6, 2023, I wasn't just giving a talk on campus about my experiences swimming against a male. I was being fed to the wolves.

• • •

The next day, Dr. Jamillah Moore, the university's vice president for student affairs and enrollment management, released the following statement to their student body:

Dear SF State community,

Today, San Francisco State finds itself again at the center of a national discussion regarding freedom of speech and expression. Let me begin by saying clearly: the trans community is welcome and belongs at San Francisco State University. Further, our community fiercely believes in unity, connection, care and compassion, and we value different ideas, even when they are not our own. SF State is regularly noted as one of the most diverse campuses in the United States—this is what makes us Gators, and this is what makes us great. Diversity promotes critical discussions, new understandings and enriches the academic experience. But we may also find ourselves exposed to divergent views and even views we find personally abhorrent. These encounters have sometimes led to discord, anger, confrontation and fear. We must meet this moment and unite with a shared value of learning.

Thank you to our students who participated peacefully in Thursday evening's event. It took tremendous bravery to stand in a challenging space. I am proud of the moments where we listened and asked insightful questions. I am also proud of the moments when our students demonstrated the value of free speech and the right to protest peacefully. These issues do not go away, and these values are very much at our core.

This feels difficult because it is difficult. As you reflect, process, and begin to heal, please remember that there are people, resources and services available and ready to receive our Gator community, including faculty, staff members, coaches and mentors who are here to support you. . . .

*The well-being of the SF State campus community remains
our priority.*[6]

When I read this statement, I nearly lost my breath. There was
no mention, much less condemnation, of the threats, the violence,
the verbal abuse, the complete lack of humanity with which the
protestors behaved. Their violence was not just condoned; it was
celebrated. SFSU leadership didn't express contempt to those who
tried to stifle free speech. It seemed to me that the well-being of
the SF State LGBTQ+ community took priority over anyone else,
especially women.

The following week, SFSU's president, Lynn Mahoney, wrote a
letter to the students:

> *Last Thursday, Turning Point USA hosted an event on
> campus that advocated for the exclusion of trans people in
> athletics. The event was deeply traumatic for many in our
> trans and LGBTQ+ communities, and the speaker's mes-
> sage outraged many members of the SF State commu-
> nity. . . . Last week was a hard one for San Francisco State.
> As we have seen here and at many universities, balancing
> these with dearly held commitments to inclusion and social
> justice is hard and painful. To our trans community, please
> know how welcome you are. We will turn this moment into
> an opportunity to listen and learn about how we can better
> support you.*

Notice Mahoney's mischaracterization of what the event was
all about. Never once have I mentioned or even thought that trans
athletes shouldn't play sports. The mischaracterization of who I

am, what I believe, and what happened that day was as shattering as the experience itself.

• • •

I'll be the first to say I think the idea of having months and/or days of visibility for certain populations does more harm than good, as it only further creates division, but during Women's History Month in March 2023, I noticed a common theme. This theme was that in places where we were supposed to honoring trailblazing women, men who said they were women were being recognized and celebrated. As mentioned previously, ESPN highlighted Lia Thomas and his achievements in a special Women's History Month segment. Rachel Levine was awarded *USA Today*'s Woman of the Year. Alba Rueda received the International Woman of Courage Award. Fae Johnstone was the honoree chosen to showcase Hershey's International Women's Day campaign using their HerShe bar. What do all these awardees have in common? They're all men.

I thought to myself, "How can we get back to honoring real women in places where that was the original intent?" I started brainstorming and came up with this idea of celebrating October 10th as Real Women's Day. Why October 10th? October 10th is the 10th day of the 10th month, denoted by 10/10. The roman numeral for 10 is X; therefore 10/10 equates to X/X. If you took fifth-grade biology, you know that XX represents the female chromosomes. After lots of elbow grease, meetings, and collaboration, I was able to pull off sending out fifty activism kits to fifty different college campuses to interactively prove the point I've been making. These kits consisted of a baseball net, a baseball, and a radar gun. Students would throw the ball into the net as they passed by and the speed of which they threw the ball (in mph) would be recorded. As you can imagine, all fifty states had the exact same outcome. The average of the speed thrown by males was significantly faster than the average speed thrown by females.

After seeing the public attention and applause this idea had garnered, Representative Lisa McClain read a bill declaring every October 10th as Real Women's Day moving forward into the US House Congressional Record.

On 10/10 I was set to speak at Penn State University. After the university canceled/blocked my speech twice, and as did a hotel close to campus, I decided I would show up to campus with a bullhorn and a soapbox and speak on their public lawn to anyone who would listen. Upon arriving to campus, I was met with the response you can probably expect. Professors and university administrators up in arms. Students and TRAs (trans rights activists) were arrested for disorderly conduct. One professor even canceled class due to the fact that "some folks may not feel comfortable" with my presence on their campus.

The real victims of the denial of free speech are the people who are hungry to hear the truth but don't get to, not the person speaking.

It's hard to imagine a world in which people who share the scientific truth that men are men and can't ever be women must be surrounded by security to ensure their safety. And certainly, I'm not alone. Instances perpetrated by trans rights activists that threaten the safety of others happen all the time, particularly in institutions of higher learning. This begs the question of, why are they so desperate to silence the message?

Selina Todd, a gender-critical feminist and professor at Oxford University, was once a supporter of transgender rights. In 2020, after researching the topic for months, she changed her stance and concluded that "this position would harm the rights of women, because so often what is being asked for is free access to women-only spaces."[7] Since then, Selina has been labeled as a transphobe by students at the university and has received daily threats and requests for her to be fired. In response, the university investigated the threats. Discovering they were valid, the school began to post two security guards in every lecture Selina gave.[8] Continuing to defend the right to voice basic truth, this professor confirmed another truth about what is at stake: "In the world today, democracy is under threat and therefore we all have to defend the right of people to have freedom of speech and freedom of debate."[9]

• • •

Around the world, academic institutions are suppressing women who advocate for women-only spaces and female faculties. From reading the stories of Dr. Hooven, Paula Scanlan, and others, you've gotten a glimpse of this reality. But there are so many more stories.

In 2018, Shawnee State University in Ohio opened an investigation into philosophy professor Nicholas Meriwether, which determined that Meriwether created a hostile environment for his students by not using the correct pronoun when interacting with a student. The university warned Meriwether he could face suspension or termination for violating the school's nondiscrimination policy. Meriwether sued, stating the university violated his First Amendment right to free speech. His lawsuit was dismissed by a federal district judge. The ruling was overturned in 2020, however, when the US Court of Appeals for the Sixth Circuit ruled that Meriwether was allowed to sue the university.[10] The court wrote:

Traditionally, American universities have been beacons of intellectual diversity and academic freedom. They have prided themselves on being forums where controversial ideas are discussed and debated. And they have tried not to stifle debate by picking sides. But Shawnee State chose a different route: It punished a professor for his speech on a hotly contested issue. And it did so despite the constitutional protections afforded by the first amendment.[11]

While Shawnee ultimately chose to settle the lawsuit with Meriwether rather than have it be heard in court, other professors and students aren't so lucky with such a favorable outcome.

Kim Russell was the head coach for women's lacrosse at Oberlin College in northern Ohio for five years. When she arrived on campus in 2018, she knew it was a perfect fit. The school was known for its progressive values, and Kim had a reputation as a "bastion for progressive politics."[12] During the 2022 NCAA Championships, Kim took to Instagram and congratulated the 2021 Tokyo Olympic swimmer Emma Weyant for being the real winner on the 500 race in the 2022 NCAA Championships, not Lia Thomas. Kim wrote, "What do you believe? I can't be quiet on this. . . . I've spent my life playing sports, starting & coaching sports programs for girls & women."[13] Kim could never have imagined the witch hunt that ensued. The next day, Kim was called into a meeting with the athletic director and assistant athletic director where she was told, "Unfortunately, you fall into a category of people who are filled with hate," and "It's acceptable to have your own opinions, but when they go against Oberlin College's beliefs, it's a problem for your employment."[14] She was forced to apologize to the lacrosse team she coached. Soon after, the athletic director scheduled a meeting with himself, Kim, the athletic department Title IX director and its diversity, equity, and inclusion (DEI) representative, as well as the Title IX director for the school. For two hours, Kim listened as her character was questioned, one person at a time. On campus, she received more of the same from students. One student athlete told her, "It's not good enough just to work for women's issues or white feminism. Your feminism has to be inclusive for everybody and work for everybody."[15] Another said, through the message she posted on Instagram, "You are genuinely trying to make an attack on me."[16] As an advocate for her athletes and having coached transgender athletes, Kim was heartbroken. "I was not just chastised, I was burned at the stake. I was stoned. I was basically told I was a horrible person."[17]

After speaking out about the backlash she received, Oberlin College removed Kim from her position as head women's lacrosse coach. She still stands firm in her views that men should only compete against men.

Kim never expected the backlash over an opinion posted on her personal social media account or the hypocrisy exhibited by what is supposed to be a liberal institution. Not only was this coach persecuted for being pro-female, but she was also told by her athletic director not to use gendered language when talking to the athletes she coached on the women's lacrosse team and their families. No differences allowed. Compelled speech and severe consequences if you don't comply? Smells a lot like Marxism to me.

As I've been going to colleges across the country to spread awareness, I've personally experienced institutions stifling my pro-woman message. Occurrences like what these women, myself, and others have had to endure is why it's so hard for some men and women to speak up and voice the truth. But if we are not allowed to talk about reality and things that should be common sense, what kind of future awaits us?

According to a poll published in the *New York Times*, 84 percent of Americans feel the burden of not being able to speak freely for fear of being criticized or canceled.[18] The threat of being canceled is real, and evident. But there's another consequence on the rise to speaking your truth that prevents many from utilizing one of the greatest freedoms in this country—the threat of physical violence. I know, I've experienced it.

The San Francisco Public Library hosted an exhibition by a transactivist group called the Degenderettes in 2018. Such a fitting name considering the group is made up of men who now identify as women and consider themselves to be lesbians.[19] The Degenderettes, who were promoted as a "humble and practical club fighting for gender rights within human reach rather than with legislation and slogans,"[20] encourage and endorse violence against women. The exhibit featured slogans like "I Punch TERFS," axes painted in the colors of the trans flag, baseball bats covered in wire, and shields with the words "Die Cis Scum," a slogan made famous by transgender white nationalist Char the Butcher.[21] The fact that the same city that accepts and celebrates people's differences is also the first to showcase blatant aggression against free-spoken women is chilling. This discrepancy is the exact reason I'm speaking out for women who are afraid to and have every right to feel that way.

Speaker's Corner is a famous area in the Hyde Park neighborhood in London. It has a colorful history of being a place where people have gathered to demonstrate for a cause. George Orwell, author of *1984*, called it a wonder of the world and wrote that he had heard a wide variety of people with different backgrounds, worldviews, and beliefs (from Indian nationalists to freethinkers to Mormons to "plain lunatics") speak in that special part of Great Britain.[22]

In 1908, in what was at that time the biggest political demonstration the country had seen, 250,000 women gathered to fight for their right to vote.[23] In 2017, another group of women gathered in that same location, but the fight that ensued wasn't the kind the women in 1908 would have ever imagined.

Sixty-year-old Maria MacLachlan and twenty to thirty other women were standing together and waiting to be told the venue for a meeting, "Let's Talk about Gender," which was to take place shortly. This meeting was a discussion in response to proposed changes to the United Kingdom's Gender Recognition Act, which offers individuals easy ways to change their sex however they identify.[24] As Maria waited with her friends, a transgender woman named Tara Wolf and others knocked the camera she was holding out of Maria's hand, hitting and kicking her several times.[25] In the background trans activists chanted, "When TERFs attack, we fight back!"[26] Keep in mind, nobody was attacking. The alleged "TERFs," the group Maria was standing with, was simply standing, and waiting around. One witness stated that at one point, the trans activists began shouting, "Kill all TERFs."[27] Wolf admitted to posting on Facebook just prior to that day: "I wanna f*** up some terfs."[28]

While the attack was traumatic to Maria, what happened in court when Wolf was on trial was even worse. Wolf was accompanied by about two dozen mostly men supporters, Dobermans and mastiffs, and speakers that blasted death metal.[29] Maria was forced by the judge to refer to Wolf as a "she" and when Maria forgot to use the "correct" pronoun, she was disparaged by the judge.[30] In an interview, Maria said, "The judge never explained why I was expected to be courteous to the person who had assaulted me or why I wasn't allowed to narrate what happened from my own perspective, given that I was under oath. His rebuke and the defense counsel's haranguing of me for the same reason just made me more nervous and so I continued to inadvertently refer to my male assailant as 'he.' In his summing up, the judge said I had shown 'bad grace' and used this as an excuse not to award compensation."[31]

Ronald Reagan once said, "Freedom is never more than one generation away from extinction. We didn't pass it on to our children in the bloodstream. The only way they can inherit the freedom we have known is if we fight for it, protect it, defend it and then hand it to them with the well taught lessons of how they in their lifetime must do the same. And if you and I don't do this, then you and I may well spend our sunset years telling our children and our children's children what it once was like in America when men were free."[32]

Violence is not the answer from either side of the debate. Common sense is. Unfortunately, little by little, truth is being drowned out by fear and intimidation. The more we allow this to continue, the less freedom we will have. And once our freedom is taken away, what do we have left?

8.

SPRINT WHEN IT HURTS

When I was in college, I developed a race strategy for the 200 freestyle. It worked well for me most of the time. My other teammates who swam the same event witnessed my success and followed my same strategy. It didn't have an official or cool-sounding name, but the overall idea was "control-build-sprint-over kick" each fifty yards. Most swimmers in short races, me included, had a habit of swimming fast right out the gate and dying out because, understandably, your body fills with lactic acid fast. Your muscles start burning and fatigue overtakes you, making it impossible to keep up your original pace and solid technique. In a 200, this burnout was typically most visibly evident in the third fifty.

The "control-build-sprint-over kick" method was to swim the first fifty controlled (we called it easy speed), then build on the second fifty so by the time you're flipping at the halfway point, you've built enough momentum to sprint all out in the third fifty, and finally overkick (exactly what it sounds like) in the final fifty.

The legs are pretty much dead on the last fifty, so if you don't put extra emphasis on straining them, then they will most likely fall off, figuratively, of course.

The key to successful implementation of "control-build-sprint-over kick" is found in the third fifty, the sprinting part. It's during this time one must, as the Navy SEALs are fond of saying, embrace the suck.

I found the more I used this strategy, the more comfortable I became with feeling uncomfortable and the better and faster I swam. My arms and legs would get used to the burn. I got to the point where I almost enjoyed that burning feeling. My body would adapt to the pain and just go. Keep in mind, I didn't develop this strategy until my junior year, so it certainly took some trial and error before being able to perform the way I wanted to and knew I could. This strategy seemed to work for more than just the 200 free. I found it worked in the 200 butterfly as well.

This brings me to the Southeastern Conference record I set in my senior year of college. First, some background. I already shared with you the honor of winning SEC Scholar Athlete of the Year in Women's Swimming and Diving my last year as a Wildcat. What I didn't tell you is how I found out.

• • •

A few minutes before it happened, my coach Lars pulled me aside at the hotel a few minutes before leaving to head back to the pool for finals to tell me I was going to be honored for this award. He cried when telling me, which shows how much he cares about our success both in and out of the pool. Normally, the recipients aren't made aware of this award prior to receiving it in front of all the fans and other swimmers from the SEC schools on the pool deck, but because the 200 fly was the first event of the session and the award was announced right before the first event, my coach decided to tell me prior to the session so I could mentally prepare and still perform to the best of my ability. As soon as I received the award, I'd have to put my swim cap on and head straight to the pool. There would be minimal prep time to get into the zone.

I had done a personal best at prelims that morning, but knowing I was racing Georgia's Dakota Luther, the 2x defending champ who broke the SEC meet record the year before, I didn't carry high hopes of winning. Really, my goal was to keep Dakota in sight as long as possible. She would be in lane 4, and I was in lane 5. If I could still see her feet at the end of the race, it would have meant I was doing a good job. She was a back-half swimmer, meaning she would almost always have the least amount of time difference between her first and last fifty when compared with the other swimmers in the pool. When everyone else was losing steam, she didn't.

About ten minutes before the race, the SEC Scholar-Athlete of the Year award was announced, and I was honored. This award was special to me because it had nothing to do with what I had accomplished athletically, which is what we, as athletes, put so much of our self-worth in. I quickly threw my cap on, handed the big trophy I had just received to a teammate, and got ready to race. The mix of caffeine from the energy drink I had and the adrenaline from receiving this award in front of so many people was the only warm-up I needed.

We dove off the blocks and I followed my normal strategy. I remember turning at the end of every lap and, with my peripheral vision, noticing that I'd touch the wall just before Luther did each time. The first fifty, I thought it was because, well, it was my first fifty. The second fifty I was convinced that Dakota was going to surpass me at any given moment. At the halfway point, I turned and gave it everything I had during the third fifty. I found comfort in being uncomfortable.

I didn't realize I had a legitimate chance of beating Dakota until we turned after the sixth lap. That's when I decided I wasn't going to lose. It came down to the touch and hardly a fingernail separated us. I had beat Luther by .14 of a second with a time of 1:51.51. This time made me one of the fastest Americans of all time in the event. I had beat my previous best time by three seconds and set a new SEC record in the process, which is an absurd amount of time to drop as a senior in college. This record still stands.

Here's the crazy thing. My coaches hardly ever let me train butterfly. Freestyle was my thing. While I was racing, I couldn't gauge in the moment how fast I was swimming, something I could easily do when racing freestyle. The only thing on my mind before I jumped into the pool was that it was my last SECs, and I had nothing to lose.

This experience parallels the cards I had been dealt, and how I responded after the 2022 NCAA Championships. I gave up a career in dentistry, something relatively safe and secure, to do something totally foreign to me. The only way pro-women advocates like me—and the countless other incredible men and women legislators, athletes, parents, and allies—are going to prevail is if we keep sprinting when it hurts. Because guess what? This race is hard, and it's far from over. We're up against violent protestors, evil conglomerates, people who want to see us and our families destroyed simply for believing what is scientifically and constitutionally true.

• • •

After I began to speak out about the injustice of the unfair competition we faced, I, naturally, was only connecting with conservative media outlets, the ones who shared similar viewpoints and opinions as I did. This was great at first because I was shedding light on the story and people began to see through the idea of "trans women" in women's sports. Before the story of Thomas, people associated the word "trans woman" with someone who has computable testosterone levels and has fully committed to transitioning by following through with the surgeries. This story enabled those same people to see how their previous assumption was entirely false because that's not what we experienced. As it concerned those NCAA female swimmers at that meet, we were competing against a male whose only physical change was that he had just grown out his hair.

Remember, I was in my last few months before heading off to dental school. My class schedule was light, I was done competing and practicing as that NCAA Championships was the final meet of my career, and I wasn't working. I figured I would just dedicate these few months to advocating for the cause before moving on with my life as a dental student and leaving this issue and the fight behind me.

The Daily Wire piece in March 2022 quickly turned into a slew of other media/speaking opportunities that I by no means felt prepared for. As I continued to gain more awareness, I began to feel like I was preaching to the choir. Most people who watch Fox News already agreed with me. How I could reach the people who *didn't* agree with me? Those were the people who needed to hear the message I was sharing.

In my own personal capacity, I began reaching out to left-leaning media sites like CNN, MSNBC, and other local outlets. Early on I messaged Matt Jones of Kentucky Sports Radio, the number one college sports podcast on iTunes that covers the University of Kentucky sports.[1] Matt is a well-known name in the Kentucky sports world and even nationally. I found it odd that he wasn't talking about the Lia Thomas debacle as the issue was close to Kentucky's heart and the story had gained national attention and traction.

I reached out to Matt via Twitter and respectfully asked if there was a reason as to why he hadn't covered it. I told him I would be happy to talk to him to answer any question he might have and reiterated how influential his platform was, especially locally. He gave a vague reply. He congratulated me for my career at UK but ultimately said this wasn't an issue he wanted to wade into, for a variety of reasons. In his message, Matt said he would be willing to have a discussion over the phone if I had any questions, and then brushed me off by wishing me success in my next endeavor. Of course, I had questions. I didn't want the exchange to end, so I called him.

During our call, Matt admitted he took time to consider both perspectives, but ultimately, he didn't agree with my stance. I told him this conversation wasn't about him having to agree with me; it was about laying the issue into the open and sharing dialogue about it. Matt was firm. "I don't share your opinion," he kept repeating. Finally, he said, "I don't like to get into politics." You may not know this, but this is the same guy who wrote the book *Mitch, Please! How Mitch McConnell Sold Out Kentucky (and America, Too)*, a scathing look into what Matt called "the ineptitude of one of Kentucky's senators." Worth mentioning, he also always covers other areas where sports and politics intersect, like kneeling for the anthem and the BLM movement.

I reiterated to him that he did in fact talk politics and that he'd have to come up with a different explanation to help me understand. But even so, this issue *wasn't* political, or at least it shouldn't be. If he thought so, he was the one making it political, not me.

The argument is about fairness and if we think women are worthy of such.

Matt asked me what I thought the perfect solution was. I admitted that I didn't know. I expressed how I was just a twenty-one-year-old girl and the solutions shouldn't be left to me to figure out, but what I did know is that the solution did not involve a scenario where women should have to compromise anything. "And there's your problem," he began. "You think there is no compromise to be had. I will not give you a platform."

Matt's comment wasn't unusual. It wasn't the first time—and it won't be the last—that my perspective was dismissed. It was, however, the first time my eyes were truly opened to media bias. Of course, I knew it existed, but I had never been personally affected by it. The rest of the other outlets I had reached out either responded similarly or simply didn't respond.

The University of Rochester recently conducted a study that determined that major US news outlets (including CNN, *Wall Street Journal*, *Washington Times*, *Christian Science Monitor*, *New York Times*, Bloomberg, NBC, *Federalist*, and *Reason*) are reporting polarizing domestic social issues along ideological lines.[2] Lead researcher Hanjia Lya noted, "We observed a lot of subtle differences in the words they choose when they cover the same high-level topics. For example, when covering abortion issues, Reason tends to use the term 'abortion law,' while CNN underscores its ideological position by using the term 'abortion rights.' On a higher level they are both talking about abortion issues, but you can feel the subtle difference in the words that they choose."[3] I can think of several instances of word choice bias of the top of my head: gun control/gun rights, illegal aliens/migrants, war in Iraq/war on Iraq. There are several ways to tell the same story, but sometimes, they end up not actually telling the same story.

Outlets on both sides are purposefully creating division through choice words, sensationalism, and spin. Make no mistake, they do not want unity. It's not unity that gets clicks and likes.

Media bias is even a thing within artificial intelligence. Researchers in Brazil and the United Kingdom created a vigorous testing method to test ChatGPT for political bias. In asking the app a survey of questions (asked one hundred times with randomized question order), they found "robust evidence that ChatGPT presents a significant and systematic political bias toward the Democrats in the US, Lula in Brazil, and the Labour Party in the United Kingdom."[4]

Dr. Fabio Motoki, lead author of the study, said, "With the growing use by the public of AI-powered systems to find out facts and create new content, it is important that the output of popular platforms such as ChatGPT is as impartial as possible. . . . Our findings reinforce concerns that AI systems could replicate, or even amplify, existing challenges posed by the Internet and social media."

When Google introduced Bard, their version of ChatGPT, to the public, executives released the following statement: "While LLMs[*] are an exciting technology, they're not without their faults. For instance, because they learn from a wide range of information that reflects real-world biases and stereotypes, those sometimes show up in their outputs. And they can provide inaccurate, misleading or false information while presenting it confidently."[5]

I just asked ChatGPT the question of "Are trans-identified males considered women?" and this was the response: "Yes. Individuals who are assigned male at birth but identify and live as women are called transgender women. It's important to respect

---

[*] research large language model

and acknowledge a person's gender and use appropriate terminology to ensure understanding, inclusivity, and respect."

We are used to hearing, listening to, and talking about the things we want to hear, listen to, and talk about. I get that. And I certainly believe both sides are guilty of it. The problem is the spin doctoring that comes into play when talking about an issue. For example, I am labeled as an extremist because I'm addressing the message of preserving female rights, female language, and female-only spaces in sports.

• • •

Standing up for women is not about spreading hate. It's about holding people in leadership who have failed women accountable. According to Dr. Linda Blade, Canadian sports performance coach, advocate for women's sports, and former elite heptathlon champion, "There is no organization more culpable for the undermining of sex-based eligibility in sports than the International Olympic Committee."[6] Sex-based eligibility has to do with policies in place regarding the women's category that revolves around biological and scientific facts.

In 2021, the IOC released what they called the "IOC Framework on Fairness, Inclusion and Non-Discrimination on the Basis of Gender Identity and Sex Variations" to determine how transgender athletes fit into Olympic competition.[7] The only problem is, they really didn't. This is the framework the IOC and the US Olympic and Paralympic Committee (USOPC) have in place under Principle 5:

5. NO PRESUMPTION OF ADVANTAGE
5.1 No athlete should be precluded from competing or excluded from competition on the exclusive ground of an

unverified, alleged, or perceived unfair competitive advantage due to their sex variations, physical appearance, and/ or transgender status.

5.2 Until evidence (per principle 6) determines otherwise, athletes should not be deemed to have an unfair or disproportionate competitive advantage due to their sex variation, physical appearance, and/or transgender status.

Yes. You read that right: the Olympic Committee says males have no proven advantage over females when it comes to athleticism or sheer strength. If they truly thought this, then why even have the women's sports category to begin with? Of course, they don't actually think male advantage is "unverified, alleged, or perceived." And if they really do, they should be fired immediately and sent back to grade school.

Rather than set specific standards or guidelines, as they had in the past, the IOC now places the onus, similar to what the NCAA has now done, on international federations of sports. As of the writing of this book, males do not have to reduce their level of testosterone to compete in Olympic sports. Nor do sporting bodies have to assume that males have an advantage over their female competitors. According to IOC policy, female athletes are now responsible for calling out and proving any advantage that a male athlete who claims the identity of a woman has. Did you get that? Female athletes are responsible, not the IOC. The IOC's framework does not give any specific rulings to follow based on scientific evidence, but it does show their priorities. They favor inclusion over both safety and fairness and definitely do not consider female athletes. It's essentially the same policy the NCAA is now in the process of implementing. The common denominator is neither governing body wants to be held responsible or accountable. Don't take my word for it. Read what Richard Budgett, IOC's medical and scientific director, said of this new framework:

> *This is guidance, not an absolute rule. So we can't say that the framework in any particular sport be it World Athletics or another is actually wrong. They need to make it right for their sport and this Framework gives them a process by which they can do it, thinking about inclusion and then seeing what produces disproportionate advantage.*[8]

Inclusion, first. Fairness, next.

Budgett has some interesting views that I'm sure has factored into creating this framework. During the 2020 Olympics he stated, "Everyone agrees that trans women are women."[9] Hmmm. So, basically the leading authority on medicine and science for the International Olympic Committee is in the same pack that can't answer the loaded question of what a woman is while also lumping the entirety of humankind in with him in his statements. This same individual has said of Laurel Hubbard, the man who competed in the female weight lifting category in the 2020 Olympics, that we ought to pay tribute to Hubbard's "courage and tenacity in actually competing and qualifying for the Games."[10] Giving homage to a man for beating out women in a weight lifting competition . . . how inspiring. It's not like millions of other men could do the exact same thing with little to no training if they wanted to, yet we don't call them courageous. Actually, we call them cheaters.

The International Federation of Sports Medicine (FIMS) and the European Federation of Sports Medicine Associations (EFSMA) released a joint statement highly critical of the IOC framework. Of specific note, the statement says:

The new IOC framework mainly focuses on a particular human rights perspective, and the scientific, biological or medical aspects are not considered. This is highlighted specifically in point 5 of the framework, which states that there should be "no presumption of advantage" due to an athlete's sex variations or transgender status. While not being named specifically in the framework but clarified in the presentation of the framework by the IOC, it is clear that this point refers to the androgenic hormone testosterone and that there should be no presumption of advantage due to high concentrations of testosterone in the male range of 9.2–31.8 nmol/L13 for long periods.[11]

This statement also presents an obvious consequence if transgender athletes are allowed into any category cart blanche:

In the other extreme case of an equally undesirable consequence of having no gender eligibility rules, that is, self-identification that amounts to a free choice to compete in any gender classification, sport would lose its integrity and near-universal support.[12]

To understand how we got here, we've got to start at the beginning. Linda Blade often talks about how gatekeeping for women competing in the Olympics began and how it led to today's IOC's lack of leadership in including males to compete in female categories. I'll show you a road map.

• • •

Women were first allowed to compete in the 1900 World Olympics in Paris. A total of 997 athletes were present, 22 of whom were women who competed in golf, tennis, equestrianism, sailing, and croquet.[13] Since 1991, a little over three decades ago at the time of this writing, the IOC determined that any new sport to be included in the Olympic programs had to include women's partic- ipations. The 2012 London Olympics were the first games in which women competed in all the sports categories. At the 2016 Olym- pics in Rio, women made up 45 percent of competitors.[14]

Linda's research has discovered at least three athletes between 1934 and 1938 who were documented males competing as females in Olympic games.[15] Sex verification for female athletes in the 1930s became necessary. Over time, it became a necessary evil. From 1934 to 1950, if someone suspected or observed an athlete was not a female, the athlete would be examined by a medical pro- fessional to confirm their sex. Then and until 1964, female ath- letes were required to participate in major competitions only if they brought with them a certificate that proved they were in fact a female.

The next verification system was undoubtedly the worst, and the most humiliating. From 1966 to 1967, female athletes were required to parade in front of physicians at the competitions so their external genitalia could be confirmed by professionals on site. In 1968, the IOC began the more reasonable gender verifica- tion via a cheek swab, which tested for the presence of only X chromosomes. Genetic testing for the SRY gene, which was more accurate, began in 1992 and ended in 1999.[16] It was found to be labor intensive and costly and there was still quite an uproar over the parading of genitalia that was done in the 1960s.

The IOC then decided it was best to abandon gender verification testing. The organization explained its reasons in an article published in *Genetics in Medicine* in 2000.[17] Some of the reasons included was that it was emotional traumatic to intersex individuals, inconvenient, and expensive. But here's the thing. During the 1996 Olympics in Atlanta, a survey was taken of 928 female athletes. They were asked if 1) testing should continue for females, and 2) whether or not they were made anxious by the testing. Eighty-two percent of the women responded that the testing should continue. An overwhelming 94 percent stated they were not made anxious by the testing procedure. Only 46 women responded they were made anxious by the testing.[18] What do these survey numbers really tell us? Most of the female athletes were okay with the testing and actually preferred it to continue.

In 2003, the IOC created the Stockholm Consensus, which allowed males to compete as females two years after gender reassignment surgery in addition to a legal change of sex.[19] Dr. Jonathan C. Reeser, a member of the IOC, wrote this after the decision: "It is not hyperbole to state that the IOC took a bold step when it decided to permit the participation of transgender athletes in the Olympic Games. Experience will eventually tell us whether they made the correct decision, and whether the modern female athletic playing field will remain level. Until such time when we can reflect on that experience with perfect hindsight, we must make the best decisions we can with the information available."[20]

Dr. Emma Hilton, a developmental biologist and fellow at the University of Manchester, was curious as to "the information available"[21] on which the IOC based their decision. Dr. Hilton concluded that in 2003, published works regarding studies of trans-identified males and performance changes post-transitions were minimal, merely a handful of studies on bone density.[22] She also found a study that was published in 2004 but presented at the IOC meeting in 2003, before it went to press, by Louis Gooren. His study tracked nineteen trans-identified males and seventeen trans-identified females over three years and noted that after three years of hormone suppression, the males lost muscle mass but retained a significant higher amount compared to the pre-treatment females in the group. The height of the males post-treatment remained the same.[23] Consider the above study by Gooren the "information available" in addition to the already established facts the committee members would have already known that males outperform females in sports, and somehow we come to the conclusion that it makes sense for men to participate as women in the Olympics as long as he is two years post–gender reassignment surgery. This is a perfect space to insert a head-scratching emoji. This decision was based on illusion and not science. It is a mockery to basic biology and those who can comprehend it. Even more detrimental is what this decision unlocked. As Linda Blade puts it, "The IOC would hence forth prioritize the male perspective in future decisions on eligibility in women's Olympic sports."[24]

This lasted until 2015, when the IOC loosened its policy to make it even easier for males to compete with females. I talked about this when I mentioned intersex and Caster Semenya's example. The requirements were basic. Surgery wasn't a necessity anymore. As long as a male could lower his testosterone below 10 nmol/L for at least twelve months prior to competing, he would be eligible to compete as a female.[25] Remember, the average female has a testosterone level of about 1 nmol/L, whereas the average male's is at least twenty times that. It was the 2015 policy change that allowed the three trans athletes mentioned earlier in the book to compete in the 2021 Olympics in Tokyo. And now, of course, that policy is discarded and replaced with the 2021 IOC "Framework on Fairness, Inclusion and Non-Discrimination on the Basis of Gender Identity and Sex Variations."

I want to address two things that led to this drastic change in policy for transgender athletes in female sports. The first development that encouraged the IOC to reverse course was being sued by Canadian trans cyclist Kristen Worley, author of *Woman Enough: How a Boy Became a Woman & Changed the World of Sport*. Worley claimed the 2003 Stockholm Consensus was a human rights violation. He had gender reassignment surgery in 2001, which put him into a menopause-like phase due to his declining levels of testosterone. Wanting to continue professional cycling, he was the first trans male to be subject to the 2003 Stockholm Consensus policy. In 2006, Worley applied to the World Anti-Doping Agency for a Therapeutic Use Exemption for testosterone, saying his health was being negatively affected.[26] Citing that regulating a testosterone limit is an abuse of human rights, Worley sued not just the IOC, but also the UCI, the Cycling Ontario Association (OCA), and Cycling Canada Cyclisme (CCC). He won. The victory scared the IOC, who then began to reconsider their policy, which came in 2015.

The second important development is when Dr. Joanna Harper, a medical physicist and avid runner, published a study of transgender athletes and performance in 2015. Harper, a trans-identifying male himself, made the case that gender reassignment surgery wasn't necessary. Harper believed that a reduction in testosterone level should be enough to equal the playing field between female athletes and male athletes. His reasoning? A study conducted of eight transgender male runners, including Harper.[27] Using their self-reported performance times and age grading methodology, Harper found that these transgender athletes who now self-identify as women had no meaningful advantage compared to female runners. One of the runners actually improved after transitioning from a male to a woman.[28] Harper concluded the study by saying,

> It should be noted that this conclusion only applies to distance running and the author makes no claims as to the equality of performances, pre and post gender transition, in any other sport. As such, the study cannot, unequivocally, state that it is fair to allow to transgender women to compete against 46,XX women in all sports, although the study does make a powerful statement in favor of such a position.[29]

This study of eight athletes (with one being himself) where all results were self-reported gave Harper an invitation to become an advisor to the IOC and influence the organization to set the bar as low as possible to allow men to participate as female athletes. To this date, Harper consults with the IOC on transgender issues as they pertain to sport. Before I get back to the IOC's policy, I must introduce a study Harper conducted that was published in the *British Journal of Sports Medicine* in 2021. The idea was to see what effect long-term testosterone-suppressing therapy had on lean body mass, muscular area, strength, and hemoglobin (Hgb)/ hematocrit (HCT). While I don't find the results of the study fascinating—the science on this issue is, after all, plain as day—I am blown away that the IOC has not even bothered to reconsider its lax guidance when it comes to allowing males to compete with female athletes. So, what did this new study conclude? After four months of hormone-suppressing therapy, trans-identified males had similar Hgb/HCT levels compared with females. A year after hormone-suppressing therapy, the males had less strength and loss in lean body mass and muscular area, yet their levels were still higher than females. The same was true even after three years of hormone-suppressing therapy.[30]

With the IOC's "Framework on Fairness, Inclusion and Non-Discrimination" released in 2021, it's clear the current policy is worse than ever. By slinking away from responsibility, what is the IOC actually doing? Empowering international sports federations? I don't think so.

In light of the barriers I've met with in both the sports and media worlds, I have built my own platform used to spread this message. Of course, I couldn't build it on my own. In just a little over a year, over 1.5 million people from all backgrounds follow me because they desperately want to be informed, equipped with the facts, and use common sense as these stories continue to happen. Some of the people looking to me for answers have already been impacted by the gender ideology madness. Some are waiting to be, as they know no one is immune.

As I continue to expose the reality of the erasure of women, the hate and vitriol increase. In times where I feel overwhelmed, I remember my race strategy that seemed to work pretty well when I needed it to: sprint when it hurts.

If you sprint when it hurts, you get to where you need to be faster. And in this case, where we all need to be. It can't happen fast enough.

9.

GET ON THE BLOCK

C ompetitive swimmers start their races with their feet positioned on starting blocks. They push off a platform to gain power to enter and move through the water. It's basically the "Ready, Set" part of "Ready, Set. Go." Before I delve into what's at stake if we choose not to get on the starting block and advocate to uphold our constitutional rights, it's important to know what we're up against. For one, the dollar. Billions of them.

When clinics, doctors, and insurance companies see transgender individuals coming, they're salivating at the thought of the dollar signs that accompany these patients' transition journeys. In 2022, the market for sex reassignment surgery (including feminization, mastectomy, hysterectomy, and chest masculinization) in the United States was estimated at $2.1 billion and is expected to increase over 11 percent in the next ten years.

During a lecture at Vanderbilt University Medical Center's gender clinic, which opened in 2018, Dr. Shane Taylor described how much money transgender patients could bring in. She said, "It's a lot of money. These surgeries make a lot of money. So, female to male chest reconstruction can bring in $40,000. A patient just on routine hormone treatment who is only seen a few times a year can bring in several thousand dollars. . . . Now these are not from the internet. But it's from the Philadelphia Center for Transgender Surgery, which has done a lot of surgery for patients. I just want to give you an idea of how much bottom surgeries are making. . . . These surgeries are labor intensive. They require a lot of follow-up. They require a lot of O.R. [operating room] time, and they make money—they make money for the hospital."[1]

This hit close to home for me, considering Vanderbilt is basically in my backyard. Shortly thereafter, the clinic stopped medically treating minors for gender dysphoria. As of July 2023, due to changes in legislature, those minors who identify as transgender in Tennessee can no longer access care in the state.

The average cost of transition for one individual is $150,000, not including necessary follow up care. Plus, the patient would require lifelong treatment, which provides a steady flow of incoming revenue. Abortions used to be a cash cow for clinics like Planned Parenthood, who from 2020 to 2021 performed 374,155 abortions that cost anywhere from $500 to $2,300, according to one regional location. One of the largest providers of cross-sex hormones, Planned Parenthood has swapped its moneymaker from abortion to transgender care as it's much more profitable.

A former employee at a Planned Parenthood in a small town admitted that "[a]bortions were the clinic's bread and butter, but trans identifying kids are cash cows, and they are kept on the hook for the foreseeable future in terms of follow-up appointments, bloodwork, meetings, etc., whereas abortions are (hopefully) a one-and-done situation."[2]

The Human Rights Campaign, an LGBTQ+ advocacy group and one of the largest political lobbying group in the United States, has a similar idea of promoting the transgender movement through what's called the Corporate Equality Index, or CEI, a benchmarking report that tracks how well they are promoting the LGBTQ community through their employee services, hiring practices, and promotion of products. The higher score, the better for the company and its investors and stockholders. For instance, although Anheuser-Busch previously had a CEI score of 100, when it didn't stand behind and defend its alliance with Dylan Mulvaney after much of the public was confused and appalled by the company's partnership with Mulvaney, the Human Rights Campaign punished Anheuser-Busch by suspending its score. While the medical community cannot control businesses like the HRC, it can pull from the wallets of parents from confused minors.

Not only that, but states who approve laws that limit or ban pro–gender identity ideology laws, like offering gender-affirming medical care to minors including life-altering and irreversible surgeries or changing definitions of words like "sex," are in danger of losing federal funding. This applies not only to state budgets but also to schools and universities and organizations like the NCAA. For example, Texas is suing the Biden administration over their unlawful interpretation of Title IX. The Biden administration claims that refusal to allow boys to compete on girls' teams and to call students by their preferred pronoun are in violation of Title IX and is threatening to withhold $6 billion in funding for elementary schools and universities in that state.[3] Corporate America, academia, the media, etc. don't follow red or blue. They follow green.

Who suffers when the gender ideology movement gains a foothold and forces American citizens to participate in its beliefs? Eventually, we all do. I'm constantly reminding myself what's at stake if we don't defend and uphold common sense—things like eliminating the word "woman" from female organizations and even the English vocabular; requiring that males be included into female-only opportunities and spaces, like competitions, scholarships, schools, shelters, prisons, and sororities; refuting science and biology so we can make males comfortable with not feeling comfortable with their biological identity; making feelings more important than *objective* truth. This should be more frightening to all of us than the very real cancel culture that we live in.

In the spring semester of the 2022–23 school year, I spoke at the University of Pittsburgh. After my message, a talk that was similar to the one I gave at SFSU, a professor stood up and spoke about how males do not pose any threat to female competition because genetic advantages naturally exist within the separate sexes. He brought up Michael Phelps as an example. This professor explained that because Phelps has Marfan's syndrome, giving him more elongation of the limbs and elasticity in joints, in any competition where he competes against another competitor who does not have these advantages, the other swimmer is inherently already at a disadvantage, making the competition unfair. I don't think he understood that this line of rebuttal supports the argument that admitting men competing against women is inherently unfair. The advantage Phelps possessed over his competitors who don't have Marfan's syndrome is a fraction of a percentage of an advantage—nowhere near the 10–12 percent performance advantage that elite male athletes have over elite female athletes who have had a similar amount of training and competed at the same level. After explaining this, I tasked the professor what subject he taught as I was curious what his area of expertise was. Anthropology, he replied.

I asked, "So if you were to dig up a human . . . two humans . . . one hundred years from now. One man and one woman. Could you tell the difference strictly based on their bones?"[4]

Now, I'm not an anthropologist nor an archeologist. I took anthropology and anatomy courses in undergrad, but I clearly wasn't an expert. I do know, however, that male and female skeletal systems are different. Males have more dense and larger bones and joint surfaces. Females have distinct pelvic structures because of biological childbearing abilities. They are deeper and wider than males. In addition, a female's thoracic cage is rounder and smaller than a male. A simple one-minute Google search or the opening of any anatomy textbook will give you even more differences.

A few seconds went by after I asked the professor the question. Finally, he blurted out with a false sense of confidence, "No."

The room burst into laughter. Some of the protestors even dropped their heads in their hands. The professor looked around the room and snapped, "I'm not sure why I'm being laughed at if I'm the expert in the room . . . I have a PhD!"

Why would a professor at a well-known and established university dispute this basic and well-studied reality pertaining to a subject he was hired to teach?

This same denial of reality is taking place across the nation and all over the world. By way of an additional example, consider the American Anthropological Association (AAA) and Canadian Anthropology Society's (CASCA) annual meeting in September 2023, where they cancelled their panel titled "Let's Talk about Sex Baby: Why biological sex remains a necessary category in anthropology." Their reason? The AAA and CASCA asserted that this panel "relied on assumptions that run contrary to the settled science in our discipline" and would harm "vulnerable members of

216 SWIMMING AGAINST THE CURRENT

our community." They further accused the panel of committing "one of the cardinal sins of scholarship" when assuming that "sex and gender are simplistically binary."[5] The panelists were accused of advancing a "scientific reason to question the humanity of already marginalized groups of people." The AAA and CASCA concluded their statement with the declaration that there is "no place for transphobia in anthropology." One of the panelists was Dr. Carole Hooven, mentioned previously as the reprimanded Harvard professor and author of *T: The Story of Testosterone, the Hormone That Dominates and Divides Us*.

The AAA and CASCA join a long list of organizations and institutions that have been captured by ideology and have therefore ceded their scientific authority. Our intellectual and scientific institutions, which used to be bastions of free speech and a safe space for the exchange of ideas, have become anti-intellectual bastions of censorship. This hypocrisy puts the very foundation of our democracy at risk. Abolitionist Frederick Douglass said, "No right was deemed by the fathers of the government more sacred than the right of speech. It was in their eyes, as in the eyes of all thoughtful men, the great moral renovator of society and government."[6]

When we are told what we can and cannot say, our basic right to freedom of speech is violated. When educational institutions— not to mention other organizations and political groups—begin to require the repression of certain opinions and beliefs, we begin to inch our way toward deep-seeded political oppression. Our constitutional republic cannot survive without the ability of all individuals to express themselves freely. Marxism, in theory, and socialism, in practice. Freedom of speech is the first right to go. Venezuela and Cuba are classic examples. These countries are in political and economic ruin. And they are not the only ones.

Now a human rights activist, Yeonmi Park fled North Korea with her mother when she was just thirteen years old. In her memoir, *While Time Remains*, she shares how life in North Korea under the regime of a dictator was steeped in hardships. Any negative talk about the government and the propaganda it spewed and forced its people to swallow resulted in interrogation and punishment. To feed his family, Yeonmi's father had to work in the black market, buying and selling goods like cigarettes, clothing, and metal. When the government found out, he was sentenced to years at a labor camp. Without money to survive, Yeonmi and her mother escaped to China, hoping to live in freedom. Instead, the two became victims in a human trafficking ring. Yeonmi was sold for less than $300, her mother for $65.

Eventually the two connected with Christian missionaries and made their way to Mongolia and then South Korea, where they could start a new life as refugees. It was there, for the first time, Yeonmi began to understand what the word "freedom" meant. Until that time, in her eyes, it just meant having an opinion or wearing jeans without the fear of getting arrested.[7] Yeonmi began to understand, little by little, that freedom had to do with the ability to create a future of her own choosing. While in South Korea, she got an education and made her way to the United States, where she enrolled in Columbia University in 2016. In her book, she describes how one of the first things she appreciated about life in America was the kindness that people showed to those who had disabilities, as well as the accommodations and opportunities that were available like ramps and advocacy organizations. She shared how the government in North Korea would discard people with special needs, expelling them to the countryside so they would starve or placing them in labor camps. Yeonmi was also enamored of the US Constitution's First Amendment, something she took to heart. Here is what it says: "Congress make no law respecting an establishment of religion or prohibiting its free exercise. It protects freedom of speech, the press, assembly, and the right to petition the Government for a redress of grievances."[8] Our founding fathers sought to protect us from what we are now enduring.

What Yeonmi encountered within academia was shockingly antithetical to this given right. Commenting on the First Amendment, she says, "For a refugee from a country like North Korea, that sentence is the very heart of freedom, a prism of cultural and political achievement, the likes of which I never thought possible for human beings not only to write on paper, but to make the very law under which hundreds of millions of individuals would live. It is a law that Columbia University teaches its students to hate—sometimes subconsciously, sometimes overtly."[9] Yeonmi was taught to look for signs of hidden systemic racism, the disease of toxic masculinity (like men holding doors for women), that "gender is a societal construct imposed by white men,"[10] and that the United States is an "inherently evil system."[11] She recalls being speechless when her Columbia professor told the class that "math was racist," as it was made by white men to control the minority.

Today, Yeonmi Park speaks all over the country working to expose the breakdown of our God-given and Constitution-endowed freedoms. She writes, "For so long, I never had the language to describe either tyranny or freedom. Now that I'm finally starting to, I need you—the reader—to help me bring attention to the fact that . . . America itself is not as safe from a similar fate as it might think."[12]

Little by little, we see an increase in restriction on the very freedoms most of us have taken for granted. Consider the relentless denial of biological reality. Consider the vaccine mandates. Consider the push for gun control.

As we witness the chronic challenge to our basic freedoms from the liberal establishment, I encourage you to open any history book and see how the steady retrenchment of individual freedom turned out for any civilization that has taken this route. Time after time, throughout history, it ends in a government that owns and controls production and distribution of all goods and services and, often, in the systematic destruction of both the systems and the people who fight to maintain democracy, and in several cases, in genocide. Have a conversation with someone who fled North Korea. Or Nazi Germany. Or China, Russia, Cuba, or Venezuela. Ask them how this style of government turned out for their home country. Ask them which direction they feel the United States is headed. This is why I feel so passionately about what I'm fighting for—it is much further-reaching than women's sports.

Nobody wants to think a free Western country is capable of evolving into a socialist regime where we are told how to think, how to feel, and what to say, but as I write these words, we are already at risk of tumbling toward this fate.

• • •

The conversation to preserve women's rights quickly (and understandably) gets centered on girls and women and we often ask ourselves the very valid question of "Where are the feminists?" Again, this is an ironically legitimate question that needs to be asked. And we should just as often be asking ourselves the question "Where are the men?" Why has this battle fallen almost entirely on the shoulders of young women like me? We *need* strong men.

There's a saying, "Hard times create strong men, strong men create good times, good times create weak men, weak men create hard times."[13] You can see this cycle play out throughout history in all human civilizations. History is known to repeat itself.

I can't help but think part of our current malaise has to do with how modern culture has crucified the male population under the banner of "toxic masculinity." The dictionary defines toxic masculinity as "a cultural concept of manliness that glorifies stoicism, strength, virility, and dominance, and that is socially maladaptive or harmful to mental health."[14] In 2019, for the first time ever, the American Psychological Association created guidelines on how to work with boys and men, claiming that "traditional masculinity is psychologically harmful,"[15] rather than point to a male's specific personality or character trait that unleashes toxicity like sociopathy, unwanted sexual aggression, and misogyny, masculinity in itself is targeted and labeled as bad.

Over time the phrase "toxic masculinity" has become distorted and diluted. Once an idea relegated to the worst parts of a man (think of a philandering drunk who beats his wife and kids and climbs his way to the top of the corporate ladder by annihilating everyone in his path), it is now a phrase flippantly thrown around in everyday circles that paints men who are confident, assertive, independent, or in control of his emotions as a threat, particularly to women. Modern culture has stretched thin the term "toxic masculinity" (as they're doing with so many previously agreed-upon definitions) to include all men who are *not* meek, mild, soft-spoken, and deferential to the opinions of women. The current cult of "toxic masculinity" teaches that we must cancel men who exhibit outwardly masculine traits because they will, no doubt, use these natural inclinations to destroy and dominate female sex. (Let me be clear. Any man who is abusive, violent, or sexist *is* toxic.)

Men who are mature and altruistic should partner with women instead of being forced to sit on the sidelines or in the penalty box simply because they were born with higher levels of testosterone. During the 2022 NCAA Championships, no men defended us when we expressed our discomfort in the locker room. Not our coaches, not our fathers, not the athletic directors. Not a single person who was supposed to be protecting (over-whelmingly men in authority) us had protected us. I desperately and naïvely waited for one of those men to step up and advocate on our behalf, but no one did.

Men, we need you to step in and step up. Your wives and your daughters are begging you to.

10.

———

TAKE YOUR MARK

When swimmers hear the words "Take your mark" before a race, it's an invitation to the calm before the storm. Everything goes silent because we need to hear the starter when he sounds the whistle. The pool becomes an echo chamber. You don't hear a thing outside the rhythmic pounding of your heart. Once everyone takes their position after stepping on the block, you cannot move. Even a muscle twitch or the slightest flinch can call for a disqualification. The seconds before the beep seem like a lifetime. Tunnel vision.

A true competitor thrives in this moment because it's when they decide whether they are going to win or lose. If there is even an ounce of doubt or self-pity or excuse-making, 99 percent of the time, the outcome is set.

When you take your mark, you know the challenge ahead. You know the risks involved. You know it's probably going to be painful. You know what's at stake. And, ready or not, you're diving into the pool.

Even a year and a half since I have retired from competitive swimming, every day I wake up and it feels like I'm taking my mark. And in the spirit of transparency, there are days in which my advocacy and activism feel much like sprinting in mud. Some days the hate I receive hurts deeper than it should. Sometimes I wonder if any of the work I'm doing is making any difference at all. It's when I get emails, text messages, or DMs from girls and women, and even men, who share their journeys of courage in standing up for themselves or others that I remind myself, no matter how slow the progress in a positive direction, progress is progress.

And it's always worth it.

• • •

So, what *is* the solution for all this madness?

The solution is what has always been, at least for the entirety of my life until my last meet. Two distinct categories based on sex still gives every single person despite their gender identity athletic opportunity and chances for success. This means some may not get to compete in the category that aligns with how they perceive themselves, but that's a consequence of the decision to transition. Every single decision has consequences, even if it's something as simple as deciding to get out of bed in the morning. You weigh the pros and cons, and you make a decision. Do what makes you happy but understand that that doesn't mean you get what you want at all times. Boys compete with boys. Girls compete with girls. Men compete with men. Women compete with women. There are only two sexes. Therefore, there should only be two categories that accommodate them. Everyone can play. And everyone *should* play regardless of gender identity, sexual orientation, race, etc. as there are truly so many benefits to playing sports outside of just athletic achievement.

Isn't the whole point of sport to set our identities aside and compete on a fair playing field? We set aside things like our race and our religion and our background to allow for a coming together that transcends our identities and unites us.

What about a third category?

I don't believe this is a realistic and feasible solution in terms of facilities, financial resources, getting enough people to compete in this division, getting enough people to watch this division, etc. Swimming already tried this. FINA created an open category for all trans individuals, with the first meet being in October 2023 at the World Cup in Berlin. There was not a single entry. Not one male identifying as a woman nor one female identifying as a man entered. If we caved and created categories based on how we identify, it would not be satisfactory to only create a league for trans individuals as it's been proven to be a slippery slope. Suddenly we must find a distinct place for those who identify as agender, pangender, gender neutral, nonbinary, genderqueer, or some combination of these things. We should not have to reconfigure all of our systems and essentially redesign society just because an extremely small percentage of the population is experiencing some sort of internal torment like gender dysphoria. A small group's torment should not become everyone else's burden. I believe it would do everyone a disservice, including trans athletes, to create a third category as the root of the problem is still not being attended to but rather affirmed.

Plus, think about it, a third category is just another category for a male to win. Another category for a male to stand atop the podium. Another category for a male to take home the prize money. Again, we already have two categories to accommodate the two sexes, and this is a sufficient solution to the problem. Everyone competes where is safe and fair. How is that controversial?

Most conversations I've had with those who disagree with my stance say a third category is not equality but rather segregation. They don't want a third category because these individuals want to be recognized for something they genetically, biologically, and factually are not. Competing in an open or trans category diminishes that not-so-invisible cloak these athletes are hiding behind. If we created a trans/open category, would it need to be further divided into males identifying as women and females identifying as men? Then would we need to divide it further by making the males-identifying-as-women category into males who began hormone suppression before puberty and males who began hormone suppression after the irreversible effects of puberty? I would bet the winner of the males would always be who changes their body and their development the least and the winner of the females would always be who changes her body the most by injecting unnatural hormones.

Can there be a solution where inclusion doesn't jeopardize safety and fairness? We'll only find out if we're willing and able to have conversations with those who disagree with us. Have the tough discussions. Consider new perspectives while also challenging them. That is how we advance and unify.

I want to challenge you as to how to wield the power you have. And yes, we all have power to influence, impact, and change. You readers are parents, coaches, athletes, students, teachers, community builders, pastors, medical professionals, Christians and advocates of faith, and ultimately sensible human beings who want to maintain the rights that women have so desperately fought for over the last several hundred years. You are passionate about upholding reality rather than a false façade that will only continue to progress in a way that's detrimental to life as we know it.

Above all else, speak the truth. It is *liberating* to do so. When you finally realize you don't have to adhere to the coercion and fear tactics used by authority figures, your own internal pressure, and the guidelines created by those who are pushing a perverse narrative, you will feel like a weight has been lifted off your shoulders. This *is* a winning issue. It is a winning issue because it is the truth—the truth of our biology, the truth of how we were formed by our infinitely wise, loving, and compassionate Creator—in His image, for the purpose of His glory.

Not only is this a winning issue among the general public, but it's a winning issue according to the truth of scripture. As a Christian, I know that these cultural issues we face are just a part of the bigger battle of spiritual warfare. The scriptures prophesy that we will live in a time where evil is considered good, dark is considered light, bitter is considered sweet. Paul warns us in the Bible that the intensity of these spiritual battles will intensify only as corruption, deception, and temptation increase. But the beautiful thing is we already know who wins—the Bible tells us. Unfortunately, it doesn't tell us how long we have to endure these times, but we know the outcome. This truth is what keeps me grounded, motivated, and unshakable in the face of backlash. I feel called to spread His message of truth, grace, and love and how these virtues work in balance with one another.

• • •

For parents . . . Stand up for your child even if it means standing against the world. Be willing to defend your daughters. If you won't, who will? They *need* you. By doing that, you show them that it's okay to question authority even if you seem alone in doing so. We can't allow this battle and psychological manipulation to fall entirely on the shoulders of young girls. Teach your sons healthy masculinity. Boys should learn the value of growing into a strong man and what that entails. Get involved in whatever way you can, whether that's attending school board meetings or coaching your child's Little League team. While you should always stick up for your kids, make sure to teach your kids how to stick up for themselves. Teach them how to make their mark on the world rather than have the world make its mark on them. The best and most effective way to teach your children this is to lead by example. To do the right thing, one must know what right is. Be their firsthand source of honesty, perseverance, good judgment, leadership, sincerity, and integrity.

For coaches and teachers . . . Be the voice of the voiceless. Create and cultivate a healthy environment where all opinions can be voiced without fear of repercussions. Don't let the greater powers above you intimidate you into submission. Remember why you started. I would bet it was to influence, empower, and inspire others. You have one of the most powerful platforms in a young person's life, I know my teachers and coaches did. You can impact more young people in a year than most people are awarded in a lifetime, so use it to the child's benefit. Be transformational rather than transactional. Seek to transform their sense of worth, value, and talent rather than using your students or players as tools to meet your own personal needs like a job promotion or for monetary gain. Great and effective leading (especially to young people) requires integrity, self-reflection, and a greater sense of obligation. That obligation includes protecting the child's safety, privacy, and opportunities. I so desperately waited for these influences in my life to stand up for me when it mattered, but they failed. Be the one they can turn to for anything.

For girls . . . Don't get discouraged. Please hear me when I tell you are worthy. And you are deserving of the same opportunities that I was fortunate enough to have. You deserve to see yourselves as champions. You are not defined by the thoughts in a man's head. Be bold. Be strong. Be brave. Hold the line. Speak up for yourselves and others when you see an injustice or feel wronged. It can be scary at times, and it may not feel like your place, but it is always within your capabilities to say "no" or "enough is enough." It's important to know when to say those things. It's easier said than done, but if you are competing against a male, weigh the pros and cons of simply not diving off that block or taking those strides when the gun goes. Know that I (and so many others) are in your corner cheering you on from afar. You are the future. And of course, play sports! I will be the first to tell you all the wonderful benefits to being on a team, setting goals, and working hard to achieve those goals. These benefits translate far beyond just sports and will teach you how to be successful in school, your career path, and within your personal relationships.

For women . . . Stop waiting for someone else to defend your rights for you. It's time to link arms with one another and show how powerful strong women can be. Nikki Haley said it best at the first 2024 Republican Party presidential debate when she proclaimed, "If you want something said, ask a man. If you want something done, ask a woman." It's due time to find the tenacity and grit to be able to mask the innate personality traits that make us such amazing mothers, daughters, wives, sisters, and friends. Raise your voice. Support one another. Get involved. Know your rights and don't surrender them for anything. It has never been on the wrong side of history to stand with women. The war on women is real and certainly among us. It's time to take back our language and our spaces. For those women who have been unapologetically speaking out, keep going. I know it can feel as if you are screaming into an empty void, but the tide is turning, and you are needed now more than ever. Oh, and stop apologizing for how you feel.

For men . . . The world and our nation are suffering from a lack of strong masculine leadership. America and the men in it are in a state of crisis. Be the change in restoring strength and success. I know the gender ideology issue doesn't as adversely affect men as much as it does women and/or children but understand we must all fight this together. Don't fall into the category of men who say, "It's up to women to solve this." Fulfill your biblical role of protecting and providing even when it feels countercultural. There is value in being a man who is selfless enough to understand his responsibilities as a husband, father, man, and leader. "Responsibility" is not a bad word, and it shouldn't feel heavy. Being responsible just means having the ability to respond which, in turn, determines the quality of life. If you put that definition into actions, it looks a lot like freedom. Use that freedom to showcase your unique characteristics and roles men play (or at least should play) in society.

For pastors, preachers, ministry leaders, and fellow Christians . . . Don't shy away from talking about cultural issues that are relevant in our intensely divisive cultural climate. As Christians, we are wired to turn the other cheek and avoid conflict. We can discuss these issues in a respectful and compassionate way that still embodies Jesus's love and purpose. He balanced truth and grace so well. All grace and no truth makes one incompetent, while all truth and no grace makes one self-righteous. Find the balance between the two when having these necessary conversations and spreading His gospel. Many of us who claim to be strong in our faith have become complacent and have forgotten what our role on this earth is, myself certainly included at times. We are here on this earth to share His word and tell others of His righteousness. God created man and woman in His image, and He doesn't make mistakes. We have a command to love our neighbors as we love ourselves. God explains love as a decision to compassionately, righteously, and responsibly seek the well-being of another in ways that lead them to their eternal good. Undoubtedly, those in opposition will disagree with this definition of love, but stay steadfast. The world says "live your truth" but our Bible says "Jesus is truth." The world says "you do you" but our Bible says "obey the Lord." The world says "follow your heart," but our Bible says "renew your heart in Christ." The world says "be your authentic self" but our Bible says "be who God created you to be." The world says "love is love" but our Bible says "God is love." Be skillful in recognizing the enemy's devices because he walks around like a roaring lion seeking whom he may devour and be prayerful against them. Know where your help and protection come from. Let me remind you of Matthew 5:10–12, "Blessed are those who are persecuted for righteousness' sake, for theirs is the kingdom of heaven. Blessed are you when others revile you and persecute you and utter all kinds of evil against you falsely ion my account. Rejoice and be glad, for your reward is great in heaven, for so they persecuted the prophets who were before you." Sound familiar? Stay the course without fear.

For **everyone** . . . Please don't wait until you're directly impacted and have to see the effects of this movement firsthand before taking a stand for truth and common sense. Be proactive rather than reactive to help minimize who falls victim to the movement. How many girls have to be injured in their sports before you take a stand? How many girls have to lose out on opportunities? Or be exploited in a locker room? How many children have to live with the regret of mutilating themselves through hormonal or surgical means before it's worth it to take a stand? Is there a magic number before this issue matters enough to take risks and make sacrifices? Courage begets courage and there is strength in numbers. You have it in you to be bold. Be mindful of the language that you use because oftentimes these words or phrases are implemented by the deceivers in a way to subconsciously normalize what should never be the norm. The words we use have more importance and influence than you may realize.

Stop giving your money to organizations and companies that hate you, because you're only funding your enemy. Hit them where it hurts. Shop your values.

I constantly refer to this phrase of true-love and what that really means. These words are synonymous, truth and love; it *is* loving to say the truth. It's not loving or kind or compassionate to deceive, manipulate, or affirm delusions. That's the exact opposite of love. Don't let the world skew your understanding of what love is.

Lastly, be able to think for yourself and be able to admit when you're wrong. I believe the absence of those two things have contributed greatly to the point we're at now. The silent majority needs to find their voice and they needed to do so yesterday.

• • •

Martin Luther King once said, "Injustice anywhere is a threat to justice everywhere. We are caught in an inescapable network of mutuality, tied in a single garment of destiny. Whatever affects one directly, affects all indirectly."[1]

Dr. King is right. Even if you don't play sports, even if you don't have a daughter, even if you're not a female, the issue of female-only spaces still affects you. And if it hasn't yet, I assure you, it will. Unfortunately, it took a crisis moment to compel me to push back and ask the necessary questions. If each one of us waits until we are directly impacted, it will be too late.

There is a common misconception around what being courageous really means. Most people believe courageousness and fearlessness are interchangeable. That is simply wrong. Of course, fearless means having no fear. Courage is quite the opposite. Someone who possesses courage understands the odds they're up against. They see the difficulties that lie ahead. They know they may withstand danger or threats or risks. A courageous person *does* have fears, but they hold the ability to face and overcome these fears while prioritizing a greater objective guided by personal values and the greater good. Mark Twain said, "Courage is resistance to fear, mastery of fear, not absence of fear."

I won't lie to you and say the risks can't become reality. They can and sometimes do as these costs come with the territory. You could be called every name under the sun like I am by those who disagree with my stance: homophobic, transphobic, racist, white supremacist, domestic terrorist, and fascist. Understand that it is just that, name-calling. It's a projection. These libelous labels are not supported with evidence, science, and common sense. It's what the opposition resorts to when they have no other means to dissuade from the argument. I agree that the reprimands are scary, but what is scarier to me (and what should be scarier to all of us) is not standing firm for the truth.

I'll remind you again of my favorite Bible verse that I thought was so perfectly relatable growing up as an athlete, Romans 8:18: "Our present sufferings are not worth comparing with the glory that will be revealed in us" (NIV). The sufferings (backlash, persecution, etc.) are worth it when you understand what and who you're fighting for, both in mortal life and eternal life.

Truth is not determined by a vote. A lie never becomes truth, bad never becomes good, evil never becomes moral just because it is accepted or embraced by a portion or even a majority of society.

Don't be scared to say the F-word: *feminist*. It's time we take back the meaning this word and intent of the movement. Be willing to face the fear. Being courageous is not the absence of fear; the very essence of courage is doing the right thing, even when you are afraid.

What are you waiting for?

Take your mark.

Beep.

ACKNOWLEDGMENTS

To my parents: Thank you for teaching me how to independently think and call out an injustice when I see it. I know you haven't always appreciated my stubbornness, but I know you do now. All the practices you drove me to. All the hours you spent in a hot, overly chlorinated pool just to watch me race for thirty seconds. All the money you spent on fast food to fill my endless pit of a stomach. You were just as invested as I was, and I realize that as I've gotten older. I wouldn't be who I am as an athlete, Christian, and woman without you.

To my husband: You had no idea what you were getting yourself into. Through all the chaos, changing of plans, tears, and unwarranted frustration directed your way, you have been a constant in a time full of ups and downs. Thank you for being my greatest supporter, most evaluative critic, and my best friend. You are truly my better half.

To my coaches: You pushed me to reach my full potential not only in the pool, but in the classroom, community, and as a person. You taught me the meaning of perseverance, fortitude, and resiliency, which has been more useful in my current life than ever before.

To those women who came before me: I would be remiss if I did not thank the individuals who have been using their voice or platform to raise concerns and pushback. While you might not feel it yet, future generations will look back and be so grateful for your ability and willingness to go against the grain in unfavorable circumstances. Onward.

NOTES

BEFORE YOU BEGIN: THE WHAT, HOW, AND WHY

1. Kathy Caprino, "What Is Feminism and Why Do So Many Women and Men Hate It?" *Forbes*, March 8, 2017, https://www.forbes.com/sites/kathycaprino/2017/03/08/what-is-feminism-and-why-do-so-many-women-and-men-hate-it/?sh=3403e3d97e8e.

CHAPTER ONE: EARLY STROKES

1. Michael Pinto, "Top 50 Greatest College Football Fight Songs of All Time," Bleacher Report, November 2, 2010, https://bleacherreport.com/articles/506606-top-50-college-football-fight-songs-of-all-time-with-video.

CHAPTER TWO: SOMETHING IN THE WATER

1. "Michael Phelps Went Five Years Without Missing a Single Day of Training," Forbes @ YouTube, October 24, 2016, https://www.youtube.com/watch?v=pkqjHRN11NM.

2. "Study Focuses on Strategies for Achieving Goals, Resolutions," Dominican University of California, news release, https://scholar.dominican.edu/cgi/viewcontent.cgi?article=1265&context=news-releases.

3. Charlotte Edmonds, "Here's How Much a Super Bowl Ring Costs," NBC Miami, February 11, 2022, https://www.nbcmiami.com/news/sports/nfl/heres-how-much-a-super-bowl-ring-costs/2687889/.

4. Spencer Penland, "Watson's 1:57 200 IM Meet Record Helps Akron Grab Lead on Day 1 of Zippy Invite," SwimSwam, December 3, 2021, https://swimswam.com/watsons-157-200-im-meet-record-helps-akron-grab-lead-on-day-1-of-zippy-invite/.

5.   James Sutherland, "Anonymous Penn Swimmer Speaks Out on Lia
     Thomas' Presence on the Women's Team," SwimSwam, December 9, 2021,
     https://swimswam.com/anonymous-penn-swimmer-speaks-out-on-lia
     -thomas-presence-on-the-womens-team/.

CHAPTER THREE: GO TIME!

1.   Dan D'Addona, "NCAA Won't Adopt USA Swimming Guidelines for
     Transgender Participation; Door Open for Lia Thomas," *Swimming World*,
     February 10, 2022, https://www.swimmingworldmagazine.com/news/ncaa
     -wont-adopt-usa-swimming-guidelines-for-transgender-participation
     -door-open-for-lia-thomas/.

2.   Mount Sinai Testosterone, accessed October 12, 2023, https://www
     .mountsinai.org/health-library/tests/testosterone#:~:text=Normal
     %20measurements%20for%20these%20tests,0.5%20to%202.4%20nmol
     %2FL.

3.   "Transgender Participation Policy," NCAA, https://www.ncaa.org/sports
     /2022/1/27/transgender-participation-policy.aspx (accessed October 12,
     2023).

4.   Katie Barnes, "NCAA Updates Policy on Transgender Participation to Let
     Sport Set Requirements," ESPN, January 20, 2022, https://www.espn.com
     /college-sports/story/_/id/33105305/ncaa-updates-policy-transgender
     -participation-let-sport-set-requirements.

5.   "USA Swimming Releases Athlete Inclusion, Competitive Equity, and
     Eligibility Policy," USA Swimming, February 1, 2022, https://www
     .usaswimming.org/news/2022/02/01/usa-swimming-releases-athlete
     -inclusion-competitive-equity-and-eligibility-policy.

6.   "FINA Inclusion Policy and Appendices," FINA (Fédération Internationale
     de Natation), https://resources.fina.org/fina/document/2022/06/19
     /525de003-51f4-47d3-8d5a-716dac5f77c7/FINA-INCLUSION-POLICY
     -AND-APPENDICES-FINAL-.pdf.

7.   Ibid.

8.   "Transgender Swimmer Lia Thomas Competes in Ivy League Women's
     Meet," CNN, February 22, 2022, https://www.cnn.com/2022/02/22/us/lia
     -thomas-transgender-swimmer-ivy-league/index.html.

9.   Ryan Gaydos, "C State Swim Star Kylee Alons Changed in Storage Closet
     during 2022 NCAA Championships," Fox News, June 22, 2023, https://

www.foxnews.com/sports/nc-state-swim-star-kylee-alons-changed
-storage-closet-during-2022-ncaa-championships-rep.

10. Ibid.

11. @dhookstead, Twitter, March 26, 2023, https://twitter.com/dhookstead
/status/1639993136230301697?ref_src=twsrc%5Etfw%7Ctwcamp%5Etweet
embed%7Ctwterm%5E1639993136230301697%7Ctwgr%5Ea4b80244426ef
06901393305bb8a5858a6a1c521%7Ctwcon%5Es1_&ref_url=
https%3A%2F%2Fwww.foxnews.com%2Fsports%2Fespn-honors-lia
-thomas-celebrating-womens-history-month-segment.

CHAPTER FOUR: A CLEAR AND UNFAIR ADVANTAGE

1. "Gender Dysphoria Diagnosis," American Psychiatric Association, https://
www.psychiatry.org/psychiatrists/diversity/education/transgender-and
-gender-nonconforming-patients/gender-dysphoria-diagnosis#:~:text=The
%20DSM–5%20articulates%20explicitly,of%20sex%20development%20(
DSD).

2. Carole Hooven, "Academic Freedom Is Social Justice: Sex, Gender, and
Cancel Culture on Campus," *Archives of Sexual Behavior*, November 7,
2022, https://link.springer.com/epdf/10.1007/s10508-022-02467-5?sharing
_token=gTPNUCpXVCqq7WzMU2n7_Pe4RwlQNchNByi7wbcMAY5rpl
xPSeiwUBnON7599x-nN5xQx3FeH6V32q5aqBxbVuS5DPZOVGgLXeaOl
OZr6g9AUNJzY-ZzYeSxjDmC8pWV-
eEP8Cf6sGBgLDN2wTMUE2QuuKXpbM2Z_ZjOphK9NwI=.

3. Emphasis mine.

4. "'Woke' Medical School Students Challenge Male, Female Terminology,"
Fox News, July 28, 2021, https://www.foxnews.com/video/6265580505001
#sp=show-clips.

5. Laura Simone Lew, Twitter, July 30, 2021, https://twitter.com
/LauraSimoneLew/status/1421128429068554250?ref_src=twsrc%5Etfw
%7Ctwcamp%5Etweetembed%7Ctwterm%5E1421128429068554250
%7Ctwgr%5Eb184ed9baed8f02c14e13d2fcad1df9a0ef31f51%7Ctwcon
%5Es1_&ref_url=https%3A%2F%2Fwww.foxnews.com%2Fus%2Fharvard
-lecturer-blasted-by-colleague-for-defending-existence-of-biological-sex.

6. Hooven, "Academic Freedom Is Social Justice."

7. Carole Hooven statement, August 3, 2021, https://s3.amazonaws.com
/media.thecrimson.com/pdf/2021/08/12/1350959.pdf.

8. "'It Destroyed Me'—Carole Hooven Reveals the Toll of Being Cancelled,"
YouTube, https://www.youtube.com/watch?v=-ECDgtGdZfU&t=169s.

9. Ibid.

10. Juliet Macur, "Caster Semenya Dominates 800 Meters; 2 Russians Thrive,"
New York Times, August 19, 2016, https://www.nytimes.com/2016/08/20
/sports/caster-semenya-800-meters.html.

11. Len Johnson, "Semenya's Improvement 'Impossible,'" *The Age*, August 22,
2009, https://www.theage.com.au/sport/semenyas-improvement
-impossible-20090822-ge81yp.html.

12. Macur, "Caster Semenya Dominates 800 Meters."

13. "Semenya Offered to Show Her Body to Officials to Prove She Was Female,"
Reuters, May 24, 2022, https://www.reuters.com/lifestyle/sports/semenya
-offered-show-her-body-officials-prove-she-was-female-2022-05-24/.

14. Rachel Savage, "Olympic Champion Caster Semenya's 11-Year Battle to
Compete," Reuters, September 9, 2020, https://www.reuters.com/article/us
-south-africa-lgbt-athletics/olympic-champion-caster-semenyas-11-year
-battle-to-compete-idUSKBN2602RM.

15. Ibid.

16. Mark Critchley, "Rio 2016: Fifth placed Joanna Jozwik 'feels like silver
medallist' after 800m defeat to Caster Semenya," *Independent*, August 22,
2016, https://www.independent.co.uk/sport/olympics/rio-2016-joanna
-jozwik-caster-semenya-800m-hyperandrogenism-a7203731.html.

17. "Questions & Answers on IAAF Female Eligibility Regulations," World
Athletics, https://worldathletics.org/news/press-release/questions-answers
-iaaf-female-eligibility-reg.

18. Molly Quell, "Olympic Runner Caster Semenya Barred over Testosterone
Rules, Prevails in Rights Case," Courthouse News, July 11, 2023, https://
www.courthousenews.com/olympic-runner-caster-semenya-barred-over
-testosterone-rules-prevails-in-rights-case/#:~:text=A%20two%2Dtime
%20Olympic%20champion,to%20those%20of%20%22a%20healthy.

19. Ibid.

20. Ibid.

21. "Genetics and Sex Differences," *Neuroscience News*, May 4, 2017, https://
neurosciencenews.com/genetics-sex-differences-6585/.

22. "A Brief History of Women in Sports," Concordia University, St. Paul, https://kinesiology.csp.edu/sports-coaches-and-trainers/a-brief-history-of -women-in-sports/.

23. D. J. Handelsman, A. L. Hirschberg, and S. Bermon, "Circulating Testosterone as the Hormonal Basis of Sex Differences in Athletic Performance," *Endocrine Reviews* 39, no. 5 (October 2018): 803–29, doi:10 .1210/er.2018-00020. PMID: 30010735; PMCID: PMC6391653.

24. David Handelsman, "Sex Differences in Athletic Performance Emerge Coinciding with the Onset of Male Puberty," *Clinical Endocrinology (Oxf).* 87, no. 1 (July 2017): 68–72, https://pubmed.ncbi.nlm.nih.gov/28397355/.

25. Carole Hooven, *T: The Story of Testosterone, the Hormone That Dominates and Divides Us*, Kindle ed. (New York: Henry Holt, 2021), 120–21.

26. Ibid.

27. "Testosterone Blockers for Trans Women: What You Need to Know," Yahoo, October 7, 2022, https://www.yahoo.com/video/testosterone -blockers-trans-women-don-230202555.html.

28. Hooven, *T*, 109.

29. "Reasons for Gender Differences in Youth Sport," Human Kinetics, https:// us.humankinetics.com/blogs/excerpt/reasons-for-gender-differences-in -youth-sport.

30. V. Thibault et al., "Women and Men in Sport Performance: The Gender Gap Has Not Evolved since 1983," *Journal of Sports Science and Medicine* 9, no. 2 (June 2010): 214–23, PMID: 24149688; PMCID: PMC3761733.

31. Gregory Brown and Tommy Lundberg, "Should Transwomen Be Allowed to Compete in Women's Sports? A View from an Exercise Physiologist," 2023, https://www.researchgate.net/publication/370600102_Should _Transwomen_be_allowed_to_Compete_in_Women's_Sports_A_view _from_an_Exercise_Physiologist.

32. E. N. Hilton and T. R. Lundberg, "Transgender Women in the Female Category of Sport: Perspectives on Testosterone Suppression and Performance Advantage," *Sports Medicine* 51, no. 2 (February 2021): 199– 214, doi:10.1007/s40279-020-01389-3; erratum in *Sports Medicine* 51, no. 10 (October 2021): 2235, PMID: 33289906; PMCID: PMC7846503.

33. "Olympian Sharron Davies—The Fight for Women's Sport," Triggernometry, https://twitter.com/triggerpod/status /1682382971829907457.

34. Hilton and Lundberg, "Transgender Women in the Female Category of Sport."

35. Julianna Photopoulos, "The Future of Sex in Elite Sport," https://media .nature.com/original/magazine-assets/d41586-021-00819-0/d41586-021 -00819-0.pdf (accessed October 13, 2023).

36. Trisha Ward, "Trans Women in Female Sports: A Sports Scientist's Take," Medscape, April 21, 2022, https://www.medscape.com/viewarticle/972250 ?uac=109711DK&faf=1&sso=true&impID=4228378&src=WNL_infocu1 _220507_MSCPEDIT#vp_1 (accessed October 13, 2023).

37. Doriane Lambelet Coleman and Wickliffe Shreve, "Comparing Athletic Performances," Duke University School of Law, https://law.duke.edu/sites /default/files/centers/sportslaw/comparingathleticperformances.pdf (accessed October 13, 2023).

38. 2023 International Women's Sport Summit—Day 2," YouTube video, 2:43:07, posted April 15, 2021, https://www.youtube.com/watch?v= pFviD7zRSAU&t=6187s (accessed October 13, 2023). See minute 16 in his talk.

39. Ibid.

40. Roger Gonzalez, "U.S. Women Bring Fun and Brave Perspective in 12–0 Elimination Loss to Wrexham in the Soccer Tournament," CBS Sports, June 2, 2023, https://www.cbssports.com/soccer/news/u-s-women-bring -fun-and-brave-perspective-in-12-0-elimination-loss-to-wrexham-in-the -soccer-tournament/ (accessed October 13, 2023).

41. "The Man Who Beat Venus and Serena Back-to-Back," Tennis Now, November 15, 2017, https://www.tennisnow.com/Blogs/NET-POSTS /November-2017-(1)/The-Man-Who-Beat-Venus-and-Serena-Back-to-Back .aspx (accessed October 13, 2023).

42. Alexandre Pedro, "Karsten Braasch: The Smoker Who Ridiculed the Williams Sisters," We Are Tennis, April 9, 2013, https://wearetennis .bnpparibas/en/news-tennis/news-results/2085-karsten-braasch-the -smoker-who-ridiculed-the-williams-sisters (accessed October 13, 2023).

43. Ian Miller, "Serena Williams Told the Truth About Differences Between Men and Women 10 Years Ago," OutKick, June 22, 2023, https://www .outkick.com/serena-williams-told-the-truth-about-differences-between -men-and-women-10-years-ago (accessed October 13, 2023).

44. @The Rubin Report, YouTube, https://www.youtube.com/watch?v= 9ajgNIHQ4Ho.

45. Ed Aarons, "Coe Warns Transgender Athletes Pose Risk to Integrity of Women's Sport," *Guardian*, March 21, 2022, https://www.theguardian.com /sport/2022/mar/21/coe-warns-transgender-athletes-pose-risk-to-integrity -of-womens-sport (accessed October 13, 2023).

46. @triggerpod, Twitter, July 28, 2023, https://twitter.com/triggerpod/status /1684942301037056000?ref_src=twsrc%5Etfw%7Ctwcamp%5Etweetembe d%7Ctwterm%5E1684942301037056000%7Ctwgr%5E8cb27742e5bb3b41d 42acfd92063cb32a435edd9%7Ctwcon%5Es1_&ref_url= https%3A%2F%2Fdailycaller.com%2F2023%2F07%2F29%2Fsharron -davies-olympic-medalist-transgender-men-competing-female-sports %2F.

47. Hooven, *T*, 128.

48. Timothy Roberts et al., "Effect of Gender Affirming Hormones on Athletic Performance in Transwomen and Transmen: Implications for Sporting Organisations and Legislators," *British Journal of Sports Medicine* 55 (2021): 577–83, https://bjsm.bmj.com/content/55/11/577.

49. Hilton and Lundberg, "Transgender Women in the Female Category of Sport."

50. "Testosterone Test," Mount Sinai Health System, https://www.mountsinai .org/health-library/tests/testosterone#:~:text=Normal%20Results&text= Male%3A%20300%20to%201%2C000%20nanograms,0.5%20to%202.4%20 nmol%2FL (accessed October 13, 2023).

51. Hilton and Lundberg, "Transgender Women in the Female Category of Sport."

52. Brenda Protz, "Cage Warrior," *Illinois Times* (Springfield), October 9, 2014, https://www.illinoistimes.com/springfield/cage-warrior/Content?oid= 11452450.

53. Alan Murphy, "Exclusive: Fallon Fox's Latest Opponent Opens Up to WHOATV," WHOATV, September 14, 2017, https://whoatv.com/exclusive -fallon-foxs-latest-opponent-opens-up-to-whoatv/ (accessed October 13, 2023).

54. Ewan Somerville, "BBC Apologises after Interviewing Transgender Athlete Who Boasted of Violence against Women," *Daily Telegraph*, July 17, 2022.

55. Matt Mercer, "With Veto Override Votes Set, Payton McNabb Shares Her Story Backing Women's Sports Bill," North State Journal Online, July 18, 2023, https://nsjonline.com/article/2023/07/with-veto-override-votes-set -payton-mcnabb-shares-her-story-backing-womens-sports-bill/ (accessed October 13, 2023).

56. Sharron Davies with Craig Lord, *Unfair Play*, Kindle ed. (Forum, 2023), 53.

57. Ibid.

58. "Doping for Glory in East Germany," *UNESCO Courier*, September 2006, 10 11. httpoı//uncodoc.uncoco.org/ark:/18223/pf0000191752.

59. Gary D'Amato, "Former Swimmer Shirley Babashoff Was Stunned by Dopers in 1976," *Milwaukee Journal Sentinel*, July 19, 2016, https://archive.jsonline.com/sports/olympics/former-swimmer-shirley-babashoff-was-stunned-by-dopers-in-1976-b99764674z1-387545691.html/ (accessed October 13, 2023).

60. Ibid.

61. "The State-Sponsored Doping Program," PBS, June 13, 2011, https://www.pbs.org/wnet/secrets/the-state-sponsored-doping-program/52/ (accessed October 13, 2023).

62. "Doping for Glory in East Germany."

63. "The State-Sponsored Doping Program"; "Doping for Glory in East Germany"; Domhnall Macauley, "Doping in Sport—a Warning from History," *BMJ* 335, no. 7620 (September 2007): 618, doi:10.1136/bmj.39343.402766.68; PMCID: PMC1988980, https://www.ncbi.nlm.nih.gov/pmc/articles/PMC1988980/.

64. Lucas Aykroyd, "Ex–East German Athletes Struggle with Health Problems Due to the Consequences of PED Taking," Global Sport Matters, November 7, 2019, https://globalsportmatters.com/health/2019/11/07/ex-east-german-athletes-struggle-with-health-problems-due-to-the-consequences-of-ped-taking/ (accessed October 13, 2023).

65. Macauley, "Doping in Sport."

66. Werner W. Franke and Brigitte Berendonk, "Hormonal Doping and Androgenization of Athletes: A Secret Program of the German Democratic Republic Government," *Clinical Chemistry* 43, no. 7 (July 1997): 1262–79, https://doi.org/10.1093/clinchem/43.7.1262.

67. Aykroyd, "Ex–East German Athletes Struggle."

68. Sarah Dingle, "Rio 2016: Former East German Athletes with Doping History Warn Russians 'It's Not Worth It,'" ABC News, August 15, 2016, https://www.abc.net.au/news/2016-08-16/athletes-with-doping-past-tell-russia-not-worth-it/7722080 (accessed October 13, 2023).

69. Ibid.

70. Jere Longman, "Drug Testing: East German Steroids: Toll? They Killed Heidi," *New York Times*, January 26, 2004, https://www.nytimes.com/2004 /01/26/sports/drug-testing-east-german-steroids-toll-they-killed-heidi .html.

71. Dingle, "Rio 2016"; Longman, "Drug Testing."

72. Free Library, S.v. "Hormonal doping and androgenization of athletes: a secret program of the German Democratic Republic government," retrieved October 13 2023, from https://www.thefreelibrary.com/Hormon al+doping+and+androgenization+of+athletes%3a+a+secret+ program+of...-a0209622275.

73. Oliver Fritsch, "Dopingopfer: Die Kinder der Dopingärzte," Zeit Online, March 26, 2018, https://www.zeit.de/sport/2018-03/doping-ddr-sport -dopingopfer-kinder-folgen-hilfe-english.

74. Longman, "Drug Testing."

75. Craig Lord, "Memories of Moscow 1980: Why Rica Reinisch Had to Retire at 15 After 3 Olympic Golds, 4 World Records," *Swimming World*, July 23, 2020, https://www.swimmingworldmagazine.com/news/memories-of -moscow-1980-why-rica-reinisch-had-to-retire-at-15-after-3-olympic -golds-4-world-records/.

76. "The Prodigy Whose Body Lasted Two Years," *Guardian,* October 31, 2005, https://www.theguardian.com/sport/2005/nov/01/athletics.comment.

77. Lord, "Memories of Moscow 1980."

78. Davies, *Unfair Play*, 43–44.

79. Davies, 8.

80. "Transgender Olympic Athletes May Face 'Huge Advantage,'" CNN, January 25, 2016, https://www.cnn.com/2016/01/25/sport/transgender -olympic-athletes/index.html.

81. A. T. Kicman, "Pharmacology of Anabolic Steroids," *British Journal of Pharmacology* 154, no. 3 (June 2008): 502–21, doi:10.1038/bjp.2008.165; PMID: 18500378; PMCID: PMC2439524, https://www.ncbi.nlm.nih.gov /pmc/articles/PMC2439524/.

82. "NCAA Banned Substances: What Caffeine Is Banned by the NCAA?" Marca, April 13, 2023, https://www.marca.com/en/ncaa/2023/04/13 /643810dae2704efe6d8b4609.html.

83. "Performance-Enhancing Drugs," NCAA, https://www.ncaa.org/sports /2016/7/20/performance-enhancing-drugs.aspx.

84. "NCAA Banned Substances," NCAA. July 13, 2023, https://www.ncaa.org /sports/2015/6/10/ncaa-banned-substances.aspx.

85. Ryan Gaydos, "Retired Cyclocross Champion Speaks Out: Trans Athletes in Women's Sports 'Not Fair Sport,'" Fox News, May 22, 2023, https://www .foxnews.com/sports/retired-cyclocross-champion-speaks-out-trans -athletes-womens-sports-not-fair-sport.

86. Supreme Court Brief Amici Curiae No. 22A800 West Virginia, et al. v. B.P.J., by next friend and mother, Heather Jackson, https://www .supremecourt.gov/DocketPDF/22/22A800/256864/20230313125831986 _Female%20Athletes%20Amicus.pdf.

87. Juliana Kim, "World Chess Just Placed Restrictions on Both Trans Women and Trans Men," NPR, August 18, 2023, https://www.npr.org/2023/08/18 /1194593562/chess-transgender-fide-pushback.

88. George Greenwood, "England Team Protest over Trans Angler," *Times*, September 25, 2023, https://www.thetimes.co.uk/article/england-team -protest-over-trans-angler-jln03r2c2#:~:text=Members%20of%20the %20England%20ladies,Hodges%20in%20the%20competition%20squad.

CHAPTER FIVE: MAKING WAVES

1. Sherri Gordon, "How Agreeableness Affects Your Behavior," Verywell Mind, April 17, 2023, https://www.verywellmind.com/how-agreeableness -affects-your-behavior-4843762.

2. P. T. Costa, A. Terracciano, and R. R. McCrae, "Gender Differences in Personality Traits across Cultures: Robust and Surprising Findings," Journal of Personal and Social Psychology 81, no. 2 (August 2001): 322–31, doi:10.1037/0022-3514.81.2.322; PMID: 11519935, https://pubmed.ncbi.nlm .nih.gov/11519935/.

3. George Orwell, *Animal Farm and 1984*, Kindle ed. (New York: HarperCollins, 2003), 90.

4. Mary Margaret Olohan, "I Left There with No Trophy: NCAA Female Swimmer Who Tied for Fifth with Trans Athlete Says Officials Put Lia Thomas Ahead of Her," Daily Wire, March 23, 2022, https://www .dailywire.com/news/i-left-there-with-no-trophy-ncaa-female-swimmer -who-tied-for-fifth-with-trans-athlete-says-officials-put-lia-thomas-ahead -of-her.

5. "Vermont School Suspended Father and Daughter for Calling a Male a Male," Alliance Defending Freedom, November 4, 2022, https://adflegal

.org/article/vermont-school-suspended-father-and-daughter-calling-male
-male.

6. "Testimony of Paula Scanlan," U.S. House Committee on the Judiciary,
July 27, 2023, https://judiciary.house.gov/sites/evo-subsites/republicans
-judiciary.house.gov/files/evo-media-document/scanlan-testimony.pdf.

7. Joe Morgan, "Lia Thomas' UPenn Teammate Speaks, Says University
Wanted Us to Be Quiet," Fox News, June 6, 2023, https://www.foxnews
.com/sports/lia-thomas-upenn-teammate-speaks-says-university-wanted
-us-be-quiet.

8. "Testimony of Paula Scanlan."

9. Morgan, "Lia Thomas' UPenn Teammate Speaks."

10. Shawn Cohen, "EXCLUSIVE: 'The Integrity of Women's Sports Is at
Stake,'" *Daily Mail*, December 15, 2021, https://www.dailymail.co.uk/news
/article-10314225/UPenn-parents-pen-poignant-letter-demanding-NCAA
-change-rules-trans-swimmer-Lia-Thomas.html.

11. Ibid.

12. "Testimony of Paula Scanlan."

13. Ibid.

14. Andrew Powell, "Riley Gaines: Open Letter to Harvard, Lia Thomas,"
Daily Caller, June 21, 2023, https://dailycaller.com/2023/06/21/riley-gaines
-harvard-lia-thomas-letter/.

15. Douglas Quan, "Not for Men, Sorry: Transgender Woman Files Human
Rights Complaint After Being Denied Brazilian Wax," *National Post*,
August 22, 2018, https://nationalpost.com/news/canada/not-for-men-sorry
-transgender-woman-files-human-rights-complaint-after-being-denied
-brazilian-wax.

16. Meghan Murphy, "Twitter Wants to Shut Us Right Down, but We Want
You to Join Us. (And We Don't Think Either of These Things Is Inevitable),"
Feminist Current, November 20, 2018, https://www.feministcurrent.com
/2018/11/20/twitter-wants-shut-right-wants-join-dont-think-either/.

17. Ibid.

18. Haroon Siddique, "Maya Forstater Was Discriminated Against Over
Gender Critical Beliefs, Tribunal Rules," *Guardian*, July 6, 2022, https://
www.theguardian.com/society/2022/jul/06/maya-forstater-was
-discriminated-against-over-gender-critical-beliefs-tribunal-rules.

19. J. K. Rowling, "J. K. Rowling Writes About Her Reasons for Speaking Out on Sex and Gender Issues," J. K. Rowling Official Website, June 10, 2002, https://www.jkrowling.com/opinions/j-k-rowling-writes-about-her-reasons-for-speaking-out-on-sex-and-gender-issues/.

20. https://www.womanalive.co.uk/opinion/women-are-being-cancelled-for-speaking-out-on-transgender-issues/12745.article.

21. @JK_Rowling, Twitter, October 17, 2023, https://twitter.com/jk_rowling/status/1714279937279160596.

22. Harriet Alexander, "University of Cincinnati Gender Studies Prof Gave ZERO Grade for Using Phrase 'Biological Women,'" Daily Mail, June 20, 2023, https://www.dailymail.co.uk/news/article-12253257/University-Cincinnati-gender-studies-prof-gave-ZERO-grade-using-phrase-biological-women.html.https://twitter.com/oliviakrolczyk_/status/1675725690900041728.

23. Snejana Farberov, "Vermont Coach Sues School After Being Fired Over Trans Views," New York Post, July 20, 2023, https://nypost.com/2023/07/20/vermont-coach-sues-school-after-being-fired-over-trans-views/.

24. Alexander Hall, "Pennsylvania Democrat Calls on University to 'Cancel' Speakers Who Question Transgender Ideology," Fox News, March 23, 2023, https://www.foxnews.com/media/pa-state-rep-threatened-calls-university-cancel-speakers-question-transgender-ideology.

25. Bobby Burack, "Eventbrite Deletes Pro-Hamas Rally Listings without Explanation after Outkicks Story, Remains Silent on Riley Gaines Event," Outkick, October 26, 2023, https://www.outkick.com/eventbrite-deletes-pro-hamas-rallies-riley-gaines/.

26. @ Riley_Gaines_, Twitter, October 29, 2023, https://twitter.com/Riley_Gaines_/status/1718812730558206050,

27. Tom Pyamn, "Transgender activist and convicted attempted murderer tells police officer 'trans rights are human rights!' as she's handcuffed and arrested for 'incitement to violence' after telling cheering crowd at Trans Pride rally to 'punch TERFs in the face,'" Daily Mail, July 13, 2023, https://www.dailymail.co.uk/news/article-12294651/Trans-activist-told-crowd-punch-TERFs-face-arrested-incitement-violence.html.

28. @MrAndyNgo, Twitter, July 9, 2023, https://twitter.com/MrAndyNgo/status/1678060752567975936/video/1.

29. Sam Montgomery, "Trans Activist Arrested After Telling Rally of Supporters to Punch Feminists," GB News, July 13, 2023, https://www

.gbnews.com/news/trans-activist-arrested-after-telling-rally-of-supporters
-to-punch-feminists.

30. "Police Probe 'Decapitate TERFs' Sign at Trans Rally," *Herald Scotland*,
    January 22, 2023, https://www.heraldscotland.com/politics/23268023.police
    -probe-decapitate-terfs-sign-trans-rally/.

31. Emily Czachor, "'Save 1 Trans, Kill 1 TERF' Graffiti Appears at Paris
    International Women's Day Event," *Newsweek*, https://www.newsweek
    .com/save-1-trans-kill-1-terf-graffiti-appears-paris-international-womens
    -day-event-1574592; https://www.vancouverisawesome.com/courier
    -archive/news/vancouver-rape-relief-targeted-with-vandalism-threats
    -over-transgender-controversy-3106045.

32. "Twitter Removes Tweets About 'Trans Day of Vengeance,'" CBS News,
    March 29, 2023, https://www.cbsnews.com/losangeles/news/twitter
    -removes-tweets-about-trans-day-of-vengeance-2/.

33. https://fairerdisputations.org/hard-lessons-in-life/.

34. Helen Joyce, *Trans: Gender Identity and the New Battle for Women's Rights*,
    Kindle ed. (London: Oneworld, 2022), 11.

35. Ibid., 7.

36. Ibid.

37. Ibid., 14.

38. K. D. Gribble et al. "Effective Communication About Pregnancy, Birth,
    Lactation, Breastfeeding and Newborn Care: The Importance of Sexed
    Language," *Frontiers in Global Women's Health* (February 2022): 818856,
    doi:10.3389/fgwh.2022.818856; PMID: 35224545; PMCID: PMC8864964,
    https://www.ncbi.nlm.nih.gov/pmc/articles/PMC8864964/.

39. National Institutes of Health, "Inclusive and Gender Neutral Language,"
    https://www.nih.gov/nih-style-guide/inclusive-gender-neutral-language
    #:~:text=Both%20pregnant%20women%20and%20pregnant,)%2C%20
    present%20an%20inclusive%20alternative.

40. "Statement on Information," Jo's Cervical Cancer Trust, June 30, 2023,
    https://www.jostrust.org.uk/press-releases/statement-on-information.

41. Gribble et al., "Effective Communication."

42. Tim Pearce, "Michigan Senate Votes to Change Breastfeeding Law to
    Remove References to 'Woman,' 'She,'" Daily Wire, October 20, 2023,
    https://www.dailywire.com/news/michigan-senate-votes-to-change
    -breastfeeding-law-to-remove-references-to-woman-she#.

43. Shannon Thaler, "Bud Light Parent Anheuser-Busch's Stock Lost $27B Over Dylan Mulvaney," *New York Post*, June 2, 2023, https://nypost.com /2023/06/02/bud-light-parent-anheuser-buschs-stock-lost-27b-over-dylan -mulvaney/.

CHAPTER SIX: IN IT TOGETHER

1. Christina Gough, "Student Athletes by Gender," Statista, March 23, 2022, https://www.statista.com/statistics/1098761/student-athletes-by-gender/.

2. "NCAA Member Schools Release Nominations for 2022 Woman of the Year Award," press release, July 14, 2022, https://www.ncaa.org/news/2022 /7/14/media-center-ncaa-member-schools-release-nominations-for-2022 -woman-of-the-year-award.aspx.

3. John Lohn, "NCAA President Mark Emmert Says Governing Body Will Continue to Allow Transgender Participation," *Swimming World*, March 28, 2022, https://www.swimmingworldmagazine.com/news/ncaa -president-mark-emmert-says-governing-body-will-continue-to-allow -transgender-participation/.

4. Ibid.

5. John Lohn, "Commentary: Letters, Lies, and Spin Reveal NCAA Mishandling of Transgender Lia Thomas Debate," *Swimming World*, March 30, 2022, https://www.swimmingworldmagazine.com/news /commentary-letters-lies-and-spin-reveal-ncaa-mishandling-of -transgender-lia-thomas-debate/.

6. "Gender Gap," Title IX Schools, July 17, 2023, https://titleixschools.com /2023/07/17/gender-gap/.

7. Ibid.

8. "A Woman's Sports Foundation Report," May 2022, https://www .womenssportsfoundation.org/wp-content/uploads/2022/05/13_Low-Res _Title-IX-50-Report.pdf.

9. U.S. Department of Education, "Title IX and Sex Discrimination," www2 .ed.gov/about/offices/list/ocr/docs/tix_dis.html.l

10. Allison Torres Burtka, "Mom Was Right: 'Title IX a Game-Changer for Daughters," Global Sports Matters, May 11, 2018, https:// globalsportmatters.com/youth/2018/05/11/title-ix-game-changer-for -daughters/.

11. Caitlyn Thompson, "Billie Jean King: The First Female Athlete-Activist," *New York Times*, August 17, 2021, nytimes.com/2021/08/17/books/review/all-in-billie-jean-king.html.

12. Bill Plaschke, "Billie Jean King Reflects on the Impact of Title IX on Women," *Los Angeles Times*, June 23, 2022, https://www.latimes.com/sports/story/2022-06-23/billie-jean-king-reflects-title-ix-impact-women.

13. Ibid.

14. "NFHS Releases First High School Sports Participation Survey in Three Years," National Federation of State High School Associations, October 10, 2022, https://www.nfhs.org/articles/nfhs-releases-first-high-school-sports-participation-survey-in-three-years/.

15. Burtka, "Mom Was Right."

16. https://www2.ed.gov/about/offices/list/ocr/docs/t9-ath-nprm.pdf?utm_content=&utm_medium=email&utm_name=&utm_source=govdelivery&utm_term=.

17. Matthew Impelli, "Judge Sides with Trans Sorority Member Accused of Inappropriate Erection," *Newsweek*, August 28, 2023, https://newsweek.com/judge-sides-trans-sorority-member-accused-inappropriate-erection-1822852.

18. Candice Jackson, "Genderizing Title IX in US Schools," Genspect, July 23, 2022, https://genspect.org/genderizing-title-ix-in-us-schools/.

19. Myah Ward, "Blackburn to Jackson: Can You Define 'the Word Woman'?" *Politico*, March 22, 2022, politico.com/news/2022/03/22/blackburn-jackson-define-the-word-woman-00019543.

20. Ibid.

21. "The Department of Justice Files Brief Defending the Constitutionality of Idaho's Fairness in Women's Sports Act," press release, U.S. Department of Justice, November 19, 2020, https://www.justice.gov/opa/pr/department-justice-files-brief-defending-constitutionality-idahos-fairness-womens-sports-act.

22. Independent Women's Forum, https://www.iwf.org/about/.

23. "Working for Women: A Modern Agenda for Improving Women's Lives," Independent Women's Forum, https://pdf.iwf.org/working-for-women-a-modern-agenda-for-improving-womens-lives-2nd-edition.pdf.

24. Virginia Legislative Information System (LIS), lis.virginia.gov/cgi-bin/legp604.exe?231+sum+HB1387.

25. https://twitter.com/JeffMBourne/status/1620189495764320256.

26. https://twitter.com/JeffMBourne/status/1620189495764320256.

27. https://twitter.com/Riley_Gaines_/status/1620513828109942784.

28. Sherman Smith, "Kansas City Democrat Risks Exile from Party after Vote on Transgender Athletes," Kansas Reflector, April 10, 2023, https://kansasreflector.com/2023/04/10/kansas-city-democrat-risks-exile-from-party-after-vote-on-transgender-athletes/.

29. "Protection of Women and Girls in Sports Act of 2023," U.S. Congress, congress.gov/bill/118th-congress/house-bill/734?s=3&r=1&q=%7B%22search%22%3A%5B%22Protection+of+Women+and+Girls+in+Sports+Act+of+2023%22%5D%7D.

30. Ibid.

31. Peter Kasperowicz, "Save Women's Sports Act Passes House with Zero Votes from Dems amid Transgender Bullying Debate," Fox News, April 20, 2023, https://foxnews.com/politics/save-womens-sports-bill-passes-house-zero-votes-dems-transgender-bullying.

32. Ibid.

33. Jim Piwowarczyk, "Wisconsin Democrat Says Girls Just Need to 'Work Harder' When Competing Against Biological Boys," Wisconsin Right Now, October 13, 2023, https://www.wisconsinrightnow.com/dave-considine/.

34. @RepGlenIvey, Twitter, April 20, 2023, https://twitter.com/RepGlennIvey/status/1649039670259376130.

35. Letter from Independent Women's Forum to Governor Charlie Baker of the NCAA, January 25, 2023, https://www.iwf.org/wp-content/uploads/2023/01/NCAA-Gov.-Baker-Letter-RGAINES-01-05-2023-_public.pdf.

36. Mark Harris, "NCAA President Charlie Baker Throws His Predecessor Mark Emmert under the Bus for Prior Transgender Policies," Outkick, October 17, 2023, https://www.outkick.com/ncaa-president-charlie-baker-transgender-athlete-policy-senate-hearing-riley-gaines-lia-thomas/.

37. Independent Council on Women's Sports, NCAA Demand Letter, January 12, 2023, https://www.iconswomen.com/ncaa-demand-letter/#icons-letter.

38. Ibid.

39. Women's Bill of Rights, https://womensbillofrights.com/wp-content/uploads/2022/04/womens-bill-of-rights.pdf.

40. Ibid.

41. https://www.iwv.org/2023/05/iwv-spokeswoman-riley-gaines-urges
    -congressional-support-for-the-womens-bill-of-rights/.

42. Jennifer Braceras et al., "We Need a Women's Bill of Rights," *The Hill*, June
    22, 2022, https://thehill.com/opinion/civil-rights/3530284-we-need
    -a-womens-bill-of-rights/.

43. Stacy Bunck et al., "Kansas Enacts Law Defining 'Male' and 'Female'
    Strictly as Sex Assigned at Birth," Ogletree Deakins, May 4, 2023, https://
    ogletree.com/insights/kansas-enacts-law-defining-male-and-female
    -strictly-as-sex-assigned-at-birth/.

44. Ryan Foley, "Arkansas Gov. Sarah Sanders Signs Executive Order Banning
    'Anti-Women' Words," *Christian Post*, October 23, 2023, https://www
    .christianpost.com/news/gov-sarah-sanders-signs-executive-order
    -banning-woke-words.html.

45. Kelly Laco, "Republicans Introduce 'Women's Bill of Rights' to Protect
    Accomplishments, Ensure Safety of Biological Females," Fox News, May
    19, 2022, https://www.hydesmith.senate.gov/republicans-introduce
    -womens-bill-rights-protect-accomplishments-ensure-safety-biological
    -females.

46. Independent Women's Voice, "IWV Spokeswoman Riley Gaines Urges
    Congressional Support for the Women's Bill of Rights," May 17, 2023,
    https://www.iwv.org/2023/05/iwv-spokeswoman-riley-gaines-urges
    -congressional-support-for-the-womens-bill-of-rights/.

47. Ibid.

CHAPTER SEVEN: BLOOD IN THE WATER

1. "Press Briefing by Press Secretary Karine Jean-Pierre and National
   Security Council Coordinator for Strategic Communications John Kirby,"
   White House, April 6, 2023, https://www.whitehouse.gov/briefing-room
   /press-briefings/2023/04/06/press-briefing-by-press-secretary-karine-jean
   -pierre-and-national-security-council-coordinator-for-strategic
   -communications-john-kirby-9/.

2. "We Have the Data to Prove It: Universities Are Hostile to Conservatives,"
   Manhattan Institute, March 3, 2021, https://manhattan.institute/article/we
   -have-the-data-to-prove-it-universities-are-hostile-to-conservatives.

3. "Riley Gaines' Visit to SF State Results in Trans Right Activist Protests,"
   Golden Gate Xpress, April 7, 2023, https://goldengatexpress.org/102298
   /latest/news/riley-gaines-visit-to-sf-state-results-in-trans-right-activist
   -protests/.

4 @TPUSA Bay Area, Instagram, https://www.instagram.com/p/CqrOkzpJ8
    TV/?next=%2Froad7819%2Ftagged%2F&hl=fr-ca.

5. Ibid.

6. @davidllamas, Twitter, April 8, 2023, https://twitter.com/davidllamas
    _/status/1644760038626713600?ref_src=twsrc%5Etfw%7Ctwcamp%5Etwe
    etembed%7Ctwterm%5E1644760038626713600%7Ctwgr%5Ea6e62a825b9
    213785f2d4b114e44d2d1abc9e3b0%7Ctwcon%5Es1_&ref_url=
    https%3A%2F%2Fwww.campusreform.org%2Farticle%3Fid%3D21906.

7. Natalie O'Neill, "Oxford Professor Gets Bodyguards After Threats from
    Transgender Activists," *New York Post*, January 4, 2020, https://nypost
    .com/2020/01/24/oxford-professor-gets-bodyguards-after-threats-from
    -transgender-activists.

8. Ibid.

9. "UK Universities Tackle Sexual Misconduct Claims," BBC News, January
    25, 2020, https://www.bbc.com/news/education-51248684.

10. Maya Yang, "Shawnee State University in Ohio Had Reprimanded
    Nicholas Meriwether, Who Then Sued on First Amendment Grounds,"
    Guardian, April 20, 2022, https://www.theguardian.com/us-news/2022
    /apr/20/professor-shawnee-state-university-wins-damages-trans-student.

11. Ibid.

12. Andrea Mew, "Oberlin College Lacrosse Coach 'Burned at the Stake' for
    Supporting Women's Sports," Independent Women's Forum, https://www
    .iwf.org/kim-russell/.

13. Gaydos, "Oberlin College Women's Coach Says She Was 'Burned at the
    Stake.'"

14. Mew, "Oberlin College Lacrosse Coach 'Burned at the Stake' for
    Supporting Women's Sports."

15. Ibid.

16. Ibid.

17. Ibid.

18. *New York Times*, op-ed, March 18, 2022, https://www.nytimes.com/2022
    /03/18/opinion/cancel-culture-free-speech-poll.html.

19. Deep Green Resist, "San Francisco Public Library Hosts Transgender Art
    Exhibit Featuring Weapons Intended to Kill," Medium, May 1, 2018,
    https://medium.com/@deepgreenresist/san-francisco-public-library-hosts

-transgender-art-exhibit-featuring-weapons-intended-to-kill
-3ccb82b34ab.

20. Julian Vigo, "The Degenderettes: The Transgender Hate Group Taking
    Aim at Women," Public Discourse, June 3, 2018, https://www
    .thepublicdiscourse.com/2018/06/21574/.

21. Isidora Sanger, *Born in the Right Body: Gender Identity Ideology from a
    Medical and Feminist Perspective*, Kindle ed. (2022), 131–32.

22. Meghan Murphy, "Historic Speakers' Corner Becomes a Site of Anti-
    Feminist Silencing and Violence," Feminist Current, September 15, 2017,
    https://www.feministcurrent.com/2017/09/15/historic-speakers-corner
    -becomes-site-anti-feminist-silencing-violence/.

23. Ibid.

24. Julie Moss, "Interview with Maria MacLauchlan: The GRA and the
    Aftermath of Assault at Speakers' Corner," Feminist Current, June 21,
    2018, https://www.feministcurrent.com/2018/06/21/interview-maria
    -maclauchlan-gra-aftermath-assault-speakers-corner/.

25. Victoria Ward, "Three Sought After 60-Year-Old Woman Beaten in
    Transgender Row," *Telegraph*, October 26, 2017, https://www.telegraph.co
    .uk/news/2017/10/26/three-sought-60-year-old-woman-beaten
    -transgender-row/.

26. Darren Boyle, "Transgender Activist Battered by Radical Feminist in
    Speakers' Corner Brawl," *Daily Mail*, April 12, 2018, https://www.dailymail
    .co.uk/news/article-5607919/Transgender-activist-battered-radical
    -feminist-Speakers-Corner-brawl.html.

27. Ibid.

28. Martin Coulter, "Transgender Activist Tara Wolf Fined £150 for
    Assaulting Exclusionary Radical Feminist in Hyde Park," *Evening
    Standard*, April 13, 2018, https://www.standard.co.uk/news/crime
    /transgender-activist-tara-wolf-fined-ps150-for-assaulting-exclusionary
    -radical-feminist-in-hyde-park-a3813856.html.

29. Jen Izaakson, "Trans-Identified Male, Tara Wolf, Charged with Assault in
    Hyde Park Attack," Feminist Current, April 27, 2018, https://www
    .feministcurrent.com/2018/04/27/trans-identified-male-tara-wolf-charged
    -assault-hyde-park-attack/.

30. Moss, "Interview with Maria MacLauchlan."

31. Ibid.

32. Progressing America, YouTube, https://www.youtube.com/watch?v=
SDouNtnR_IA&t=3s.

CHAPTER EIGHT: SPRINT WHEN IT HURTS

1. Kentucky Sports Radio, https://www.talk104fm.com/shows/kentucky
-sports-radio/.

2. Jinsheng Pan, Weihong Qi, Zichen Wang, Hanjia Lyu, and Jiebo Luo, "Bias
or Diversity?" University of Rodchester, https://workshop-proceedings
.icwsm.org/pdf/2023_25.pdf.

3. "Study of Headlines Shows Media Bias Growing," University of Rochester
Newscenter, 2023, https://www.rochester.edu/newscenter/study-of
-headlines-shows-media-bias-growing-563502/.

4. F. Motoki, V. Pinho Neto, and V. Rodrigues, "More Human than Human:
Measuring ChatGPT Political Bias, *Public Choice* (2023), https://doi.org/10
.1007/s11127-023-01097-2, https://link.springer.com/article/10.1007/s11127
-023-01097-2.

5. Sissie Hsiao, "Try Bard: Exploring State-of-the-Art AI in Real Time,"
Google Blog, March 21, 2023, https://blog.google/technology/ai/try-bard/.

6. "International Women's Sports Summit Day 1," YouTube, July 21, 2023,
https://www.youtube.com/watch?v=5iHvRgNaw5U&t=5180s; see 1:26:39.

7. "IOC Releases Framework on Fairness, Inclusion and Non-Discrimination
on the Basis of Gender Identity and Sex Variations," International Olympic
Committee, November 16, 2021, https://olympics.com/ioc/news/ioc
-releases-framework-on-fairness-inclusion-and-non-discrimination-on
-the-basis-of-gender-identity-and-sex-variations.

8. Rich Perelman, "LANE ONE: Sports Medicine Federation Pushes Back
(Hard) against IOC's Framework on Transgender Inclusion," Sports
Examiner, January 18, 2022, https://www.thesportsexaminer.com/lane
-one-sports-medicine-federation-pushes-back-hard-against-iocs
-framework-on-transgender-inclusion/.

9. Sean Ingle, "IOC Praises Weightlifter Laurel Hubbard Ahead of
Transgender Athlete's Olympic Debut," *Guardian*, July 29, 2021, https://
www.theguardian.com/sport/2021/jul/29/ioc-praises-weightlifter-laurel
-hubbard-ahead-of-transgender-athletes-olympic-debut.

10. Ibid.

11. F. Pigozzi, X. Bigard, and J. Steinacker on behalf of the International
Federation of Sports Medicine (FIMS) and the European Federation of

Sports Medicine Associations (EFSMA) et al., "Joint Position Statement of the International Federation of Sports Medicine (FIMS) and European Federation of Sports Medicine Associations (EFSMA) on the IOC Framework on Fairness, Inclusion and Non-Discrimination Based on Gender Identity and Sex Variations," *BMJ Open Sport & Exercise Medicine* 8 (2022): e001273, doi:10.1136/bmjsem-2021-001273, https://bmjopensem .bmj.com/content/8/1/e001273#ref-1.

12. Ibid.

13. "When Did Women First Compete in the Olympic Games?" Olympics. com, https://olympics.com/ioc/faq/history-and-origin-of-the-games/when -did-women-first-compete-in-the-olympic-games#:~:text=Women %20competed%20for%20the%20first,%2C%20croquet%2C %20equestrianism%20and%20golf.

14. Ibid.

15. @Coachblade, Twitter, April 10, 2020, https://twitter.com/coachblade /status/1248475180113911808.

16. @Coachblade, Twitter, April 11, 2020, https://twitter.com/coachblade /status/1248835401877348352/photo/1.

17. L. Elsas et al., "Gender Verification of Female Athletes," *Genetics in Medicine* 2 (2000): 249–54, https://doi.org/10.1097/00125817-200007000 -00008.

18. Ibid.

19. Statement of the Stockholm consensus on sex reassignment in sports, https://stillmed.olympic.org/Documents/Reports/EN/en_report_905.pdf.

20. J. C. Reeser, "Gender Identity and Sport: Is the Playing Field Level?" *British Journal of Sports Medicine* 39 (2005): 695–99, https://bjsm.bmj.com /content/39/10/695.

21. "Dr. Emma Hilton reviews the science supporting the IOC decision to let male-born transgender athletes into female competition." Fair Play for Women, July 14, 2019, https://fairplayforwomen.com/emma_hilton/.

22. Ibid.

23. L. J. Gooren and M. C. Bunck, "Transsexuals and Competitive Sports," *European Journal of Endocrinology* 151, no. 4 (October 2004): 425–29, doi:10.1530/eje.0.1510425; PMID: 15476439, https://pubmed.ncbi.nlm.nih .gov/15476439/.

24. "2023 International Women's Sport Summit—Day 1," You Tube, July 21, 2023, https://www.youtube.com/watch?v=5iHvRgNaw5U&t=5485s, see 1:34:07.

25. "IOC Consensus Meeting on Sex Reassignment and Hyperandrogenism November 2015," https://stillmed.olympic.org/Documents/Commissions _PDFfiles/Medical_commission/2015-11_ioc_consensus_meeting_on _sex_reassignment_and_hyperandrogenism-en.pdf.

26. "Athlete Health and Fair Play: Kristen Worley Case Puts Women's Sport Policy in the Dock," The Conversation, July 20 2017, https:// theconversation.com/athlete-health-and-fair-play-kristen-worley-case -puts-womens-sport-policy-in-the-dock-81361.

27. Joanna Harper, "Race Times for Transgender Athletes," *Journal of Sporting Cultures and Identities* 6, no. 1 (January 2015): 1–9, https://www .researchgate.net/publication/307766116_Race_Times_for_Transgender _Athletes.

28. Ibid. (runner #7)

29. Ibid.

30. J. Harper et al., "How Does Hormone Transition in Transgender Women Change Body Composition, Muscle Strength and Haemoglobin? Systematic Review with a Focus on the Implications for Sport Participation," *British Journal of Sports Medicine* (2021): 1–9, doi:10.1136 /bjsports-2020-103106, https://bjsm.bmj.com/content/bjsports/early/2021 /02/28/bjsports-2020-103106.full.pdf.

CHAPTER NINE: GET ON THE BLOCK

1. https://tennesseestar.com/the-tennessee-star/vanderbilts-gender-clinic -doctor-trans-surgeries-make-money-for-the-hospital/sberry/2022/09/21/.

2. Abigail Shirer, "Employee: 'Trans-Identifying Kids Are Cash Cows' for Planned Parenthood," *Federalist*, February 11, 2021, https://thefederalist .com/2021/02/11/employee-trans-identifying-kids-are-cash-cows-for -planned-parenthood/.

3. Press release, office of Texas attorney general Ken Paxton, June 14, 2023, https://www.texasattorneygeneral.gov/news/releases/texas-launches -lawsuit-against-bidens-unlawful-title-ix-guidance-forcing-transgender -policies.

4. https://www.campusreform.org/article/i-have-a-phd-pitt-anthropologist -ridiculed-after-claiming-men-women-have-same-bones/21828.